THE
PMDD
PHENOMENON

THE
PMDD
PHENOMENON

Breakthrough Treatments for Premenstrual
Dysphoric Disorder (PMDD)
and Extreme Premenstrual Syndrome (PMS)

❧

Diana L. Dell, M.D., FACOG

Department of Psychiatry, Department of Obstetrics and Gynecology,
Duke University Medical Center

and Carol Svec

Contemporary Books

Chicago   New York   San Francisco   Lisbon   London   Madrid   Mexico City
Milan   New Delhi   San Juan   Seoul   Singapore   Sydney   Toronto

The McGraw·Hill Companies

Library of Congress Cataloging-in-Publication Data

Dell, Diana L.
　　The PMDD phenomenon : breakthrough treatments for premenstrual dysphoric disorder (PMDD) and extreme premenstrual syndrome (PMS) / Diana L. Dell and Carol Svec.
　　　　p.　　cm.
　　Includes bibliographical references and index.
　　ISBN 0-07-140075-3
　　　1. Premenstrual syndrome.　　2. Generative organs, Female—Diseases—Treatment.
　I. Svec, Carol.　　II. Title.

RG165 .D45　　2002
618.1′72—dc21　　　　　　　　　　　　　　　　　　　　2002067295

1 2 3 4 5 6 7 8 9 0　DOC/DOC　1 0 9 8 7 6 5 4 3 2

ISBN 0-07-140075-3

McGraw-Hill books are available at special quantity discounts to use as premiums and sales promotions, or for use in corporate training programs. For more information, please write to the Director of Special Sales, Professional Publishing, McGraw-Hill, Two Penn Plaza, New York, NY 10121-2298. Or contact your local bookstore.

The information in this book is not intended to be a substitute for the medical advice of physicians. The reader should consult with his or her doctor in all matters relating to health. Although every effort has been made to ensure that the drug doses and other information are presented accurately in this book, the ultimate responsibility for proper medical treatment rests with the prescribing physician. Neither the authors nor the publisher can be held responsible for errors or for any consequences arising from the use of information contained here.

This book is printed on acid-free paper.

For my father, who taught me never to judge others.
For Evelyn, Pat, and Donna, who taught me not to judge myself.
And for the hundreds of women who have taught me their wisdom by sharing
their stories during difficult and vulnerable times in their lives.

—DIANA L. DELL

For Bill, as always.
And for those remarkable and inspiring women in my family:
Harriet, Marina, Teresa, and Ann.

—CAROL SVEC

Contents

Acknowledgments

WE WOULD LIKE TO JOINTLY thank the people who helped bring this book from concept to reality, in particular: our agent, Jo Fagan of Jane Dystel Literary Management, who has a way of making everything come together; Jane Dystel, who is fanatically supportive; our editor, Judith McCarthy, whose enthusiasm and responsiveness were always greatly appreciated; Susan Moore, editorial team leader, who did an outstanding job guiding the manuscript through the process of becoming a book (and where did you get your keen eyes?); and Michele Pezzuti, who took care of the details.

Special thanks to Khris Sherlock for her tireless efforts in researching and scheduling. She handled everything so efficiently that we could barely keep up.

D.L.D. also owes special thanks to Phyllis Dye, who helps in multiple ways, great and small; and to Caroline Haynes, who cares for my patients when work on this and other projects takes me on the road. And many thanks to Carol and the brightness she has brought to this project.

C.S. thanks her lucky stars for Joanna Jones, Alan Lee Jones, and Wendy Potkay, whose keen eyes and minds helped shape early drafts of the book. Thanks once again to Sid Kirchheimer—friend, mentor, top-notch editor, and all-around good guy. A note of appreciation for Jay Lawrence and Gene Potkay—you know why. And thanks beyond measure to Diana for her wisdom, dedication, tirelessness, and compassion. I'm fortunate to have met her and grateful for this chance to call her a friend and colleague.

We would also like to thank all the women who agreed to tell their stories to us. Their names and identifying details are changed in the book to respect their privacy, but their stories are faithfully re-created. Their participation was fueled by their desire to help other women. Almost all, at some point in the interview, asked us to make sure we let women who suffer from PMDD know that they are not alone.

Finally, we both wholeheartedly thank Bill Svec for his interest, support, humor, and good restaurant selections. P.S.—Thanks for understanding all these years.

Introduction

PREMENSTRUAL DYSPHORIC DISORDER (PMDD) is a new name for a condition that has been described both by physicians and by women for centuries. Most women experience some emotional or physical symptoms during the week or two before their menstrual periods, including irritability, sadness, mood swings, bloating, breast tenderness, and difficulty concentrating. For about 40 percent of women, these symptoms are strong enough to be troubling and cause moderate discomfort. If medical attention is sought, the diagnosis is likely to be premenstrual syndrome (PMS), because it is so common. But between 3 and 9 percent of menstruating women experience symptoms so severe that they interfere with personal, social, or work relationships, leading to a diagnosis of PMDD. For some part of every month, their lives—and the lives of the people around them—are turned upside down. Women with PMDD commonly describe feeling as though they have two personalities: the "nice" one, which is their usual self, and the angry, "crazy," "evil," or out-of-control one, which is their premenstrual self.

The concept of difficult premenstrual symptoms has been around longer than there has been formalized medicine. Since the time of Hippocrates, healers and physicians have described women's premenstrual discomfort in terms that are still being used today: mood changes, sadness, depression, weepiness, anxiety, irritability, psychosis, impatience, and nervousness. Despite the long history of reports of premenstrual suffering,

PMS was not commonly recognized as a medical condition by physicians or by women themselves. Although first described in American medical literature in 1931, little progress in the study or treatment of this phenomenon immediately followed. In 1945, Dr. S. Charles Freed wrote in the *Journal of the American Medical Association*, "It is quite possible that the reason for this general unawareness . . . is the acceptance by the woman herself that these disturbances are a normal part of a woman's fate and thus she makes little effort to seek relief unless they are severe."

Premenstrual syndrome remained a relatively obscure diagnosis until the 1970s when the lay press began writing extensively about the disorder. As women read magazine stories about PMS, they began to recognize their own symptoms. They began to understand that their monthly turmoil wasn't simply a normal part of being female. But as awareness of the disorder increased, the concept of PMS changed. What started as a medical diagnosis evolved to become part of the vernacular to describe any woman's ill-tempered behavior. Then came the jokes. Hundreds of them. Whole books of nothing but PMS jokes.

On the medical front, there was a marked increase in research about the disorder. Unfortunately, that research was hampered by the lack of a consistent definition of the syndrome itself. Without such a consistent definition, studies were conducted as if PMS scientists were trying to fit together puzzle pieces from different puzzles; no clear picture could ever emerge. In 1987, amid much controversy about "political correctness," the third edition of the *Diagnostic and Statistical Manual of Mental Disorders (DSM-III-R)*—a book that lists criteria for diagnosing various psychiatric conditions—outlined research criteria for the most severe form of the disorder, calling it "late luteal phase dysphoric disorder." That name never gained popularity among the lay press or medical practitioners, but it gave enough structure to the disorder so that research scientists were finally all working on the same puzzle.

With the 1994 edition of the *Diagnostic and Statistical Manual of Mental Disorders*, the name was changed to "premenstrual dysphoric disorder." (*Dysphoria* is the opposite of *euphoria* and simply means an emotional state of anxiety, depression, or unease.) In both *DSM* editions, the condition was listed in the appendix as a condition requiring further research before being listed as a "real diagnosis" like major depression or generalized anxiety disorder.

It wasn't until the summer of 2000 that PMDD leapt into national consciousness. That was when the U.S. Food and Drug Administration (FDA) approved fluoxetine hydrochloride as the first drug to be used specifically to treat PMDD symptoms. Soon afterward, Eli Lilly, the pharmaceutical company that manufactures the medication under the brand name Sarafem, began running television ads that struck a note of familiarity for millions of women. While showing realistic portrayals of highly irritated, depressed, or bloated women, the ads asked, "Think it's PMS? Think again." And with those five words, the world was introduced to PMDD.

Response to the ads was mixed, to say the least. Many women who had experienced severe PMS (and their loved ones) rejoiced that there was finally a serious diagnosis for their sporadic but volatile symptoms, and—better yet—that there was something to treat them. Women rushed to their physicians and spent $14.6 million the first five months the medication was sold.

Other people were less excited. Some called it a marketing scheme because Sarafem is the same medication as the antidepressant drug Prozac, and Prozac was due to lose its patent protections. It was argued that by creating a new brand name for the same medication, Eli Lilly could create a whole new market for the same drug. Others called it an antiwoman political move designed to create yet another diagnosis that could be used to treat women as second-class citizens. Still others believed that creating a new diagnosis for premenstrual symptoms is akin to calling every woman abnormal, because every woman menstruates. The one common thread that ran through all the opposing arguments was that women were being duped because PMDD wasn't a real disorder.

Premenstrual dysphoric disorder *is* a real disorder. Millions of women can attest to the physical, mental, and spiritual suffering they experience the week or so before their periods. These women, and the millions more who have the milder symptoms of PMS, know that what they feel is not caused by any political, sociological, or marketing phenomenon. They know that there are days when a woman with PMDD feels like there's an angry stranger living in her head . . . days when she feels out of control . . . days when her husband threatens divorce because he cannot stand the mood swings anymore. "If you want to know if PMDD is real," these women say, "walk a mile in my shoes. Spend a month in my skin."

Premenstrual dysphoric disorder is real. We know because we've treated or studied PMS and PMDD for years. We can (and will) point to the medical literature and show how research has been fitting together the puzzle pieces of these disorders to give us an inkling of what really is going on. Although no one knows exactly what happens physiologically to cause PMDD or PMS, we do know that women who have severe premenstrual symptoms differ from women who don't have premenstrual symptoms in ways that can be measured in a laboratory.

We also know PMDD and PMS exist, because we, the authors, both have experienced some form of these disorders ourselves. One of us (C.S.) traced back and discovered that for both corporate jobs she quit, she gave notice the week before her period—and then regretted her decision a week later once her premenstrual phase passed. She also spent years torturing her husband once a month, eating pounds of chocolate and pasta, and questioning her sanity before she came to understand that millions of women share her problem. Even now, on these pages, she finds it difficult to admit to such potentially embarrassing personal details. But keeping quiet only enhances the stigma of the disorder and does not promote dialogue about the important issues surrounding PMDD. As you can see, our interest in and approach to this topic are both professional and highly personal. We understand the symptoms and the frustrations, we've followed the research, and we're committed to sharing what we know to help other women understand the disorder and what treatment options are available—and which work best.

For women who have endured the mood swings, irritability, depression, low self-esteem, or any of the other symptoms of PMDD, our message is simple: You are not crazy, you are not losing your mind, and you are not alone. There's an explanation for what you are going through. There is medical research that points to targeted treatments. There is hope.

This book is divided into two parts. The goal of Part I is to provide a thorough explanation of what is currently known about PMDD and severe PMS. We include theories about the physiologic mechanisms behind these disorders, an explanation of what happens in a normal menstrual cycle, and a description of symptoms. (In Appendix B is a chart for you to keep track of symptoms to see if what you are experiencing is really PMDD.) Also in Part I, we include real-life stories of women with PMDD to illustrate the variety of forms the disorder can take and give a picture of how serious the problem can be for women with symptoms.

Part II is all about feeling better. Each chapter discusses a different type of treatment, including the latest information about newly approved prescription medications, nutrition, complementary therapies, and stress reduction. We include a PMDD game plan—guidance on the best steps to take to reduce or eliminate symptoms.

It's important to understand that although symptoms of PMDD or PMS can be eliminated or greatly reduced by using one or more of the treatments discussed in this book, not every treatment will work for every woman. One woman may respond well to taking a prescription medication, but another may have too many side effects to continue. One woman may get total relief by changing her diet and lifestyle, but another may need to take two or three different medications to treat all her symptoms. With a little trial-and-error, virtually every woman can find relief with the right combination of treatment options. This book is designed to help you find the best possible treatments *for you*. Think of this process as an exploration, a small time investment to reclaim that missing portion of your life you've been losing to premenstrual dysphoria.

From Dr. Diana Dell

In the course of my academic life, I received grant support from a number of sources, including Berlex, GlaxoSmithKline, and Pfizer. I have served as a consultant to both Eli Lilly and Pfizer as they attempted to get FDA approval for treatment of PMDD with their respective products, fluoxetine and sertraline. I take very seriously my commitment to educate both professionals and the lay public about hormonally related mood and anxiety disorders, so I am a frequent lecturer on the topic of PMDD and related subjects. Some of these lectures receive pharmaceutical industry support; others are unsponsored. I currently serve on the Speaker's Bureau for Berlex, GlaxoSmithKline, Eli Lilly, Pfizer, TAP Pharmaceuticals, and Wyeth-Ayerst.

I have wanted to write this book for the past five years, but time and circumstances have prevented the project. I will be forever grateful to Carol Svec for seeking me out and teaming up to produce this scholarly but readable book for the thousands of women who have been ridiculed or maligned for recurring symptoms that affect so many aspects of their lives.

Part I

UNDERSTANDING PREMENSTRUAL DISORDERS

I

Is PMDD Real?

Sometimes I would just snap. There was so much anger, I felt like I just wanted to grab something breakable and slam it down and break it and shatter it and just explode.

—Toni

EVER HAD A HEADACHE? Really? Prove it.

Imagine if only 2 percent of all the people in the world ever got headaches. How would you prove to doctors and scientists that your headaches were real? There are no blood tests, x-rays, or body scans that can be used to diagnose a headache, except for the exceptional few, such as headaches due to brain tumors. Pain itself cannot be seen on a monitor. What if the other 98 percent of the world didn't believe that you could just wake up in the morning with pain in your head, or go home after a day of work with throbbing temples? Or, what if other people believed that the pain you felt was psychosomatic and that you were just using the so-called headache as an excuse to get out of work . . . or that aspirin companies had brainwashed you into thinking you had a headache just so they could sell more pills . . . or that you should accept your fate and suffer in silence so that you wouldn't be branded as "sick"?

Are headaches real? Of course they are. Everyone has had at least one, so there is no debate. And they come in different intensities, from a mild working-at-the-computer-too-long variety to the extreme pain of a full-blown migraine. What causes migraines and most headaches is still unknown, but there is no doubt that they exist, and people who have them need and get sympathy and treatment.

Is premenstrual dysphoric disorder (PMDD) real? Of course it is. As with headaches, there are no specific diagnostic tests for PMDD, it comes in different intensities and varieties, and the actual cause is still unknown. But because PMDD has been experienced by only a small fraction of the world's population, there is considerable debate and controversy about the diagnosis.

The discussion often becomes quite heated. If you or a loved one has PMDD, or even if you've just tried to talk about the topic, you've likely heard at least some of the controversy from friends or your health care practitioner. One woman reported that she had to listen to a male nurse go on a tirade about how PMDD was a "made-up disease" while she was in the hospital in labor giving birth to her second child. Although that may not have been the appropriate time or place for a discussion of the merits of PMDD as a diagnosis, many of the concerns are well intentioned and the issues deserve attention and responses. Here are some of the most commonly heard questions and arguments.

Question 1: PMDD is a modern invention, perhaps caused by the stresses of modern times. Otherwise, why haven't we heard about it until now?

Actually, premenstrual symptoms have been reported in medical writings for centuries. During the fifth century B.C.E., Hippocrates wrote that retained menstrual blood could cause serious symptoms, including delusions, mania, and thoughts of suicide. Writings from the time of the late Renaissance show that premenstrual suffering was commonly reported, and a survey conducted in the 1800s showed that 20 percent of all women experienced serious psychological troubles premenstrually. Those physicians of old described symptoms such as nervous over-excitation, sensory disturbance, mood changes, sadness and depression, involuntary fits of weeping, anxiety, psychosis, irritability, impatience, and being "difficult to live with"—words that sound familiar even today.

In the 1900s, physicians began scientific research of this complex of symptoms. The disorder has been named and renamed several times in the past seventy-five years, and each name change reflected a greater understanding of the problem. It has been called "premenstrual tension," "menstrual molimina," "premenstrual intoxication," "premenstrual distress," "premenstrual syndrome," "late luteal phase dysphoric disorder," and "premenstrual dysphoric disorder." Although we've come to define *premenstrual syndrome* (the familiar "PMS") as referring to milder symptoms, the initial intent was the same for all of these diagnoses, regardless of name. They were intended to describe a group of cyclic changes in personality and distressing physical symptoms that, according to a 1938 article by Dr. S. Leon Israel, "appears abruptly from 10 to 14 days prior to the expected menstruation and terminates dramatically with the onset of the flow."

Medical literature about premenstrual symptoms published in the early 1900s reflects the colorfully descriptive writing consistent with that time in scientific reporting. The condition was described as "indescribable tension and a desire to find relief by foolish actions difficult to restrain" (Frank 1931); "a feeling of the sensation of wanting to jump out of one's skin, with marked physical unrest and constant irritability, and with the forbearance of the patient's family taxed beyond endurance by her unnatural and extreme annoyance with trifles" (Israel 1938); "a clinical picture of depression, hyper-irritability, irascibility, and a hair-trigger temper," among other symptoms (Stieglitz 1949); "a distressing impairment of the sufferer's psychic and physical well-being" (Morton 1950).

Women themselves have always known that they felt different premenstrually, but they didn't always talk about it. In a 1949 article published in the *American Journal of Medical Science*, Drs. Edward J. Stieglitz and Seruch T. Kimble wrote that symptoms were often ignored by physicians and women alike because "they have come to feel that it is an unavoidable evil, an inevitable part of the distress of menstruation . . . these patients suffer for years in silence on the assumption that because their mothers and elder sisters suffered, they too must endure this distress."

Throughout the 1900s, scientists endeavored to describe and understand women's premenstrual symptoms. As science progressed, the name for this phenomenon kept changing. As it became obvious that psychological symptoms were a major cause of distress, it was called "premenstrual tension." When a physiologic chemical was hypothesized to cause the change in personality, it was called "premenstrual intoxication." When it was noted that there was a cluster of potential symptoms that followed a typical pattern, it was called "premenstrual syndrome." In an effort to create a more specific and scientifically descriptive name, the name was changed to "late luteal phase dysphoric disorder." And finally, in 1994, when it became obvious that there were different patterns of symptoms that might also involve the early luteal phase, the disorder became known as "premenstrual dysphoric disorder," a term that gives appropriate weight to its predominant mood-related symptoms.

So why didn't you hear about PMDD earlier? You did. Only then it was called premenstrual syndrome (PMS). Most people outside the medical profession only heard about this new term when television commercials for Sarafem, the first medication approved for treatment of PMDD, were aired in 2000. The commercials were new, but the disorder has been around forever.

Question 2: If PMDD is nothing more than PMS, why create another category of disorder?

Although the term *premenstrual syndrome* was coined in the 1950s, most women didn't hear about it until the 1970s. By then, television and other mass media outlets were more common and pervasive than in the 1950s, and the concept of PMS became popularized because information could be disseminated more easily. Back then, knowing that there was such a thing as PMS was a relief for many women. Finally there was a name for the bloated, puffy, achy, tender transformation our bodies underwent each month, and recognition of the emotional tortures and plummeting self-esteem some women suffered. Having a name for the disorder gave us a common language we could use to discuss our problems with other women and with our doctors. There was strength in labeling that bad time of the month because if we could name it, we could understand it and perhaps fix it.

But as the concept of PMS caught on and found acceptance, it lost its original meaning. Every time a woman raised her voice in anger, there was the danger that her actions would be labeled as part of PMS. Humor, too, helped trivialize the syndrome. It was one thing for women to joke amongst themselves, but when talk show hosts, television sitcoms, husbands or lovers, and bosses started joking about PMS, the power behind the name became diluted. In time, *PMS* became a term of ridicule. Any emotion, passion, or argument—at home or in the workplace—could be labeled PMS by others, and therefore dismissed. By separating PMDD from PMS, the medical community is acknowledging that it recognizes that there are some women with very severe, potentially disabling symptoms who need an appropriate diagnosis and treatment.

Question 3: PMDD is strictly a problem of women in the United States. If it's real and biological, why don't we find PMDD in other parts of the world?

In fact, premenstrual symptoms have been reported in many other countries, including Great Britain, Italy, India, Pakistan, Nigeria, and China. In nearly every country in which premenstrual symptoms are found, PMDD or severe PMS can be diagnosed in approximately the same number of women as has been found in the United States—3 to 9 percent. A study conducted in Italy found that even women who were generally unaware of the concept of PMS still had the standard, or classic, symptoms of breast tenderness, tension, and avoidance of social activities premenstrually.

One of the reasons critics argue that PMDD doesn't exist everywhere is because women across the globe don't spontaneously report the same set of symptoms. For example, studies show that in other countries, particularly in less industrialized parts of the world, women report physical symptoms more often than emotional symptoms. It's important to remember, however, that in many of these countries, it is not as accepted or typical to talk openly about emotions. When these women are asked directly, they often admit to premenstrual depression and irritability.

In extremely underdeveloped nations, where premenstrual symptoms are not reported as often as in developed nations, the very hardship and harshness of the lives of women there may explain the lack of PMS. It is known, for example, that exercise can help alleviate premenstrual symptoms, and women in underdeveloped nations must expend considerable energy just to get through their days. Their day-to-day activities could very well be protecting them against PMS. Social expectations in various nations may also play a part in which symptoms get reported and which do not. Not all women have the same freedom to acknowledge and express their anger and irritability as do women in the United States. Future research will undoubtedly focus on which symptoms are common to all women, which symptoms are culturally based, and what factors might protect some cultures from the full effects of PMS.

Question 4: PMDD "medicalizes" a normal female function and will cause hundreds of thousands of women to be labeled "sick." Being irritable and emotional is part of life; why should we take pills to dampen normal emotions?

Premenstrual dysphoric disorder is not your average mood swing. Anyone who has experienced PMDD or severe PMS knows how far from "normal" this disorder is. Yes, menstruation is a normal female function. Yes, hormone fluctuations are part of normal female physiology. And yes, some premenstrual symptoms are common and normal. But the symptoms of PMDD make women feel like something is terribly wrong. When asked to describe the feelings they have during their premenstrual week, women with PMDD have said, "I feel like someone else is living in my skin," "I'm not myself," "it's like Jekyll and Hyde," "I turn evil," "I can't stand myself," "it's like having severe sunburn of your emotions, everything hurts." For that one week, lives are turned upside down.

As an analogy, consider acne in puberty. Hormonal shifts are a normal part of adolescence, and acne is common among teenagers. But there are a few people who have acne that is so severe it scars the skin, lowers self-esteem, and makes a tremendous impact on their ability to have "normal" social lives. Because acne is visible, no one says, "Hey, it's a few pimples. It's a normal part of growing up; you'll outgrow it." Everyone can see the devastation. Therefore, for very severe acne, doctors prescribe medications that can make a real difference in a teenager's life.

The symptoms of PMDD are not as apparent, but they are just as real. And if women with symptoms are having a tough time functioning, they deserve to be treated. No one is talking about medicating an entire generation of women, just the ones who need help. If that's one woman or one million women, treatment should be offered when needed.

Question 5: How can PMDD be a "real" disorder when there are no physical differences between women with PMDD and women without PMDD?

In the early days of research, scientists did studies to see if there were any differences in what seemed like the obvious problem area: women's hormones. They found no difference in circulating levels of estrogen or progesterone, which led them to believe that there were no physiologic differences. More recent research, however, has turned up some important differences between women with and without PMDD.

The most significant difference involves the neurotransmitter serotonin. Dr. Andrea Rapkin of the UCLA School of Medicine and her colleagues measured the amount of serotonin in the blood of women with and without premenstrual syndrome. In women without premenstrual symptoms, the amount of serotonin increased the last ten days before their periods; but in women with PMS, the amount of serotonin *decreased*. In all people, serotonin is the precursor for melatonin in the brain. Dr. Barbara Parry of the University of California, San Diego, has performed many experiments that show that women with PMDD have lower levels of melatonin than women without PMDD throughout the menstrual cycle. The assumption is that lower levels of melatonin means lower levels of serotonin. Since low levels of serotonin are associated with feeling depressed and/or aggressive, these studies suggest a strong link between the mood symptoms of PMDD and low levels of serotonin.

Because PMDD and PMS are complex conditions, the research often focuses on subtle differences. For example, women with premenstrual symptoms have been shown to have lower levels of allopregnanolone in the luteal phase of their menstrual cycles compared with women without premenstrual symptoms. (Allopregnanolone is a by-product of the metabolism of the female hormone progesterone.) And women with PMDD have been shown to secrete some hormones, such as the stress hormone cortisol, at different times compared to women without PMDD.

As research into the causes of PMDD and PMS progresses, other physiologic differences will come to light. But even the limited data available in this area now give a clear indication that there is something special going on biologically with women who experience premenstrual symptoms.

Question 6: Wasn't PMDD made up by the drug companies to sell more drugs to women? Eli Lilly was about to lose its patent on Prozac, so it created a new disorder, repackaged the drug, and now stands to make billions of dollars.

The drug companies did not "make up" PMDD. Unless they've been in business for the past 2,000-plus years, they couldn't have made it up. Women have been suffering for centuries.

And, fortunately, pharmaceutical companies don't have a magic wand they can wave to make scientists, government officials, and physicians all do exactly what is best for the company. It's a long, involved process to get to the point where a new drug can be marketed. The process starts with drug testing to show that a particular medication works as a treatment. Scientists don't randomly choose drugs and test them to see if they work on various disorders. Fluoxetine hydrochloride (the generic name for Prozac) is a selective serotonin reuptake inhibitor (SSRI), a type of medication that makes the neurotransmitter serotonin more available in the brain. Because one of the working theories about PMDD is that women with the condition may have lower levels of serotonin, it made sense to test Prozac as a treatment for PMDD.

Fluoxetine spent years in testing, and, according to experts, it was the first drug that actually helped improve symptoms. Dr. Meir Steiner of McMaster University in Hamilton, Ontario, Canada, testified in U.S. Food and Drug Administration (FDA) hearings that "As old as I am and [for as long as I] have been in this field, this is the first time that something works. This is the first time that the clinic got flowers from husbands. We treated something that sort of restored life in some of these households. Clinically, this was so impressive that it was almost unbelievable." After reviewing the research, the FDA approved fluoxetine as a treatment for PMDD.

Was it good timing for the pharmaceutical company? Sure. But this wasn't a last-ditch effort to save a source of revenue. The drug had been in testing for treatment of premenstrual symptoms for years. If the tests had proven it wasn't helpful, the company would have been out of luck.

What worries some critics is that Eli Lilly took Prozac, renamed it "Sarafem," and then repackaged it in lavender and pink capsules. The critics object to this mainly because they felt that women were being misled— if women knew Sarafem was the same drug as Prozac, they wouldn't take it.

Physicians have made no secret of the fact that Sarafem is fluoxetine and that the drug is available as a generic. Some women request the generic, and other women specifically request Sarafem—not because of successful marketing, but because they don't want to be taking a drug they perceive to be specifically for depression when they don't suffer from depression. As one woman said, "My doctor offered me generic Prozac, but I'd rather have my pharmacist fill a prescription for Sarafem. I live in a small town; I see my pharmacist at the grocery store. I'm not depressed." Another woman said that she gets generic Prozac, "but I tell everyone I'm taking Sarafem. It's just easier. They know what it is and what it's for. It's less explaining I have to do."

Finally, no pharmaceutical company can force a physician to prescribe a medication that does not work, nor can clever advertising brainwash women into thinking they have symptoms if they don't. If a medication works, then it is a valid and important treatment option for women with PMDD, regardless of what name it is sold under.

Question 7: If you start giving out pills to women to make them feel better, won't everyone want to take them?

Most people don't want to take medication. Even when some people are suffering from rather serious diseases, it's tough to get them to take their pills regularly, if at all. Few people will continue to take pills that don't solve the problem. That's why it's so hard to get people to continue to take medication for high blood pressure or cholesterol—these disorders have no symptoms, so it's impossible for the patient to get any indication that the drugs are working.

Selective serotonin reuptake inhibitors work for many, but not all, women with PMDD. Women will continue to use the drug if the medication relieves their most severe symptoms and helps them feel "normal." But as with just about any medication, there are side effects. Every woman must decide whether the side effects are worth the difference in her monthly moods. Not everyone will decide in favor of the medication.

Women without PMDD will not experience any sense of "feeling better" if they take fluoxetine or most other antidepressant medications (unless they have major depression, anxiety disorder, or another undiagnosed problem). Some drugs—such as Valium, cocaine, or amphetamines—affect anyone who takes them; SSRIs do not. If a well person takes these types of antidepressant medications, they don't get "high." They are not "happy pills" in the sense that many people imagine, and they are not the modern equivalent of "mother's little helper," as Valium was colloquially known. There is virtually no reason anyone would want to take Sarafem if it wasn't needed, and there would be virtually no reason for a physician to prescribe it if there wasn't a problem.

Question 8: If PMDD is real, why is it listed only in the appendix of the DSM-IV instead of in the body of the text with other "real" disorders?

Premenstrual dysphoric disorder is listed in the appendix of the fourth edition of the *Diagnostic and Statistical Manual of Mental Disorders* as a disorder that is in need of additional research. It is categorized as an example of a "depressive disorder not otherwise specified," and is therefore separated from the more familiar depression types, such as major depression or bipolar disorder. Indeed, more research into PMDD was needed back in 1994 when the manual was published. Its listing in the *DSM* gives a coherent and consistent definition of the disorder, assuring that researchers in Maine and researchers in Mongolia will be using the same criteria for their investigations.

Considerably more research has been done since then, and we now have a body of literature based on these common criteria. No doubt the placement of PMDD in the manual will be discussed when the editors plan for the next revision.

Question 9: I have PMS, and it's not so bad. My friends' PMS is not so bad. Isn't it just that these other women don't know how to handle their periods?

It is difficult for anyone who has not experienced true PMDD to comprehend the emotional and physical pain that can be involved. That's understandable. If you've only had tension headaches, it is going to be impossible for you to truly understand the pain of a migraine headache. Trust us, it's bad for us. We ask not to be judged because of this physiologic disorder. We ask for the understanding and support of the general public and medical community as we continue to search for treatments that allow us to be *ourselves* all month long.

2

What Is PMDD?

There's so much negative stereotyping when it comes to this. It is definitely real. It is a disorder. Nobody would be making this up for any reason. You know, I'm not just trying to pull a fast one on anybody.

—Marisa

EACH WOMAN'S EXPERIENCE of the physical aspects of monthly menstruation is different. We all know that some women's periods are longer or shorter than our own, that the flow of blood may be heavier or lighter, and that cramping may be stronger, weaker, or nonexistent.

Similarly, the very real effect of monthly cycling on emotional and physical premenstrual symptoms differs from woman to woman, as well. Most women have a few minor, tolerable complaints just prior to their periods—perhaps a little bloating, increased moodiness, breast tenderness, insomnia, or cravings for certain types of foods. These are natural responses of the body to the hormonal and other physiologic changes that occur in all women of childbearing age. Between 20 and 40 percent of women have moderate premenstrual complaints, with symptoms that are more uncomfortable, distressing, or annoying than the average, but that are still tolerable and don't affect the way these women function or relate to people. These women are said to have premenstrual syndrome (PMS), a diagnosis that acknowledges that changes are occurring and that the discomfort is not merely in these women's minds.

When PMS is severe . . . when the premenstrual symptoms cause so much anguish, irritability, or depression that women feel out of control . . . when these symptoms affect relationships with spouses, lovers, children, friends, and coworkers, then we're no longer talking about simple PMS. Then we're talking about a mood disorder called premenstrual dysphoric disorder (PMDD). This diagnosis recognizes the overwhelming and sometimes debilitating physical, mental, behavioral, and emotional responses a woman may have in the ten to fourteen days prior to menstruation, and which disappear entirely within a day or two after menstrual bleeding begins. (For a full list of symptoms, see Chapter 3.)

It is estimated that between 3 and 9 percent of menstruating women have PMDD—that equates to between two million and six million women in the United States alone, and several million more worldwide. Although PMDD can affect any menstruating woman at any age, it is most commonly seen by physicians in women in their midthirties. One study found that more than 50 percent of adolescents report premenstrual symptoms that they consider extreme, but this group is not likely to seek treatment for their symptoms, and parents are likely to attribute moody behavior to just "being a teenager." Some women report that their symptoms began or got worse after the birth of their first child. Women with PMDD find that their symptoms get progressively worse as they get older until menopause, when both menstruation and premenstrual symptoms disappear. Clinical observations suggest that women with premenstrual symptoms are more likely to have postpartum emotional issues and more difficulty with the changes that accompany the transition to menopause.

There appears to be a genetic component to PMS and PMDD. Women with premenstrual symptoms generally have mothers with premenstrual symptoms, and most women without premenstrual symptoms had mothers who also didn't have symptoms. It is difficult to know, however, whether this commonality is due to a direct genetic link or to a shared environment—after all, most daughters grow up living in the same household as their mothers. If there is something in that home situation, whether it is diet or learned behavior, chances are it will affect both mother and daughter. This question has been addressed, in part, by studies that looked at twins. Identical twins share identical genes and usually have identical environments, whereas nonidentical (or fraternal) twins share different genes but usually have identical environments. By comparing these two groups of women, it is possible to get an idea of how much premenstrual symptomatology is due to genes and how much is due to environment. These studies have suggested that at least a portion, perhaps about 35 percent, of PMS is due to genetics, but because of the complex nature of personality and this disorder, exactly how much of PMDD is inherited remains uncertain.

Most researchers believe that PMDD is simply an extreme form of PMS. They believe that there is a continuum of symptom severity, from no symptoms at one end (about 10 percent of women), to mild-to-moderate PMS-type symptoms in the middle (about 85 percent of women), to PMDD-level severity at the far end (about 5 percent of women).

There is also a third diagnostic category called premenstrual exacerbation (PME). Any underlying disorder worsens premenstrually, including migraine, depression or other mood disorders, anxiety disorders, diabetes, asthma, arthritis, lupus, fibromyalgia, irritable bowel syndrome, diabetes, chronic fatigue syndrome, and even allergies. What may feel like severe PMS or PMDD may be the result of one of these underlying conditions, which gets much worse premenstrually. Of the large number of women with all the preceding conditions, PME affects more women than PMDD does. But similar treatment strategies can be used for women with PME, as we will discuss in later chapters.

No one knows why some women have certain symptoms or more intense symptoms than other women have. Physicians don't know whether PMDD reflects an extreme of the normal range of expected symptoms, or if there is some other underlying problem—or set of problems—that causes a more intense reaction of the body to premenstrual changes. Research hints that the latter might be true. But before we can begin to talk in detail about what happens in the body to cause PMS, PME, or PMDD, we need to have a basic understanding of what happens in a typical menstrual cycle.

The Mechanics of the Menstrual Cycle

Few of us really consider the exquisite timing and coordination required by the body to bring on monthly menstruation. Most people know the basics of a typical menstrual cycle: Every month, a woman's body produces a mature egg. When the time is right, the egg is released from a sack (or follicle) in an ovary, a process called ovulation. The egg travels down the fallopian tube to the uterus. If the egg is fertilized by sperm, it attaches itself to the uterine lining (the endometrium) and develops into a baby. If the egg is not fertilized, the endometrium is shed from the uterus in the form of menstrual blood.

It all seems to happen somewhere "down there" in the body. But when we look at the details, we see that menstruation occurs only because of an intricate communication system between the brain and the reproductive organs, with all messages in the communication system carried by hormones.

Hormones are complex chemicals that are produced in various organs of the body, travel through the bloodstream to other organs, and signal that some action needs to take place. Interestingly, hormones are produced in response to signals from other hormones, and sometimes hormones are produced because of the lack of another hormone, so there is a constant give-and-take of hormonal messages in the body. Menstruation requires and is guided by five major hormones that carry communication between the brain, the pituitary gland, the ovaries, and the uterus.

The average menstrual cycle lasts twenty-eight days, although "normal" cycles can run from twenty-one to thirty-five days. The following description assumes a twenty-eight-day cycle.

Day 1 of a new cycle starts the day menstrual bleeding begins. Starting at Day 1 and continuing to about Day 14 is the *follicular phase* of the menstrual cycle. In the follicular phase, a portion of the brain called the hypothalamus releases a hormone called gonadotropin-releasing hormone (GnRH). Gonadotropin-releasing hormone sends a message to the pituitary gland (located at the base of the brain), which releases follicle-stimulating hormone (FSH). Follicle-stimulating hormone travels through the bloodstream to the ovaries where it stimulates the growth and maturation of eggs in little sacks called follicles (hence the name follicular phase). Although many eggs may start ripening, usually only one outpaces the others and becomes a mature egg. The arrival of the FSH hormone messenger also prompts the ovaries to produce estrogen, one of the two primary hormones responsible for "femaleness." This estrogen enters the bloodstream and signals the uterus to start the process of thickening the lining in preparation for the mature egg.

The rising level of estrogen in the blood is detected by the pituitary gland. This signal prompts the pituitary gland to do two things: (1) cut back on its secretion of FSH (the job of that hormone is virtually done because the follicle is nearing full maturation); and (2) secrete luteinizing hormone (LH), which causes the mature egg to be released from the follicle. The release of the egg, known as "ovulation," occurs at about Day 14. This begins the portion of the menstrual cycle known as the *early luteal phase*, from about Day 15 to Day 21.

The empty follicle (now called the corpus luteum, which gives the luteal phase its name) starts producing estrogen and large amounts of progesterone, the other primary hormone responsible for femaleness. The rising levels of both estrogen and progesterone in the bloodstream signal the uterus to continue to build and thicken the uterine lining. Additionally, when the pituitary gland senses the high hormone levels, it stops secreting FSH and LH.

The corpus luteum needs FSH and LH to continue to work, so when circulating levels of these hormones fall, the corpus luteum begins to disintegrate and stops producing estrogen and progesterone. Once estrogen and progesterone levels begin to fall, we enter the *late luteal phase* of the menstrual cycle, when premenstrual symptoms occur. This occurs about Day 22 to Day 28. Without a steady and abundant supply of estrogen and progesterone, the uterine lining cannot be maintained. It separates from the uterus and appears as menstrual blood. On Day 28, just before bleeding starts, estrogen and progesterone levels are at their lowest. The low levels of these hormones are detected by the hypothalamus, which responds by secreting GnRH, and the cycle begins again.

Theories About What Causes PMDD and PMS

As is probably obvious from the description of a typical menstrual cycle, there are a multitude of factors that have the potential to cause or contribute to premenstrual symptoms. And if the picture doesn't seem complicated enough yet, consider this: as hormones circulate in the bloodstream, they affect more than just the organs involved in menstruation. The effects are felt systemically (meaning "throughout the body," the whole anatomical system). Numerous other body processes are affected by these normal hormonal signals.

Through decades of research, scientists have come up with various theories or models to explain what might be happening in the body to cause premenstrual symptoms. These models provide scientists with a place to begin, a way to think about the problem, which allows them to formulate experiments that can test out the limits of the model. Each experiment provides one small piece to the puzzle, and it is hoped that, when all the pieces are complete, a full image of PMDD will emerge. Today, the model that best fits the available data is that PMDD is a function of biochemical changes in the brain secondary to fluctuating levels of ovarian hormones (estrogen and progesterone). Lines of research contributing to knowledge about premenstrual symptoms include (1) special sensitivities, (2) stress and cortisol, (3) dysfunctions in the production or response to "feel good" chemicals, and (4) a biopsychosocial complex. All these lines of research contribute valuable information to the PMDD puzzle, and they each show a different way of looking at the problem and understanding what may be causing it all.

PMDD as a Biochemical Change in the Brain

It seemed obvious to early practitioners with an interest in premenstrual changes that because the menstrual cycle is driven by hormones, premenstrual symptoms must be related to some imbalance or abnormality in the production of these hormones. It was suggested that some change in the production of estrogen or progesterone (or both) must be responsible for the symptom cycles. Those theories have been disproved. For example, research has already shown that women with PMDD and women without premenstrual symptoms have similar levels of circulating estrogen and progesterone—the main female hormones—throughout the month. Further, there is no difference in the levels of another hormone called adrenocorticotropic hormone (ACTH)—a hormone that helps regulate the release of other hormones that increase blood sugar levels and help the body resist the effects of stress—or testosterone (the typically "male" hormone that is present in small amounts in women and seems to affect sex drive).

Although abnormal amounts of hormones have not been found in women with PMDD, hormones still contribute to the problem in ways that are not fully understood. One important study by Dr. Peter J. Schmidt of the National Institute of Mental Health and his colleagues demonstrated the importance of ovarian hormones in precipitating premenstrual symptoms. In this study, women with premenstrual symptoms and women without premenstrual symptoms took a medication that artificially stopped their bodies' production of estrogen and progesterone. In women with PMS, stopping the production of these hormones caused a complete cessation of their premenstrual symptoms. When the women were then given supplemental estrogen and progesterone, symptoms started right back up again.

The current and most popular theory is that the changing levels of estrogen and progesterone—not the overall levels, but the *change* in the levels—cause changes in the neurotransmitters in the brain, and those neurotransmitter changes are responsible for the symptoms women experience. Neurotransmitters are the chemical messengers that allow nerve cells to communicate with each other. The neurotransmitter that is the primary "suspect" for premenstrual symptoms is serotonin. In general, serotonin is associated with calmness and a sense of well-being. People who are deficient in serotonin tend to be depressed, irritable, and/or angry (sound familiar?). People with clinical depression are often helped by medications that allow greater amounts of serotonin to be available in the brain, such as Prozac, Zoloft, and others. Therefore, it was hypothesized that the changes in brain chemistry probably cause the symptoms of PMS and PMDD.

It made sense, then, to test women with PMDD to see how well their serotonin systems worked. Research suggests that women with PMDD suffer from a dysfunction of some facet of the serotonin pathway, perhaps in how much serotonin is produced or how quickly it is broken down, or perhaps in how sensitive the nerve cells are to its effects. An abundance of research has shown that some women with PMDD can get complete relief from their premenstrual symptoms by taking medications that make serotonin more available in the brain, and up to 70 percent of women with PMDD get at least some relief from those serotonin-enhancing medications. Serotonin production and availability are influenced by a number of different factors, including hormones, diet, and psychological or social factors, so a combination of treatment options may be appropriate.

Another example of how hormones play a role in causing premenstrual symptoms is shown in research involving a steroid called allopregnanolone, one of the metabolites of progesterone. The effects of allopregnanolone are seen throughout the body, including the brain, where, among other things, it reduces anxiety levels. One study by Dr. Susan Girdler of the University of North Carolina at Chapel Hill and her colleagues found that women with PMDD who experience high levels of premenstrual anxiety and irritability had lower levels of allopregnanolone than women with PMDD who had less premenstrual anxiety and irritability. This makes sense, that the women with the greatest anxiety had lower levels of an anxiety-reducing chemical. Interestingly (and confusingly), women with PMDD had overall *higher* levels of allopregnanolone than women without PMDD, which, the researchers say, may be an indication of the dysregulation, or "out-of-controlness," of this aspect of women's physiology.

Special Sensitivities

Scientists' current best guess about what causes premenstrual symptoms is that symptoms are triggered by the change in the overall levels of estrogen and progesterone. Remember, in the luteal phase just before menstrual bleeding starts, estrogen and progesterone levels plummet to their lowest monthly levels. This happens in all women. So why don't all women have premenstrual symptoms? Actually, most women do, but their symptoms are mild. The extreme response of some women is probably due to a special inborn sensitivity to hormonal changes or hormone-influenced neurotransmitter changes that other women don't have. That would explain why, for example, women with PMDD are more likely to have difficulties during the postpartum period and during the transition to menopause, other life-cycle changes that are accompanied by large hormonal shifts.

The study by Dr. Peter Schmidt mentioned earlier is a classic illustration of this phenomenon. Ten women with PMS and fifteen without PMS had their menstrual cycles artificially stopped with a drug called leuprolide, which basically halts ovarian function. This treatment also stopped all premenstrual symptoms in the women with PMS. Then, all the women were given artificial estrogen and progesterone at levels that were controlled by the researchers. The women who had PMS before the leuprolide had a return of their PMS. The women who did not have PMS before the leuprolide did not begin having PMS when estrogen and progesterone were added. This is significant because women with and without PMS clearly had a different set of reactions to the *same levels* of estrogen and progesterone. There must be, therefore, some type of special sensitivity at work to create symptoms in one group of women but not in the other.

Stress and Cortisol

Other research suggests that cortisol could also be an issue. Cortisol is our so-called stress hormone. Levels of cortisol rise in response to either physical or emotional stressors. In response to stress, the hypothalamic-pituitary-adrenal (HPA) axis is activated. These three organs—the hypothalamus, the pituitary gland, and the adrenal glands—set in motion a complex series of interactions involving corticotrophin-releasing hormone (CRH), the glucocorticoids (cortisol, cortisone, and corticosterone), and adrenocorticotropic hormone (ACTH).

Ever miss a period because of extreme stress? That's because the stress hormones released during HPA axis activation cause a huge hormonal communication glitch. With HPA axis activation, CRH is released, which stops the release of GnRH, the hormone usually responsible for getting the whole menstrual cycle going; and the glucocorticoids suppress luteinizing hormone (LH) and the secretion of estrogen and progesterone by the ovaries. Basically, the whole process gets jammed up, leading to a lack of menstruation.

Now add in hypersensitivity. Imagine the hormonal havoc of a woman who is highly sensitive to HPA activation *and* has a lot of stress in her life. Clinically, women with PMDD report that their symptoms get worse when they are under stress. And a few studies have shown that women with PMDD have altered reactions to stress compared to the reactions of women with no premenstrual symptoms. Women with premenstrual symptoms not only show heightened sensitivity to stress, but sometimes with a seemingly contradictory physiologic response. For example, studies have found that heart rate—which usually goes up in times of stress—goes *down* in women with PMDD in response to stress. This could be an adaptation of the body to long-term or continual stress, or simply an example of how "disconnected" certain regulatory systems might be in women with PMDD.

Dysfunction of "Feel-Good" Chemicals

Brain chemistry, which has such an important role in the menstrual cycle and stress reactions of the body, also controls our moods. Endorphins are neurotransmitters that act like a natural opiate with a similar (but much weaker) effect as morphine. Namely, they make you feel happier and act as pain relievers. Some studies have shown a difference in endorphin levels that may relate to premenstrual symptoms. These studies show that women with PMDD have lower levels of endorphins premenstrually than women without PMDD. Lower endorphin levels mean greater physical discomfort or pain, more anxiety, and more food cravings. These results are not universal—at least one study showed no difference in endorphin levels, which still leaves open the possibility that it is the response to endorphins that is different in women with PMDD, not pure blood levels. Looking at it from a real-world perspective, endorphins are released during exercise, and exercise has been shown to decrease premenstrual symptoms for most women, regardless of premenstrual symptom severity.

A Complex of Multiple Factors

Because we are all more than just the sum total of all our body chemicals, some researchers believe that premenstrual symptoms are the result of an interweaving of *bio*logy, *psycho*logy, and *social* factors (a *biopsychosocial* complex). As hormones are produced and nerves are sparking, the inner physiology is influenced by a combination of family history, learned behaviors, societal expectations or pressures, and our own personalities.

This is not to say that women are to blame for their symptoms. The physiologic part of premenstrual disorders is real; the hormonal shifts and inherent sensitivities in women with PMDD are part of their biology. But external factors can have dramatic and very real effects on the body as well. For example, every emotion is associated with some chemical reaction in the body, so everything we think, feel, or experience causes physiologic changes. How might this work in PMDD? If the luteal phase makes us biologically more vulnerable, we may react more strongly to things in our environment at that time. Because every emotion causes some biochemical change in our bodies, our stronger premenstrual emotions might create a bigger biochemical change. Of course, biochemical changes can affect our moods and stress affects our moods, which will make more changes in the body . . . ad infinitum, until we get our periods again and our bodies reset themselves. And that doesn't even take into account the ways we may have learned to react by watching how other women act premenstrually, or how we feel about ourselves, or what else is going on in our lives. Researchers are currently looking into how psychological and social influences may modulate premenstrual symptoms.

The lesson we learn from all these different models is that premenstrual disorders are the result of complex biochemical, social, psychological, and genetic factors. Although the most promising hypothesis is that hormonal changes create changes in brain chemistry that affect mood, other factors—such as stress hormones and endorphins—probably also play at least some role. It is likely that the interaction of many factors leads to the extreme symptoms of women with PMDD. As more studies are conducted and refined, more of this medical puzzle will become clear, and better treatments can be created.

3

Do You Have PMDD?

I felt like I had failed some piece of myself by having to seek treatment. I'm the type of person, if there is something around the house that needs to be fixed, I'll go get the power tools. Admitting that there was a part of my life that I couldn't control was very difficult. At the time it felt like I was throwing up my hands and saying, "I can't do this." Sort of like admitting defeat at that point. But in hindsight, it was taking control of the situation. I wasn't being weak by admitting I couldn't do it myself. Once it was explained to me what was going on and why—that it isn't the same thing that affects the majority of women, it's cranked up several notches. I know now it is not an admission of weakness to seek the help, because it's not the same thing that my girlfriends have.

—BONNIE

THE AVERAGE premenstrual dysphoric disorder (PMDD) sufferer "loses" between three and seven years of productive life during her childbearing years due to highly symptomatic days. According to Dr. Kimberly A. Yonkers, a PMDD expert from Yale University, a woman who develops PMDD by age twenty-six will likely experience more than 200 symptomatic cycles between then and menopause, or somewhere between 1,400 and 2,800 symptomatic days. Divide 2,800 by 365 days in a year, and you find that this hypothetical woman will experience, at the upper range, 7.6 years of tension, irritability, anger, depression, low self-esteem, and a general feeling of being out of control. One week out of each month sounds manageable, but up to seven years out of a lifetime sounds like cruel and unusual punishment. Getting a diagnosis and making a commitment to finding relief for your symptoms is the first step toward reclaiming lost time.

By the simple act of reading this book, you are already taking positive steps toward getting your full life back. It means that you have recognized that your symptoms are tied to your menstrual cycle. Some women understand the connection immediately; others take decades to come to that realization. Still others never realize it and may spend their lives thinking that they are mentally unbalanced or physically ill. You also have a good sense of self and understand the factors that affect your well-being. Despite the life difficulties caused by premenstrual symptoms, research shows that most women underestimate the extent of the disorder's interference in their lives. Because of this underestimation, many women never seek treatment. They tell themselves that "it's not so bad." Sometimes, that spirit of toughing-out a bad situation can come back to haunt them. One woman with PMDD says she distinctly remembers specific opportunities that she let slip through her fingers simply because, with her intense premenstrual depression and anxiety, she couldn't follow through. She left graduate school, and she turned down high-profile jobs that required traveling. Now, years later, after finally seeking treatment, she recognizes everything she lost. In retrospect, toughing it out was not a good option for her.

Another reason women may not see a doctor is embarrassment. Research into women's attitudes shows that many women are embarrassed to discuss premenstrual symptoms with a professional. And if they get up the nerve to talk with their doctors, many women are wary of the results. In 2000, the Society for Women's Health Research found that nearly one-quarter of women surveyed felt that their doctor wouldn't take their symptoms seriously. And about 40 percent believed that there was nothing that the doctor could do to help them.

In addition, a great many women tend to see their symptoms as a personal weakness, something they should be able to control if only they had enough mental and physical fortitude. They may look for cures in magazines or other anonymous venues, but they find it difficult to talk with their doctors. Let us say right now: *fortitude has nothing to do with it.* Premenstrual symptoms, in whatever form they take, are driven by biology. There is no reason for any woman to suffer with symptoms, pain, and regret for three to four decades of her life.

Common Premenstrual Symptoms

Mood Symptoms

- Depression
- Sadness
- Feeling hopeless
- Anxiety
- Tension
- Being "on edge" or "keyed up"
- Mood swings
- Oversensitivity
- Tearfulness
- Irritability
- Anger
- Agitation
- Nervousness
- Restlessness

Cognitive Symptoms

- Feeling out of control
- Difficulty concentrating
- Forgetfulness
- Strained personal relationships
- Increased interpersonal conflict
- Avoidance of social situations
- Decreased interest in hobbies or other activities
- Perceived poor performance
- Decreased self-image
- Change in sexual interest

Physical Symptoms

- Breast tenderness or pain
- Abdominal bloating
- Abdominal cramps
- Migraine/other headaches
- Back pain
- Muscle or joint pain/aches
- Fluid retention/edema in hands, legs, or feet
- Acne
- Constipation

Other Symptoms

- Food cravings/appetite changes
- Binge eating
- Fatigue, tiredness
- Sleeping more than usual
- Insomnia or difficulty sleeping
- Weight gain

Because there are more than one hundred different possible symptoms, premenstrual disorders can look and feel different to different women. (See the sidebar "Common Premenstrual Symptoms.") Currently, there are no blood tests, x-rays, or body scans that can be used to make a definitive diagnosis because there are no known consistent, overt physiologic changes that can be measured objectively that correlate with premenstrual symptoms.

Diagnosing PMDD

Although most women are familiar with premenstrual syndrome (PMS) and are learning about PMDD, there are actually three diagnostic possibilities for premenstrual symptoms: PMDD, PMS, and premenstrual exacerbation (PME).

The criteria for diagnosing PMDD are highly specific in terms of type, timing, and severity of symptoms. In fact, many women who think they have PMDD actually don't. When women are recruited for medical studies, fewer than half of the women who think they have severe PMS meet the criteria for having PMDD. Those who don't meet the criteria usually have milder symptoms and can be classified as having "just PMS." Some women experience some symptoms throughout the month but find that their symptoms get worse premenstrually. These women are categorized as having premenstrual exacerbation (*exacerbation* basically means "worsening"). Although the differences may seem trivial on the surface, the particular diagnosis made in each case is important because finding the right name for your condition means that you and your physician can design the best treatment plan for you. Plus, the actual "label" that gets put on the symptoms is necessary because insurance companies need a specific diagnostic code before they will cover the costs of treatment and prescriptions.

Unlike most other medical conditions, there is no single defining complaint to help a doctor make the diagnosis. Instead, the timing of symptoms is key. All women with PMDD or PMS have symptoms that appear only in the luteal phase of the menstrual cycle (after ovulation) and then disappear entirely within a day or two after their periods begin. Women with PME have some symptoms throughout the month, but their symptoms get much worse and more difficult to manage in the luteal phase. Physicians must therefore rely on women's personal accounts of symptoms and their timing before deciding if the symptoms are due to a premenstrual condition or some other disorder.

Research Criteria for Premenstrual Dysphoric Disorder

A. In most menstrual cycles during the past year, five (or more) of the following symptoms were present for most of the time during the last week of the luteal phase, began to remit within a few days after the onset of the follicular phase, and were absent in the week postmenses, with at least one of the symptoms being either (1), (2), (3), or (4):

 (1) markedly depressed mood, feelings of hopelessness, or self-deprecating thoughts

 (2) marked anxiety, tension, feelings of being "keyed up" or "on edge"

 (3) marked affective lability (e.g., feeling suddenly sad or tearful or increased sensitivity to rejection)

 (4) persistent and marked anger or irritability or increased interpersonal conflicts

 (5) decreased interest in usual activities (e.g., work, school, friends, hobbies)

 (6) subjective sense of difficulty in concentrating

 (7) lethargy, easy fatigability, or marked lack of energy

 (8) marked change in appetite, overeating, or specific food cravings

 (9) hypersomnia or insomnia

 (10) a subjective sense of being overwhelmed or out of control

 (11) other physical symptoms, such as breast tenderness or swelling, headaches, joint or muscle pain, a "bloating" sensation, or weight gain

B. The disturbance markedly interferes with work or school or with usual social activities and relationships with others (e.g., avoidance of social activities, decreased productivity and efficiency at work or school).

C. The disturbance is not merely an exacerbation of the symptoms of another disorder, such as major depressive disorder, panic disorder, dysthymic disorder, or a personality disorder (although it may be superimposed on any of these disorders).

D. Criteria A, B, and C must be confirmed by prospective daily ratings during at least two consecutive symptomatic cycles. (The diagnosis may be made provisionally prior to this confirmation.)

The research criteria set clear standards and guidelines for defining PMDD. They require that the symptoms begin sometime after ovulation, disappear soon after menstrual bleeding begins, and not reappear until after ovulation again. If, for example, feelings of depression or mood swings occur throughout the month but get worse premenstrually, then PME—not PMDD—would be diagnosed. In order for PMDD to be diagnosed, there must be a window of time after menstrual bleeding begins and before ovulation occurs when there are no mood symptoms at all.

To get a true PMDD diagnosis, each woman must keep a two-month daily record of what symptoms she experiences and at what intensity. This prospective diary is the key to proper diagnosis because it allows women to record symptoms while they are happening, rather than having to rely on memory, which sometimes can be imprecise. Most women who keep a diary find that their ability to recall their previous symptoms has been faulty— usually they have *more* symptoms than they originally mentioned to their health care provider, and the duration of their most intense symptoms is shorter than they thought. A daily symptoms diary helps women see the pattern of their symptoms, clarifies the differences that will determine the diagnosis, and allows physicians to find the best appropriate treatment for each individual.

The research criteria also require that the premenstrual symptoms significantly interfere with work or school, or with personal or social relationships. There must be some negative effect on your life. What qualifies as a negative effect? If you can answer "yes" to any of these questions, you've had a negative effect:

- Do you regularly cause or pick fights with your husband or partner premenstrually? Have the people in your life brought this type of premenstrual combativeness to your attention? Do your actions premenstrually confuse or frighten your family members?
- Do you become visibly angrier around your children during that week or two before your period? Do you find yourself spanking or yelling at them more? Have you ever had to explain to your children why you may have acted badly?

- Have you ever cancelled a party or declined an invitation that fell during your premenstrual time because of your symptoms? Do you tend to isolate yourself during that time?
- Do you take days off work or skip school because of your premenstrual symptoms? Have you ever rescheduled a meeting because it fell in that premenstrual time?
- Do you have to schedule vacations around your menstrual cycle because of premenstrual symptoms?
- Do people at work or school know they have to be careful of what they say around you at certain times of the month?
- Have you lost friends due to something you said or did premenstrually?
- Have you ever gotten into legal difficulties because of your premenstrual behavior?
- Do you drink more alcohol or take more illicit drugs during your premenstrual time?

You'll notice that work performance was not included on this list. Although there may be problems at work, the problems are usually in the realm of work relationships—the work itself doesn't suffer. Women with PMDD may think they do not perform as well on tasks and tests during their premenstrual times, but research has shown otherwise. Women *perceive* that they do worse, but in fact they perform at the same level as at all other times of the month. There is no increase in absenteeism, and they perform no worse than women without premenstrual symptoms. So although it may be harder for women to motivate themselves to work when they are feeling fatigued and depressed, the product of their work is just as good as it always is.

This is different from what has been seen with other mood disorders, especially depression, where people are more easily distracted, tend to have slower work performance, and are prone to giving up on difficult tasks more readily. None of these patterns have been shown with women who have premenstrual symptoms. This is good news, indeed, for women with PMDD who experience lower self-esteem during their premenstrual days and might be more inclined to judge their own work harshly; and also for employers, who might be worried about the productivity of their women workers. No cause for worry—we do our work just fine.

Diagnosing PMS

Premenstrual syndrome, a milder form of premenstrual distress, is relatively simple to diagnose. Most women can recognize PMS in themselves, their colleagues, or their girlfriends simply by noticing when behaviors start to change and then matching those days to a menstrual calendar. If you believe that you or a loved one has some form of PMS, you are probably correct. Researchers estimate that up to 90 percent of menstruating women experience some symptoms premenstrually.

Ideally, the diagnostic process should be the same for PMDD, PMS, and PME. Women who don't meet the strict criteria for PMDD but still experience significantly annoying premenstrual symptoms will receive a diagnosis of PMS. A conscientious physician will require that each woman complete two months of a daily symptoms diary to confirm that the symptoms fall in a predictable premenstrual pattern, with at least one week that is symptom-free. However, an official diagnosis by a physician isn't always necessary. Some women can manage their symptoms without medication, and any woman who feels that she has mild to moderate premenstrual symptoms can begin making healthful changes that might offer relief, such as starting an exercise program or taking calcium supplements.

Because there are no specific symptom criteria for diagnosing PMS, it runs the risk of becoming a catchall diagnosis for women with a variety of complaints. There is a risk of diagnosing (or misdiagnosing) PMS when some other disorder is actually causing the symptoms. So what's the value of the PMS label? Assuming that a physician has ruled out the possibility of another disorder causing the symptoms, having the diagnosis of PMS available allows doctors to assure women that the symptoms they are feeling are within a range of what is normal for the menstrual cycle. Understanding the nature of the symptoms and when to expect them gives women a greater sense of control and helps eliminate the common fear that something more serious may be causing their discomfort. And differentiating between PMS, PMDD, and PME allows women and their physicians to come up with the best treatment strategies.

Diagnosing PME

If a woman experiences significant premenstrual symptoms yet does not fit the diagnostic categories of PMDD or PMS, she may have PME. Again, a prospective symptoms diary will show what your personal pattern of symptoms is. A typical symptoms pattern for women with PME would be a low level of symptoms throughout the month, with an increase in the severity of symptoms premenstrually, but with no consistent symptom-free interval. It is known that most physical and emotional conditions get worse premenstrually. This means that any undiagnosed condition can flare up premenstrually, and that low-grade depression or anxiety disorders, which are manageable most times of the month, become unmanageable premenstrually. Proper diagnosis of PME allows physicians to treat the underlying or coexisting condition, while also controlling premenstrual symptoms. This might mean, for example, that a woman will take medication for the full month, instead of just the week or two she has premenstrual symptoms. (See Chapter 4 for more information about PME.)

Cyclicity Patterns

A two-month symptoms diary helps to verify that the cyclic symptoms a woman perceives are actually related to her menses. For example, one woman who was convinced she had PMDD tracked her symptoms and discovered that they were, indeed, cyclical—but not related to her menstrual cycle. She had extreme irritability, anger, and other symptoms every six weeks, exactly coinciding with visits from her field office supervisor. (Needless to say, she did not need treatment for PMDD, but learned a valuable lesson about how much stress those visits caused her. After brief therapy that helped her understand her responses and find strategies to deal with this difficult person, she was able to keep her stress and anger in check.)

Each woman has her own set of premenstrual symptoms and her own pattern of when symptoms appear and disappear each month. This pattern tends to remain remarkably stable over time. Although a few studies suggest that symptoms get worse as a woman gets older, on a basic month-to-month or year-to-year comparison, symptoms appear consistent and timed like clockwork.

There are five possible distinct patterns of symptom presentation across the menstrual cycle, as illustrated in the following graphs (adapted from Reid 1985).

Spike

This is the most common pattern. Symptoms begin three or four days before a woman's period is due. Their intensity increases sharply until the day before menstrual bleeding begins and then disappears within hours or a couple of days. In total, symptoms are experienced for about five days each month.

Spike Pattern

(dotted line = day of ovulation; solid line = first day of menstrual bleeding)

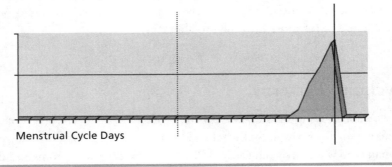

Menstrual Cycle Days

Peak and Spike

In this pattern, there are a few mild symptoms at the time of ovulation that last about forty-eight hours, followed by more severe symptoms that begin about a week before a woman's period is due. Their intensity again increases, although a bit more slowly than with the spike pattern, reaching their peak the day before menstrual bleeding begins. Symptoms disappear entirely within three days. In total, symptoms are experienced for about twelve days each month.

Peak and Spike Pattern

(dotted line = day of ovulation; solid line = first day of menstrual bleeding)

Menstrual Cycle Days

Peak and Mesa

In this pattern, there are again symptoms at the time of ovulation that last about forty-eight hours. But then more severe symptoms kick in almost immediately and last until two or three days after menstrual bleeding begins, when they disappear entirely. In total, symptoms are experienced for about fifteen days each month.

Peak and Mesa Pattern

(dotted line = day of ovulation; solid line = first day of menstrual bleeding)

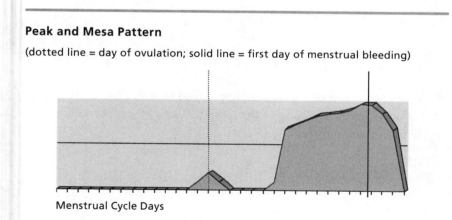

Menstrual Cycle Days

Butte

In this pattern, symptoms are relentless. They start at the time of ovulation, reach a severe level very quickly, and remain at high intensity until about four days after menstrual bleeding begins, after which they disappear entirely until the next ovulation. In total, symptoms are experienced for about twenty days each month. Careful clinical evaluation will almost always indicate that this is a form of premenstrual exacerbation of an underlying physical or emotional condition.

Butte Pattern

(dotted line = day of ovulation; solid line = first day of menstrual bleeding)

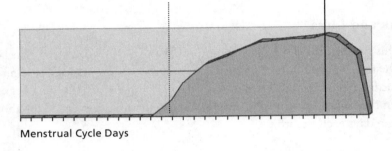

Menstrual Cycle Days

PME Pattern

In PME, some low level of symptoms appears all month, with no symptom-free period. The actual timing of the spike and level of symptoms may differ from those depicted here.

PME Pattern

(dotted line = day of ovulation; solid line = first day of menstrual bleeding)

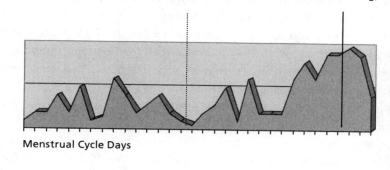

Menstrual Cycle Days

Steps to a Diagnosis

If you feel that you might have a premenstrual disorder, the best first step is to make an appointment with your favorite health care practitioner. It should be someone with whom you have a good partnership, someone you trust and can talk to easily. Psychiatrists and gynecologists are most likely to understand the pattern of symptoms and be open to treating premenstrual symptoms, but primary care physicians, nurse practitioners, and other health professionals are becoming increasingly aware of the disorder and should be able to make an appropriate diagnosis or refer you to a specialist.

Immediately, even before your appointment, begin keeping a daily diary or checklist of your premenstrual symptoms. Chances are your physician will ask you to keep such a symptoms diary for at least two months, so you might as well start early. (Several months of blank diary pages, instructions for completing them, and a sample completed page are included in Appendix B.) There are several different diary forms available, and your health care provider may use one that is different from the symptoms diary provided here. This form is quick and simple to complete and allows easy visualization of symptom patterns. Studies of similar diary scales have shown that they can be used reliably to diagnose and rate PMS severity, and that they can differentiate between PMS, PME, and other mood disorders.

When completing the diary, keep it in a convenient spot and choose a specific time each day to review your symptoms. Most women prefer to complete it each night, after a full day of symptoms, but you can choose the time that's best for you. Don't wait until the end of the week or the month to complete the diary. Women who do that tend to underreport important symptoms, and they may receive an inaccurate diagnosis. Also, be entirely honest. Don't mark boxes for symptoms you don't have, or neglect to mark boxes just because you think they will somehow mess up your results. You and your health care practitioner will want to track your symptoms precisely so that you can start on a treatment appropriate for your condition. For example, if you decide to try one of the medications for PMDD, your doctor may prescribe continuous dosing (in which you take the medication all month long) or intermittent dosing (in which you take the medication only during your premenstrual phase) depending on which pattern of PMDD symptoms you experience. An accurate and honest symptoms diary will help you and your physician make the best and most appropriate choices for treatment for your particular needs.

NOTE: If you feel so depressed or anxious that you cannot function, or if you are having thoughts of suicide, see your health care provider immediately. If you can't get an appointment, go to the emergency department of your local hospital. These are serious symptoms that should not be ignored. There are treatments that can help you regain control of your life.

At the Health Care Office

During your first appointment, your health care practitioner will take a medical history. This is a chance for you and the practitioner to talk about your concerns, your symptoms, and any other relevant health information. Again, be entirely honest and open, and don't leave out details just because you think they may not "fit" with the symptoms of PMDD. Remember, you want to select the treatment that will relieve your symptoms most effectively.

Start the conversation by saying that you are concerned that you might have PMDD. Once your health care practitioner knows what your worries are, he or she can focus questions more precisely and order the appropriate tests. Other information you'll need to talk about may include:

- **Your symptoms.** Use the symptoms list on page 29 as a guide, but add any symptoms that are specific to you. Include every symptom you experience, even if you think it doesn't have anything to do with PMDD. Each symptom is a clue about what is going on in your body, and with enough clues, the right diagnosis can be made.
- **When the symptoms appear and how long they last.** If you've begun filling out a symptoms diary, bring it along to show to your health care practitioner.
- **Other diseases, conditions, or illnesses you have.** Most disorders, both physical and emotional, get worse premenstrually. Your health care provider needs to understand your total physical condition to pinpoint which symptoms might be due to PMDD and which might need different types of treatment.
- **When the symptoms started, and how long you've had them.** Some women start having PMDD symptoms as teenagers, while others aren't bothered until their thirties, and still others don't have any problems until after they have children. Knowing the amount of time a woman has been experiencing symptoms can reveal a lot to a physician. For example, if a woman in her forties seeks treatment for symptoms that only recently developed, her health care provider may want to check to see if the symptoms might be early signs of menopause, rather than PMS.
- **Other life stress or changes you are experiencing.** The menstrual cycle and premenstrual symptoms are strongly affected by stress. Although stress won't cause PMDD, it can make symptoms feel worse.

After taking a medical history, the next step is to rule out other disorders that can mimic PMDD or that have similar symptoms. Blood should be drawn to test for thyroid problems (hypothyroidism), anemia, and diabetes. In addition, your health care provider will likely order additional tests or ask questions to try to rule out depression, anxiety disorder, eating disorders, seizure disorders, chronic fatigue syndrome, systemic lupus erythematosus, or other conditions. Diagnosing PMDD requires not only that you have premenstrual symptoms that meet the criteria but that other conditions have been ruled out. Be patient with the questions and testing, they all have a purpose.

Depending on your physician and the type of insurance you have, several things can happen at this first office visit: (1) you may be given an order for blood work or other tests (unless the blood was drawn at the office); (2) you may be given symptom checklists to complete for the next two months; (3) you may be given a referral to a specialist, such as a psychiatrist or a gynecologist, who might be able to diagnose PMDD better; (4) you may be given a follow-up appointment with the same health care provider; (5) you may be asked to alter your diet or lifestyle habits; or (6) you may be given a prescription for an antidepressant medication (see Chapter 6).

Diet and lifestyle changes can be helpful for many women, and no one would argue against trying them and sticking with the ones that work. Different strategies work for different women. Special attention to diet, exercise, and stress reduction will improve anyone's health if adopted in the long term. They do, however, require time and some sacrifice. In Part 2, we review all the different strategies.

Medication is a different story. In an ideal world, a primary care physician or nurse practitioner would refer you to a PMDD specialist, and you would already have two months of daily symptoms ratings before beginning medical treatment. But the realities of health care are less than ideal. There are not many PMDD specialists, and women want relief now! Many physicians find it easier to start a patient on medication immediately. If the drug works, the prescription will be renewed; if the drug doesn't work, another reason for the symptoms will be sought. Although this is not good clinical practice, it says more about the relative safety of the medications and the realities of health maintenance organizations than it does about physicians. For women who have no health insurance or restrictive insurance, this kind of shortcut is usually only harmful if it delays getting treatment for another illness that is masquerading as PMDD. For example, women with depression may be given intermittent dosing instead of continuous treatment.

If you are given medication without having to complete a symptoms diary or take other medical tests, it's a good idea to keep monitoring your symptoms and keep a careful record on diary pages as you start the medication. This will quickly show if the medication is working or if some symptoms still need to be addressed. Medications for PMDD work almost immediately for most women, so a difference in symptom severity may be seen and felt the first month you begin taking them. If you don't feel any difference after the first cycle or two on medication, go back to your doctor.

The key point we'd like to make is that premenstrual symptoms should not be ignored. If they affect your health, your life, or your sense of well-being, you owe it to yourself to get help. Get a diagnosis, and then look for the right kind of treatment for you.

4

Premenstrual Exacerbation (PME)

One thing I have also had happen is I get cold sores. I've been getting them ever since fourth grade when I'm under stress or I eat eggplant. But I also get them almost every month just before I get my period. I have three of them on my lip right now. I don't know if it's correlated, but it must be because it happens at about the same time every month, three or so days ahead of time.

—Marisa

Women with premenstrual symptoms sense that things get worse just before their menstrual periods. Stress seems more stressful, pain seems more painful, and they become more easily irritated with little or no provocation. Situations they could have handled without breaking a sweat just days earlier can seem insurmountable and overwhelming premenstrually.

Health care professionals who study premenstrual disorders have confirmed those feelings. Everything really does get worse premenstrually. Physical illnesses, emotional struggles, and mental disorders all get worse—a phenomenon known as premenstrual exacerbation (PME). This happens to some degree for all women, even those who experience few premenstrual symptoms; but for women with severe premenstrual symptoms, the level of exacerbation can make a normally manageable disorder unmanageable.

The reason why this across-the-board exacerbation occurs is unclear. We do know that hormones have broad effects in the body and the cyclical changes in hormone levels influence multiple body systems. Immune function is decreased in women premenstrually, which means that women in their luteal phase may have a harder time fighting off diseases. When a woman's estrogen level falls premenstrually, it has an overall negative effect on her well-being. This change in estrogen has been associated with migraines, asthma exacerbation, multiple sclerosis flares, and other health concerns. Estrogen also seems to influence the number and function of serotonin receptors in the brain, and thereby influences mood. And those are just the basic actions we know about. The functions of estrogen and other hormones are under active investigation, and undoubtedly many new effects are yet to be discovered.

Premenstrual exacerbation is more common than premenstrual dysphoric disorder (PMDD). Consider this: The lifetime incidence of depression for women is about 21 percent, and about 8 percent of all Americans have anxiety disorders. Those depressed or anxious women are going to get worse premenstrually. Then consider the total number of women with asthma, diabetes, migraines, arthritis, irritable bowel syndrome, chronic fatigue syndrome, lupus, multiple sclerosis, seizure disorder, or any other chronic illness. Those women are going to get worse premenstrually, too. By virtue of the sheer number of women with all these other disorders, PME is a major health concern.

Because the relation between luteal phase changes and other physical and emotional disorders is not well known or understood, most women don't seek help for PME. What typically happens is that a woman goes to see her physician and says, "I think I have PMS." She is correct in identifying that she feels bad premenstrually. But when she keeps a prospective symptoms diary, many times the diary reveals that she has the same symptoms throughout the month, although usually at a lesser intensity. That is a clear signal to a savvy physician that the woman has PME—a physical or psychological condition that gets worse during the luteal phase of her menstrual cycle. That is why the diary is so critical to proper diagnosis. By keeping a daily log of the symptoms you experience and their intensity, you and your physician will have a clear record of your individual pattern of symptoms.

For women who know they have a physical disorder, undiagnosed PME can be distressing because they may feel unable to control their health. This can lead to feelings of incompetence and can cause women considerable concern about their lack of health stability. For example, women with diabetes often find it more difficult to keep their blood sugar levels under control premenstrually, despite maintaining their usual insulin and diet regimens. Simply understanding the connection between the menstrual cycle and their illness can help put symptoms in perspective. And by tracking and monitoring symptoms across their menstrual cycles, women can work with their physicians to find a way to keep the worst symptoms in check and maintain overall wellness.

It is also possible that a woman might have PME *and* PMDD. A woman with PME of asthma could very well also have the affective symptoms of PMDD. This type of diagnosis might require two different medications—one for the illness that causes physical symptoms and one for PMDD. Some researchers have raised the question of whether it is possible to have PMDD and another affective disorder (such as major depressive disorder), or whether that pattern should only be called PME. For affective disorders, the distinction is of lesser importance because medications that treat affective disorders often can be used to treat symptoms of PMDD. If, however, a woman who is being treated for major depressive disorder tracks her symptoms and finds that she is getting worse or has breakthrough symptoms premenstrually, it may be necessary to switch or adjust the dosage of her medication. Once again, it all comes back to the importance of the symptoms diary.

Physical Illness PME

How the menstrual cycle affects health depends on the underlying disorder. Premenstrual exacerbation of physical illness is a well-recognized phenomenon among physicians and scientists but is less often recognized among women themselves. Any woman who perceives a periodic deterioration in her medical condition can benefit from keeping a symptoms diary for two or three months, adding her physical symptoms to the list provided on the standard diary sheets. Many women are surprised to learn how much of an effect their menstrual cycles can have.

Research is currently being conducted to reveal how women with particular disorders are affected premenstrually. The following sections cover what we already know.

Migraine

The most prominent of the physical disorders affected premenstrually is migraine. Scientific evidence consistently supports the theory that migraine headaches are linked to estrogen withdrawal—the effect of rapidly falling estrogen levels, which occurs in the late luteal phase of the menstrual cycle. If you look at the incidence of migraine headaches, a pattern emerges that suggests a hormonal link: (1) migraines, although relatively rare in children, occur equally in boys and girls before puberty; (2) migraines increase in incidence and number after menarche; (3) women are two to three times more likely to experience migraine headaches than men; (4) a majority of women who experience migraines link their attacks to their menstrual cycles; (5) 70 to 90 percent of women who experience migraines note an improvement while pregnant, and many experience a worsening postpartum; and (6) after natural menopause, migraine activity decreases.

One theory about the hormone-migraine connection is that women who get migraine headaches have a special sensitivity that makes the blood vessels in their head respond dramatically to hormone changes. With the withdrawal of estrogen just before a woman's menstrual period, the blood vessels in her head constrict (become narrower), leading to intense pain. For some women, estrogen therapy via a patch seems to be most helpful because the patch provides a low, steady level of estrogen. But estrogen cannot be taken by all women with migraines, because of concerns about whether there may be some increased risk of stroke. Oral estrogen therapy or oral contraceptives, on the other hand, can make migraines worse for many women. Other preventive medications, such as ergot alkaloids, are available for women with particularly severe or long-lasting migraines. One study found that ergonovine (Ergotrate maleate), taken premenstrually, reduced the severity and duration of migraine attacks in about 60 percent of women.

Epilepsy

Premenstrual exacerbation of epilepsy is also quite common. By even the strictest definition, about 12 percent of women with epilepsy have most of their seizures clustered around their menstrual period, a condition called catamenial epilepsy. Women who have catamenial epilepsy usually experienced their first seizures at or near the time of their first menstrual period. This form of epilepsy is thought to be related to the body's reaction to falling levels of progesterone, which lowers the threshold for seizure activity.

Although catamenial epilepsy is specifically tied to the menstrual cycle, all types of epilepsy are exacerbated premenstrually. What further complicates the picture is that a woman's body metabolizes anticonvulsant medications differently premenstrually than at other times of the month. In fact, metabolism of these medications, which are designed to prevent or reduce seizures, is faster, which means the drug is not available in the body as long. This, in turn, means that there is a greater chance that seizures will occur. So not only is epilepsy exacerbated, the effectiveness of medication to prevent seizures is reduced. Ideal treatment, then, requires careful monitoring of blood levels of the medication, with supplemental medication given as needed during the luteal phase.

Asthma

As with migraine, the hormone connection with asthma is seen early. Asthma is equally common in boys and girls until puberty, after which asthma is more common in women than in men. Research shows that approximately 40 percent of women with asthma have PME, with increases in both the severity and the frequency of asthma attacks. Women with PME of asthma are more likely to be hospitalized for a severe asthma attack than women with asthma who don't show a premenstrual pattern of exacerbation. Understanding the connection between the menstrual cycle and asthma attack severity and frequency is key to prevention. Researchers are currently investigating preventive medications that can be taken on an intermittent basis. For example, in one study conducted by scientists in Israel, more than half the women with PME of asthma prevented exacerbations by using a long-acting bronchodilator during the ten days before menses.

Diabetes

Women with insulin-dependent diabetes tend to have a difficult time maintaining healthy blood sugar levels during their luteal phase. Insulin reactions and ketoacidosis, which can lead to coma or death, are more likely to occur premenstrually than at any other time of the month. The reasons why this happens are still unclear because estrogen and progesterone play a very limited role in metabolism. We recommend that every woman with diabetes track her blood glucose levels and look to see if glycemic control is worse premenstrually. If so, she should talk with her physician about the possibility of adjusting her insulin dose according to her menstrual cycle.

Irritable Bowel Syndrome

This common gastrointestinal disorder affects women between three and twenty times more often than it affects men. Irritable bowel syndrome (IBS) is not a serious disorder in that it doesn't progress and is never life threatening, but its symptoms—diarrhea and/or constipation, bloating, and abdominal pain—can range from barely noticeable to severe enough to disrupt a person's ability to function. Symptoms tend to increase premenstrually and around the time of ovulation. Although progesterone is known to have effects on the gastrointestinal system, exactly what happens to affect IBS premenstrually is not known. There are no medications currently available that are highly effective for treating IBS. The most common "treatment" is education about which foods might be more likely to trigger an episode of IBS and a recommendation to avoid those foods. Women with IBS may want to keep their diets particularly free of trigger foods premenstrually.

Eating Disorders

Overeating and bulimia are almost always exacerbated premenstrually. With food cravings and increased calorie intake being two possible symptoms of

PMDD, it's easy to see the link between the luteal phase and eating disorders. In women with bulimia, the urge to purge is strongest premenstrually. In fact, some women may only binge and purge during their worst premenstrual days.

Other disorders that have been demonstrated to show a cyclic worsening of symptoms in some women are fibromyalgia syndrome, multiple sclerosis, chronic fatigue syndrome, rheumatoid arthritis, and systemic lupus erythematosus. But these are just the disorders that have been studied. It is possible that eventually every disease will be shown to be susceptible to PME. The best recommendation now is to keep a symptoms diary, maintain an awareness of how your body feels throughout the month, and consult your physician if you notice cyclic changes. There may be ways to prevent or lessen these premenstrual effects for your particular disorder.

Psychological Disorder PME

Right from the beginning, Dr. Katharina Dalton, the physician who coined the term *premenstrual syndrome* (PMS), noted that women who have a serious psychiatric condition are more likely to be hospitalized the first couple of days before or during their menstrual periods than afterward. Premenstrual exacerbation of psychological and psychiatric disorders is very common. It is so common, in fact, that it can be difficult to distinguish "pure" PMDD or PMS from PME, if the underlying disorder is mild. Women with low-grade underlying depression or anxiety disorders have a certain steady-state level of dysphoria, which they get used to but which—like everything else—gets worse premenstrually.

As with physical symptoms, recognition of these disorders is key to proper treatment and future well-being. There is a phenomenon known to mental health professionals as the theory of "kindling." This theory suggests that every time we get depressed, our brains are affected in such a way that depression becomes more likely in the future. In effect, the brain "learns" the signature chemistry of depression and therefore can re-create it more easily. This is why it is easier to treat people experiencing their first-ever episode of depression, rather than long-standing depression. The brain is not as entrenched in its depression chemistry the first time as it is after a

The Stigma of Mental Illness

It wasn't that long ago that no one would speak the word *cancer.* We called it "the C word" or "the big C" because of the stigma that diagnosis held. Now, cancer survivors are rightfully celebrated, and a new cancer diagnosis is a call for social support and family togetherness.

Mental illness is a medical condition that is still highly stigmatized. In part, this is because of the images we hold in our imaginations from movies and television programs that tried to dramatize a story by exaggerating or misrepresenting mental illness. Also, it was not that long ago that people with severe mental illnesses were assumed to have a moral failing, not a medical illness, and were locked away. Plus, psychoactive drugs to treat mental illness have been around only a few decades. To this day, the thought of "crazy" people in "insane asylums" makes many people back away from any hint of mental illness.

The causes and mechanisms of mental illness are hidden and complex and therefore seem mysterious. We can't look inside a brain to see what causes mental illness the way we can look inside just about every other body part and see what is going wrong. The workings of the brain are at the molecular and cellular level—neurotransmitters helping nerve cells communicate with one another. It is harder, therefore, to believe in mental illnesses as something physical. We can't hold the evidence in our hands or see it on an x-ray. Still, the changes are physical changes.

There are signs, tiny inklings, that the tide is turning for mental illness. With the advent of fluoxetine, there was, for the first time, an effective treatment for depression that didn't cause onerous side effects, was much safer to use than previous agents, and didn't require frequent visits to a psychiatrist. (Originally fluoxetine was sold exclusively under the brand name Prozac, but it is now also available as a generic.) Newer antidepressant medications are so easy to use that general practitioners are comfortable diagnosing and treating their patients with depression. Plus, consumer advertising has helped make several psychotropic medications commonly known by their brand names, effectively changing the stigma of depression via familiar television commercials. The net effect was that between 1987 and 1997, the number of people in the United States treated for depression rose from 1.7 million to 6.3 million, not necessarily because more people were getting depressed, but because more people were willing to seek help for their feelings of depression. Tak-

continued

The Stigma of Mental Illness (continued)

ing an antidepressant is no longer broadly stigmatized. In some circles, Prozac and other antidepressants are now appropriate topics of conversation at dinner parties and even in offices.

Eventually, this normalization will spread to other mental illnesses. Already, television commercials are introducing the public to other disorders they were likely unfamiliar with, including PMDD, generalized anxiety disorder, panic disorder, and social anxiety disorder. Although some people argue that this makes people more likely to seek treatment for a nonexistent illness, others believe that awareness can only bring benefits. The greater the awareness, the less "different" or "crazy" we'll feel, whatever our symptoms, and the more comfortable we'll be asking for help. Admitting to and getting treatment for any mental illness should not have to be a matter of courage.

few episodes. Early identification and treatment of depression is key to preventing recurrences. Although many women find it difficult to admit to and seek help for depression, proper treatment is critical to decrease the potential for lifetime recurrence of mood disorders. If, after keeping the symptoms diary for two months, you discover that you have some mood symptoms that don't entirely go away after you get your menstrual period, it is highly recommended that you talk with your doctor about the possibility of having an underlying mood disorder that gets worse premenstrually. You and your physician can work out the kind of treatment that solves your health problem all month long.

Depression

Premenstrual symptoms are closely related to other affective disorders, especially depression. In general, women have a higher incidence of depression than men at every point in their adult lives except old age. In their lifetimes, 21 percent of women will have at least one episode of major depression. It has been estimated that about half of all women with PMDD have a history of major depressive disorder (MDD). One study from London found that 77 percent of women with PMDD had experienced some major affective or psychiatric disorder, compared with only 17 percent of women without PMDD. The two disorders can be so closely aligned that studies were conducted early on to determine whether they are a single disorder or two separate entities. The results showed that even after depression was successfully treated, premenstrual symptoms remained, putting them in a class of their own.

As with physical disorders, PME makes everything worse for women with depression. Women with depression are more likely to be hospitalized for their depression premenstrually than at any other time of the month. And among women who are suicidal, more suicide attempts are made premenstrually or during menstruation.

In an interesting twist, some researchers suggest that PMDD may actually predispose a woman to future episodes of full-blown major depression. A small preliminary study showed that a woman with PMDD is fourteen times more likely to have an episode of major depression than a woman without PMDD. The likely reason for this goes back to the theory of kindling, that women become sensitized to the biochemical changes that occur each month when they have premenstrual depression and eventually become at risk for depression throughout the month. This is another reason why appropriate treatment is so important. If "toughing out" premenstrual symptoms predisposes you to other disorders, then not seeking help is a little like ignoring a dirty cut. Sure, it seems harmless now, but if infection takes hold, you'll wish you hadn't ignored it.

What does this mean for treatment? For PME of depression, women need to be treated with antidepressant medications all month long, not just during the luteal phase. Sometimes the depression is difficult to recognize, particularly if it is a chronic low-grade depression. Because of the length of time women with that diagnosis have been depressed, they may have gotten to a point where they can manage their symptoms, except premenstrually. Taking medication every day, with a possible increase in medication premenstrually, can help keep the PME in check.

Seasonal Affective Disorder

Seasonal affective disorder (SAD) is a cyclic form of depression that occurs most commonly in the winter months. Symptoms are thought to be triggered by a lack of sunlight as daylight hours get shorter in winter. This affects our internal body clock, which in turn affects hormone production and secretion. (See Chapter 10 for more information about the body clock and its relation to PMDD.) Symptoms typically include sadness, lethargy, excess sleepiness, and carbohydrate cravings. Because of the cyclic nature of SAD and because its symptoms are remarkably similar to those of PMDD, it was logical to examine the relationship between the two disorders. Studies have shown that about 40 percent of women with PMDD also experience seasonal affect changes. Scientists speculate that the two disorders might be linked by a common dysfunction in the body's serotonin system. Clinically, this may mean that women with SAD may only experience premenstrual symptoms during the winter months, or that their symptoms get noticeably worse in the winter months.

Anxiety Disorders

The term *anxiety disorders* encompasses generalized anxiety disorder, panic disorder, social anxiety disorder, obsessive-compulsive disorder, posttraumatic stress disorder, and other conditions. As with depression, PME of anxiety disorders is very common. Studies show that between 30 and 60 percent of women with PMDD also report having an anxiety disorder.

But the relationship is a little more complicated. It has been suggested that there may be a biological link between anxiety disorders and PMDD. The evidence for this comes from what are known as "challenge studies." In these studies, scientists attempt to induce panic attacks in women with PMDD by using the same stimuli they use to induce panic attacks in people with panic disorder. The theory is that if panic attacks can be induced in women with PMDD (who are free of any anxiety disorder) by the same stimulus that induces panic attacks in women with panic disorder, then both disorders may be caused by similar physiologic sensitivities. Indeed, studies have shown that women with PMDD are much more likely to respond to the stimulus challenge with a panic attack than are women without PMDD. This may be one explanation why some women with PMDD respond well to treatment with medications designed to reduce anxiety.

5

What Does PMDD Feel Like?

WHILE WRITING this book, we interviewed several women with severe premenstrual syndrome (PMS), premenstrual exacerbation (PME), or premenstrual dysphoric disorder (PMDD) to hear their stories firsthand. We've included four of the stories here. There are striking similarities in how they describe their symptoms, but each woman has a slightly different story to tell. Each woman talks about her personal pain and how her premenstrual disorder affected her personal and work relationships. Perhaps you can hear your own story echoed here.

Although many of the women we interviewed are currently taking medication for their symptoms, we did not specifically seek out these stories. Perhaps the women who are taking medication are those who recognized their problem and therefore sought help from a doctor. Perhaps some women only feel comfortable telling their stories once their symptoms are under control. Our intent was to paint a picture of what PMDD feels like from the inside. These are their stories, in their own words.

Bonnie, age 38

Bonnie, a working mother of two girls, has what could be called "classic" PMDD, with a spike pattern of symptoms. Like many women, her symptoms worsened after each pregnancy.

Ever since my early twenties, I've noticed some type of PMS. After I had my first daughter seven years ago, I noticed all my symptoms becoming worse—irritability, loss of patience, being overly sensitive, and being highly emotional. I would cry at the drop of a hat. My husband noticed the difference, but we never really discussed it. He never put it together that it was in any way related to my menstrual cycle. He just assumed that with the new baby, sometimes my disposition would change.

At that time, it was manageable. It really didn't cause any problems between us. Every now and then, he'd say, "Whoa, what happened to you?" But at that time it was not so severe that it overly bothered me. I made a concerted effort, when it was getting close to my period, to try and mentally override it. And I read anything that I could find about PMS in the magazines, and if there were suggestions about what to try, I would try them. I tried them all. And everything I tried, I tried for a minimum of about four months. I tried calcium and magnesium supplements because I heard they helped. They didn't. I tried exercise and meditation. I tried changing my diet, but one article would say eat a diet high in complex carbohydrates, another would say eat a diet low in carbohydrates. I tried them both. I tried black cohosh. I would go to the health food store or the vitamin store and ask, "What have you got?" I tried aromatherapy. Everything smelled nice, but it didn't do anything to change my disposition.

Irritability and other symptoms started becoming a real problem after the birth of my second daughter, which was about two and a half years later. I think my husband attributed my difficulties to having another baby. But it wasn't all the time. I could time it down to the seven days before my period would start. And every day would just become worse and worse during those seven days. Every day of that week, I was like a spring being wound tighter and tighter. And that last day before I would get my period, the spring was just a little too tight and it went.

The thing that really made me notice how bad it was getting was the yelling. I'm generally a very even-keeled person. I didn't grow up in a household where there was ever any yelling. My parents never yelled. That's not to say we didn't have a cross word here and there, but there was never a raised voice. That just wasn't done. The week before my period, I would find myself yelling and screaming at my children, at the dog, at my husband. Something as minor as the kids not getting their shoes on fast enough, or just a comment that my husband would make that normally, during any other week of the month, would just be swept away and not even thought about.

It came out as anger, oversensitivity, crying jags, self-doubt. It got to a point where I was just dreading that week. I would start the countdown early—OK, I've got two more weeks of being normal. Once I got to those last seven days, I would try to withdraw from my family to keep them out of the line of fire. I didn't get married and have children to avoid them, but during that time I would avoid them. I would just go out into the yard and pull dead flowers off of plants.

And I would hate myself. The looks, especially from my kids, the looks on their faces after I would yell. Knowing that that's not how you treat children. I never did any name-calling or anything that would be that hurtful. I was cognizant of that. But while I was yelling, I knew that what I was doing was wrong. I knew that I was being irrational, but there was nothing I could do to stop it. That week of the month, I would wonder, why did I have children? Why did I get married? It would have been better off for everyone if I had just remained alone in my life.

My husband didn't realize that it was tied to my cycles. And I was very reluctant to tell him that it was associated with my period because I didn't want it thrown back at me at any other week in the month, at any time that we had just a normal disagreement about something. I couldn't stand to hear him say, "Oh, is it that time?" Plus, I didn't want to really admit that it was something I couldn't handle. Every woman gets her period. Why am I whacked out? Why is everyone else handling it and not me? I did not want to make that admission to him.

It got to a point where I could predict the night before that my period would come. I didn't have a regular twenty-eight-day cycle, it was between twenty-four and thirty days, but I would know the night before I would get my period because I would be emotionally raw. I'm the type of person that normally will do anything to avoid an argument. But the night before I would get my period, without variance, I would wind up picking a fight with my husband. It would end with me screaming, crying to the point of hyperventilation, and he would be looking at me like a deer in headlights. It would be over something insignificant, something like what to watch on TV. Something as innocuous as that. It would pretty much end with him saying, "What do you want from me?" And me, hyperventilating and crying and just going to bed, both of us wondering what was going on. Then

I'd wake up in the morning and there would be my period, and I would feel normal. That very day. Everything would be fine, aside from guilt feelings about my behavior the previous week.

The worst point was when my husband and I had a business trip for his company to Hawaii. The last night that we were there, I can't remember exactly what the argument was about, but I definitely instigated it. He was completely innocent, but he just got blasted. We had just had three or four great days in Hawaii, but that ruined the whole trip. I knew that I was completely and totally in the wrong—and there are few occasions when I will admit that I am completely and totally in the wrong. I knew, but I just could not back off from it. I can remember during the argument he said, "I don't like what is going on here, and I'm tired of it." I was never fearful that he would leave me—our marriage is way too strong for that. But to me, that was the jab that I needed to realize that I obviously couldn't do this by myself.

I was completely unaware that there was anything, any treatment, I hadn't tried. A few years ago, my doctor called me at home with some test results from my annual exam. Before we got off the phone, he said, "Is there anything else I can do for you today?" I'd just been thinking that morning, OK, I've got another two weeks before all hell breaks loose again. Offhandedly I said, "Well, if you've got anything new for PMS, I'd certainly be interested in trying it." I said it in kind of a joking manner, but he stopped cold and asked me what my symptoms were and what was going on. We made an appointment for me to see him the next day to talk about a new medication.

That night, I told my husband that all the craziness was connected to my menstrual cycle. His reaction was, "Jeez, why did you wait so long? If the doctor can help, why did you wait so long?" I warned him not to use that as ammunition at any time in the future and that it was hard enough for me to admit to needing the help.

When I went to see my doctor, after the exam and the history, he said that I had all the classic earmarks of PMDD. He explained what PMDD was, and he told me that the U.S. Food and Drug Administration (FDA) had approved a new drug. He said he wanted to make sure that I didn't have any qualms about taking an antidepressant for this kind of condition. He explained about serotonin and how it's not all in your head, it's a physical thing going on in your body. At that point, I was at the end of my rope. If he had told me that standing on my head for three hours a day would change it, I would have done it. I would have done anything. He gave me samples and sent me home. Two and a half weeks later, when I got my period, I was shocked. No symptoms beforehand. No week of hell. It was that fast.

I've been taking medication for two years now. I do not feel the tension. I'm not hyperemotional. I no longer yell. But I'm not a Stepford wife or anything. It wasn't like being on the medication wiped out all of my emotions. Things that would upset me the normal weeks of the month still upset me. I still get angry at my husband, I still get angry at my kids, but I do it in a productive manner, in a way that is not hurtful to anybody, and in a way that I do not hate myself afterward. Now I feel like myself four weeks of the month instead of three.

Caren, age 43

Caren seems to have typical PMDD, with clear interference with personal, work, and social relationships. She has rearranged her life to accommodate the disorder.

When I think back, I remember having symptoms as far back as adolescence. I had difficult teenage years, to say the least, and I wonder now how much of that was due to premenstrual stuff and how much was because of normal teenage stuff. The problem is, I didn't recognize it for what it was for a long, long time. I'm embarrassed to say it took me until my late thirties before I understood the correlation between my periods and "the crazies." I just thought I was semi-insane. When I got my first job after college, I got one week of vacation and one week of sick time per year. I remember talking with other women at the company and asking them how they did it. I needed at least one day in bed each month because of how bad I felt. They looked at me like I was crazy, and it made me *feel* crazy.

Because I hadn't figured it all out, anything structured was really hard for me. Work was a chore, even though I loved my job. And it was hard for me to commit to even fun stuff, like volunteer work or parties or vacations, because I never knew when the crazies would hit. I would make plans to go out but cancel at the last minute because I couldn't bring myself to go. Of course, I couldn't say why—that I was feeling so horrible emotionally—so I made up excuses that I thought made me sound like a more stable person.

My symptoms are all over the place. Irritability big-time. Ask my poor husband. The guy is a saint. I'll snap at him for no reason. He could ask where the crackers are and I'll go off on why he should know where the crackers are and that I shouldn't have to be at his beck-and-call to find crackers whenever he wants them. That kind of stupid stuff. He has to walk on eggshells for a couple days, for the two or three days before my period. I know when I'm saying it that it is nasty, but the emotions boil over, totally uncontrollable.

I also get into a lot of self-loathing. That time before my period, my body looks ugly, my face looks ugly, my hair, my clothes, my house. I'm stupid, I'm lazy, I'm a failure. It doesn't help that I get really, really bloated, to the point where my pants don't fit. I have two sets of clothes now—one for most of the month and ones with bigger waists for my premenstrual days. Of course, that just makes me more irritable and depressed. The very day I get my period, poof, I'm normal again. The sun is shining, life is good, and my husband can breathe again.

When I finally figured out that this was all related to my periods, I felt, well, relief. It was like I could say, "OK, it's just a physical reaction. I'm not losing my mind." I started arranging my life to make things easier on me. I took a job with flextime so I could choose the hours and days I work. I don't schedule any important meetings or parties the week before my period. I once made the vice president of a company reschedule a lunch meeting because the date she suggested fell the day before I was due to get my period. I claimed to be out of town, got the meeting moved, and then didn't answer my phone for two days in case someone at the company called. Scheduling vacations is an ordeal. I have to count out the days in advance, add in a fudge factor in case one of my periods comes a little early or a little late, add in the number of days we'll be away—and then hope I got it right by the time the trip comes along.

As I've gotten older, the symptoms actually seem to be getting worse. More intense. I finally talked with my OB/GYN this past year, and she suggested medication. I know other women who are on it. It helped them and it would probably help me, but I decided not to take it. I don't like the idea of the types of sexual side effects she said could happen. Hey, my libido has been in the pits for the past few years anyway; I don't want to take anything that will make it worse. Plus, I'm almost at menopause. I figure if I've gotten this far without medication, I can make it another few years. I'm exercising a lot now and taking calcium, and I'm learning to meditate. It's a little better, but I still feel it. On a scale of zero to ten, with ten being totally out of control, I've gone from about an eight to a five.

Probably the biggest help was just recognizing it for what it was. Now I can talk with my husband, let him know to prepare himself, and then try to be aware of my actions. And while opening up to my girlfriends, coming clean about why I cancel out so much, I found out that one of them has the same thing. Now we call each other when we're feeling bad and laugh and cry on the phone, talk about how horrible we feel, talk about the latest irritation, make jokes about being crazy. And it all seems a little less . . . I feel reconnected.

Marisa, age 32

Marisa is a single professional. She appears to have PME—premenstrual exacerbation of an underlying depressive disorder. Although her medication keeps her feeling well most of the time, she still has breakthrough symptoms that occur premenstrually. But because of her continuous treatment, her premenstrual symptoms are now manageable.

I hadn't had any emotional symptoms that were that drastic with PMS or PMDD—I didn't even know what they were. Not until two and a half years ago. I had a job that was a little stressful. And for about three months, I chalked it up to that. What happened was my body just really started to change—physically, emotionally, mentally, every single way. One day, I was at work and cried in the middle of my office in front of my boss. It was a stressful situation about something that I had to do at work, but I have never cried at the office in my life. I'm completely different at work than at home. I mean, I'm emotional at home. But at work, I'd never been like that. I literally lost it. I remember going to the bathroom and having to compose myself. I was overwrought emotionally, and that led into these physical feelings of exhaustion. I was so tired.

This is a good time to be talking about this because I'm about four days away from my period right now, so I not only recall it, I'm living it right now. It's utter fatigue. I am completely and utterly exhausted to the point where I can actually lie and watch TV or lie in bed for hours and hours and hours. Anybody who knows me can tell you that that just doesn't happen when I'm not premenstrual. Normally, I get bored and restless, and I have to eat while I'm watching TV, or jump up every five minutes. But about a week, sometimes a week and a half, before my period I'm just utterly exhausted.

So after crying in front of my boss, I got fired. I don't know if it was because of my emotionality or not. I think that may have been a factor. The guy I worked for was older, sixty-five maybe, not somebody who would understand me very readily as a young woman. Also, my tendency is to be more flippant and more reactionary when I'm about to get my period, even at work. I also think the job wasn't right for me. It may be coincidence, I don't know, but I did end up losing that job, and that was all around the same time. "We don't think this is the right fit," they said. They asked me to go.

That's when I knew I had to get help. I went to my doctor, and she diagnosed me. "You have severe PMS/PMDD." She said it's sometimes hard to tell the distinction. She asked if I'd be interested in medication. I asked what kind, and that prompted this whole discussion about how long my symptoms had been going on and what they were like. At that time, I would say it had been happening for about four months. It took me a while to get clued in that it was happening the same time every month.

The lowest time I can remember was when I was curled up in a fetal position on the bed, laughing and crying, and then laughing and then crying. The littlest thing would set me off. Screaming in rage at somebody or something, and then crying. It would go back and forth between yelling, ranting and raving, and feeling remorseful and guilty and sad and then sobbing. And then laughing at myself because I felt like such an idiot. It ran the gamut. Part of me was thinking about how ridiculous it was, and the other part would think, "Oh my God, you're losing your mind." I really thought I was going crazy sometimes.

That in itself was exhausting, not to mention the physical effects. There's always one day that's the worst. I get obsessive. I don't know how else to explain it. I mean, fixated on a depressing thought, and it will not go away. It usually comes from something unreal, almost paranoid. It escalates or snowballs into this ridiculous huge thing. The thing I'm thinking of in particular is my ex-boyfriend and I got into an argument, and I was so convinced, all because of this dumb little thing, all of which stems from me being a freak. I was convinced he was going to leave; he was going to break up with me. All the next day at work, I couldn't do any work. I was in the bathroom constantly, not to get sick or anything like that, I was just crying, and going in there to think and sit by myself. And when I was back in my office, I would call him on the phone. I probably called him ten times that day about absolutely nothing.

This has absolutely affected my relationships. The relationship with my ex-boyfriend, for example. This happened four months in a row, and he had no clue why I was flipping out at certain times. He ended up not being that understanding a person, so he never really got it anyway. Even currently, I live with my new boyfriend now. We've been together for about a year and a half. He's a friend, he knows all about me, he knows this is real. But at the same time, it is very exasperating for him. The physical stuff, the cramps, and even the lethargy don't bother him, but the bitchiness is not pleasant.

When my doctor suggested Prozac, I was surprised, but I wasn't scared off. I had a history of depression. About two years earlier, my therapist had put me on Prozac. It virtually saved my life. I have no fear of therapy or medication. I thought that might be what was going on again, that I was getting depressed. But it was just the timing. It was so predictable, and I finally figured it out. My doctor put me on a really low dosage of Prozac—I'm still on it—10 milligrams. I'm a little emotional, still a little crazy every month, but nothing I can't handle. It's sort of gone from this uncontrollable level to a level that I can manage, one where I just get sort of weepy and cranky, and my food cravings are there.

Initially, my doctor said I could take the medication a week before my period, or I could take it all the time. Since I was prone to depression in my life—I'd had more than one episode—I decided to take it every day. It's been really good. I feel better throughout the month. I haven't been depressed, the really bad stuff, for a while. I had touches of it more frequently before than I do now that I'm on the medication. It's evened me out. I really don't have a problem taking this drug—I don't care if I'm on it the rest of my life.

Faith, age 27

Faith has classic PMDD symptoms with premenstrual and menstrual migraine. She's being treated for premenstrual symptoms, but the migraine headaches remain a problem.

I first noticed problems when I was twelve. It was around then that I used to always get headaches. I didn't really know what they were. But I sort of figured out as I got a little bit older and did more reading that they were migraines. I started tracking them. I get two every month. One comes two days before I bleed, and then one comes two days after I start bleeding. It was mainly migraines for a long time. I didn't notice mood changes so much, until . . . I think that to notice mood changes you have to have someone else point it out to you. So I think it wasn't until I was in college and I was in relationships and people would be like, "OK, what is wrong with you?"

Three or four days before I bleed, my brain starts going really, really fast. I can tell that it's sort of like spinning almost, so many thoughts just going. The really bad things stick, and they sort of pile up, and I think *paranoid* is the best word. Like I think my partner—I'm a lesbian—I'm convinced my partner really doesn't love me, that we're just sort of together, and she doesn't like me, and this is bad and that's bad. And I know . . . I can sit there and think, OK, this stuff is all crazy, and I am just crazy right now, but I can't stop it. And so, I can even warn her and say, "My mind is starting to spin, so I'm not really responsible for anything that happens in the next forty-eight hours." It's like, before I started taking medicine, it was . . . on a scheduled basis, I would try to end our relationship. And I did a pretty good job a few times, almost.

There would always be one particular thing that would be the really bad thing that was going on right then, and I would expect for her to know what was wrong, and then when she didn't, then that obviously meant that she didn't care at all. There was always some big blowup. There was some sort of fight. And then there was always crying. And then we'd make up right away, especially since she knows I'm sort of insane at that time and that none of it is real. After the big crying thing happens, everything sort of goes away, and I generally don't really remember what it was that I was so mad about anyway. It's just gone. Usually, four days beforehand is when my head starts spinning, and then the next day is usually when the big ugliness happens. The day before, or the same day as the ugliness, is when I'll get a really bad migraine. It's always one or two days, usually two days, before I bleed. I also get the standard bloating stuff, but I think everyone gets that.

Back in April, I went to the doctor and got Sarafem. But I was not doing such a good job of keeping track of the calendar, and I would wait until my head started spinning to take it. And so sometimes I wouldn't really be paying attention, and I'd be sitting there at my desk reading E-mail and I would have tears streaming down my face, and there wasn't any real reason, nothing was really sad. Then of course someone asks you what's wrong and it makes you really cry. I think on a couple of different occasions I've called my partner and asked her, "Can you bring my medicine to work?" So I get started on it, and it's just amazing how it slows my head down, and I feel like a normal human being.

I decided I was going to start taking the medicine on day 25, before my head was spinning at all. I did have a day where I felt a little glum, but glum is OK. You can live with glum. But it was just amazing. I still get the migraine, but I'm thinking about talking to my doctor about a migraine medication.

My partner can definitely relate better [than a man might]. For the past three, maybe four months, we've both started bleeding within twelve hours of each other. She has, I guess, what you would consider to be standard PMS grumpiness. She's not a joy to be around, either. She has general irritability. Small things that happen during the day, small things that might be an inconvenience become more than just an inconvenience. They make her really, really angry. I know what her normal personality is, and I know when it's just something like that. You can't just say to someone, "Hey, you're just doing this because of hormones," so you just try going to a different room or something. The difference between the way it affects her and the way it affects me is I get "psychotic." Normally I'm really . . . I think *perky* is a good word to describe me. That time of the month, I'm just . . . I'm horrible. I hear things coming out of my mouth, and I think, why am I saying this? This is insane. But there's no stopping. I've been on the medicine almost the whole time we've been in sync. Of course now, my personal opinion is I've been almost normal and she's been the crazy one.

It doesn't really affect my work because I tell everyone about it. I'm a teary person anyway. My whole family is teary. So anything, happy, sad, exciting, whatever, tears come to my face. Everyone sort of expects me to be teary. I don't have any qualms about telling people that I take the medicine, either. I know how much it has helped me. I sort of feel like I work better during that week, but maybe it's because the medicine calms my head down in general. I've noticed that in the past couple of months I've gotten more work accomplished during that week than I have any other week— sort of like power surges.

My mother is the same way. She's never done anything about it, but I've talked to my dad since then about it. I just really, really feel bad for my dad, because growing up, there were two of us in the house. I remember my dad just going in and closing the door. Mom and I would have some serious girl-shrieking going on. I didn't understand what was going on then, but it's the same thing, all the nonlogical thinking.

What I'd like other women to know is just if they think something is going on, it really is. They need to look into trying to help themselves. It's a quarter of your life you spend feeling it, having this horrible thing, and then recovering from it. And then trying to mend whatever you broke.

Part II

TREATING PREMENSTRUAL DISORDERS

6

Serotonin Reuptake Inhibitors

The way I see it, if you've got a vitamin deficiency, you take your vitamin. If you've got hay fever, you take your allergy pill. I view taking medication as, I've got a serotonin problem. For one week out of the month, my hormones send me out of whack, and this is what needs to be done to correct it, just as you would for any other condition.

—Bonnie

In the summer of 2000, the U.S. Food and Drug Administration (FDA) approved the use of fluoxetine hydrochloride (generic Prozac) for the treatment of premenstrual dysphoric disorder (PMDD). This medication, sold under the brand name Sarafem, was the first drug approved for this use after clinical trials showed that it was an effective treatment, capable of reducing or eliminating all premenstrual symptoms in a majority of women who used it. Official approval meant that the FDA finally caught up with what clinicians had known for years—that there was a class of medications that could successfully treat the intense symptoms of PMDD, premenstrual exacerbation (PME), and premenstrual syndrome (PMS). The approval also created a renewed sense of hope in women who had sought medical treatment for their premenstrual disorders earlier but found that none had been available. In 2002, sertraline (Zoloft) was also approved by the FDA for this use, and other medications may also be submitted for approval once clinical trials documenting their effectiveness for premenstrual symptoms are completed.

Both fluoxetine and sertraline belong to a class of drugs known as selective serotonin reuptake inhibitors (SSRIs), a group of medications primarily thought of and used as antidepressants, but which are also effective in the treatment of a broad spectrum of anxiety disorders. To understand how and why they work for women with premenstrual symptoms, you need to understand a little about brain chemistry and emotions.

Basic Brain Chemistry

Everything we do, think, or feel is controlled by the brain's intricate network of nerves. Nerve pathways are sometimes referred to as the brain's "wiring," but that analogy can be misleading. With a wired electrical circuit, the wires are all connected so that they form a single, continuous pathway. As electricity flows through the wiring, any break in the circuit will disrupt the flow and stop the electrical signal. Nerve cells (also called neurons), however, are not all connected. They have tiny gaps between them called synapses. To keep the flow of communication going from one nerve cell to the next, the signal must cross this synapse. This is done by means of chemical messengers called neurotransmitters.

As a neuronal impulse travels down the nerve cell, it eventually comes to a dead end where the nerve stops, also known as the terminal. Beyond the terminal is the synapse, and then another one or more nerves begin. The arrival of the neuronal impulse at the nerve terminal sets in motion a chemical change that allows neurotransmitters, which are stored in that terminal end of the nerve, to be released into the synapse. The neurotransmitters cross the synaptic gap and bind to special receptors (like tiny docking ports) at the end of the next nerve or set of nerves. Once the receptors are filled, chemical changes set off a neuronal impulse in the next set of cells. In effect, the binding of the neurotransmitters to the receptors in the second set of nerve cells is like completing a circuit so that signals can continue through the wiring.

The neurotransmitters don't stay locked in the receptors. They are removed by one of three mechanisms: (1) the neurotransmitters are broken down by enzymes, (2) the neurotransmitters simply move away by diffusion, or (3) the neurotransmitters are sucked back into the original nerve cell—the one that released them in the first place—in a process called reuptake.

So now the name of this class of medications begins to make sense. Selective serotonin reuptake inhibitors selectively block (or inhibit) the reuptake of a specific neurotransmitter called serotonin, without having much effect on other neurotransmitters. The overall result is an increase in the amount of serotonin in the brain. This serotonin-enhancing effect has been used to treat a number of conditions in which serotonin deficiencies are suspected, including depression, generalized anxiety disorder, social anxiety disorder, posttraumatic stress disorder, and obsessive-compulsive disorder. Other classes of antidepressant medications affect levels of other neurotransmitters, such as norepinephrine or dopamine, or may nonselectively block the breakdown of all neurotransmitters.

The Case for SSRIs

When serotonin is blocked experimentally, leading to decreased levels of this neurotransmitter in the brain, both laboratory animals and people experience heightened irritability, aggression, and a craving (or preferred feeding, in the case of animals) for carbohydrates—the same symptoms experienced by women with PMDD. The similarity is striking. These and other studies led scientists to believe that PMDD is caused by some dysfunction that results in women having lower levels of brain serotonin. Indeed, studies have shown that women with PMDD have lower amounts of serotonin in their bloodstream compared with women without premenstrual symptoms.

This observation spurred researchers to look at the effects of serotonin-enhancing medications on premenstrual symptoms. The first SSRI, fluoxetine hydrochloride (Prozac), was approved for use in the United States in 1987. And the first study showing the effectiveness of this agent for relieving premenstrual symptoms was published in 1990. The impetus for that research was based on the observations of Dr. Elias Eriksson and his colleagues at Göteborg University in Sweden. They found that one antidepressant from the older class of medications called tricyclic antidepressants helped relieve premenstrual symptoms. That tricyclic antidepressant, clomipramine, was the only tricyclic antidepressant to have a significant impact on serotonin levels *and* the only one shown to alleviate premenstrual symptoms.

In the first study of the effects of fluoxetine on premenstrual symptoms, Dr. Andrea B. Stone of the University of Massachusetts Medical School and her colleagues found that more than 80 percent of women treated with the SSRI felt better after treatment. These early studies confirmed that the serotonin system was somehow involved in premenstrual disorders. Since then, many more studies have investigated the effects of SSRIs, and in virtually all of them women had significantly fewer premenstrual symptoms while taking medication.

The landmark study (by virtue of its size and design) of the effects of an SSRI on premenstrual symptoms was published in 1995 in the *Journal of the American Medical Association* by Dr. Meir Steiner of McMaster University in Ontario, Canada, and his colleagues. In this study, more than 300 women with prospectively diagnosed PMDD (or "late luteal phase dysphoric disorder," as it was called when the study was conducted) received one of three different treatments for six menstrual cycles: (1) a placebo, a "fake" pill that does not affect physiology; (2) 20 milligrams of fluoxetine daily; or (3) 60 milligrams of fluoxetine daily. All women were regularly evaluated for premenstrual symptom severity.

The researchers found that fluoxetine helped relieve symptoms almost immediately—within the first menstrual cycle after starting treatment. More than half the women who received fluoxetine, in either dosage, had moderate to marked improvement in symptoms throughout the six months of the study. Here, "moderate improvement" was defined as 50 percent improvement over how the women typically felt, and "marked improvement" was defined as 75 percent improvement over what was typical. The response was approximately double the improvement felt by women who took the placebo pill. (Placebos always have some initial effect, in part because of optimism, attention to the problem, and the relief of finally having a treatment available. This is called the "placebo effect," and it usually wears off within a couple of months. The effect seen with serotonin-enhancing medications does not wear off like the placebo effect does.)

It seems logical that antidepressant medications would alleviate emotional symptoms. After all, they are designed to help people with depression; but SSRIs also improve premenstrual physical symptoms. Along with improvements in depression, mood swings, and irritability, studies have shown that many women who take SSRIs also have less discomfort from breast tenderness and bloating and have reduced food cravings. These and other studies have left little doubt that serotonin is a major player in the cause of premenstrual symptoms, and that SSRIs are a valuable treatment option. But the research didn't end there.

Medication Timing

One of the most fascinating—and puzzling—aspects of SSRI treatment of premenstrual symptoms is how quickly the medication starts to work in women with PMDD. When SSRIs are given to people who are depressed, it takes three to six weeks for the medication to start to work. But when the same medication is given to a woman with PMDD, she usually will feel a difference very quickly. In fact, some studies show that the medication can start having an effect within one or two days. Clinically, women say the same thing. By the time they seek medical treatment for their severe symptoms, many women are so discouraged by the lack of improvement after trying self-help treatments that they don't expect the medication to work, either. When their next menstrual period comes with none of their usual premenstrual symptoms, they report being shocked and delighted. This quick mode of action may be due to different mechanisms involved in causing and treating depression and premenstrual symptoms.

When a person takes the first dose of an SSRI, serotonin levels begin to increase over the next twelve to twenty-four hours. This is not enough to treat a major depression, but it seems to be enough to relieve symptoms in women with PMS or PMDD. Treatment of depression involves a process called down-regulation of serotonin receptors in the brain, in which nerve cells change their sensitivity to serotonin in response to increased serotonin levels. This process takes four to six weeks in most people. Alleviation of premenstrual symptoms does not seem to require down-regulation but is brought about simply by the increase in serotonin. This difference provides further proof that women with PMS or PMDD are not simply depressed. This condition is different from depression. There is something else going on, something that makes the drug act differently (and quicker) for premenstrual symptoms than it does for depression.

Once this difference was noticed, researchers began another line of testing. Scientists speculated that, given how quickly the drugs work, perhaps women could take the medication only when they need it. Studies were done to determine whether women need to take SSRIs continuously throughout the month (continuous dosing), or if they could get just as much relief by taking the medication only during the luteal phase, when they experience symptoms (intermittent dosing). Nearly all studies have shown that intermittent dosing with an SSRI is as effective—if not more effective—than continuous dosing in controlling or relieving premenstrual symptoms in women with just PMDD or PMS. Women with PME, however, will get better results by taking medication continuously throughout the month, although some may need to increase their dose in the luteal phase to keep their worst symptoms under control.

All of the research to date on intermittent dosing has been done using medication through the whole luteal phase (the second half of the menstrual cycle). In clinical practice, however, many women effectively use "symptom phase" dosing. This means that they begin taking an SSRI when they start having symptoms and stop as soon as menstrual bleeding starts. Women with the spike pattern of symptoms (see Chapter 3), who experience symptoms only the week before getting their menstrual periods, often do well if they start taking the medication seven days before they expect their period to begin and stop taking it the day menstrual bleeding starts. Women with the peak and spike or peak and mesa patterns, in which there are some symptoms midcycle at ovulation and more intense symptoms just before getting their menstrual periods, often do well if they start taking medication throughout the entire luteal phase—beginning about two weeks after menstrual bleeding begins and ending the day after menstrual bleeding begins. Women with the butte pattern don't do well with intermittent dosing and should take medication continuously throughout the month. Clinically, some women say that they can never remember exactly where in the cycle they are. They use their symptoms as a reminder, take the medication at the first sign of trouble, and usually get relief within one or two days.

Intermittent dosing, when appropriate, has significant benefits beyond relief of premenstrual symptoms. The primary benefit, obviously, is cost. Taking medication for only part of the month is less expensive than taking medication every day. Cost should not guide your decision—that should be based on your pattern of symptoms—but it is an advantage for some women. Second, SSRIs used for the treatment of depression have a tendency to stop working after they've been taken for a long period of time, a phenomenon colorfully known as "poop-out." No one knows why this occurs, and for any depressed individual, no one knows how long the medication will remain effective. Poop-out has not been reported when SSRIs are used for treatment of PMS or PMDD, but if that potential exists, then it is hoped that intermittent dosing will delay or even eliminate the poop-out phase. (Not to worry—there are several SSRI medications available. Evidence suggests that if a person with depression has a medication that poops out, switching to a different SSRI will likely relieve symptoms again.)

A third benefit is reduced side effects. All medications carry some risk of side effects. Although SSRIs are usually well tolerated by most people who take them, there are side effects. By taking the medication only part of the month, women are likely to experience fewer side effects thanks to the reduced number of days they are exposed to the medication. Since the drug is in their system a shorter amount of time, they may even avoid certain side effects altogether. (See the next section for more information about side effects.)

In short, SSRIs are a targeted treatment for PMDD, PME, or severe PMS. SSRIs are, currently, the best medical treatment available for these disorders. A 2000 review and meta-analysis of all studies then published about SSRIs in the management of premenstrual symptoms found that SSRIs are effective in controlling both emotional and physical symptoms (although the effect on emotional symptoms was stronger), that intermittent dosing is as effective as continuous dosing in women with PMDD or severe PMS, that side effects are generally mild, and that the studies are free from bias, even when funded by pharmaceutical companies. And studies that compared SSRIs to other medications—including other antidepressants, antianxiety medications, and vitamin therapy—found SSRIs to be superior to all in terms of symptom relief.

Taking SSRIs: Decisions and Side Effects

Physicians prescribe SSRI medications for women with premenstrual symptoms that are so intense that their ability to function normally is short-circuited every month. There are no specific criteria for deciding who *really* needs treatment with medication. There is no yardstick for measuring distress and disability. If you feel that your premenstrual symptoms are ripping your life apart, talk with your physician about the possibility of taking an SSRI.

As good as they are, these medications are not right for everyone. Because SSRIs interact with other drugs, make sure your doctor knows all medications, supplements, vitamins, or herbal medicines you are taking. It may not be possible for you to take an SSRI because of potentially dangerous interactions with other medications you are using.

Some women hate the idea of taking any medication and will do anything to avoid it. If that's you, try some of the other treatment options described in later chapters to see if you get some relief from your symptoms. Some strategies, such as exercise, will help almost everyone feel better. If that's good enough to make your premenstrual symptoms manageable, then you don't need to consider medication. Don't let anyone intimidate you into taking a medication that you are not comfortable taking.

On the other hand, don't let anyone intimidate you out of taking a medication that might help. Years ago, rumors circulated in the media that Prozac might have caused some people to become more aggressive or commit suicide. *Those rumors are not true.* Some women still remember those stories and are fearful of trying the medication for that reason. There is absolutely no cause for concern, and that fear should not be part of your decision making. In 2001, researchers from Ireland reviewed all published medical papers about the relationship of SSRIs and violent or suicidal behavior. They found that there was no increased susceptibility to aggression or suicide and stated that SSRIs may even result in *lower* levels of aggression.

Every medication has potential side effects, and SSRIs are no exception. In every study on SSRIs and PMDD, at least some women drop out because they are particularly sensitive to some of the side effects. Typical side effects of all SSRIs include gastrointestinal disturbances (such as dry mouth, nausea, diarrhea, or constipation), headache, sleepiness, insomnia, agitation, weight gain or weight loss, impaired memory, excessive perspiration, and sexual dysfunction.

You may have noticed that both sleepiness and insomnia are on the list, as are weight gain and weight loss, and constipation and diarrhea. People respond to medications differently, for reasons no one understands. At the same dose of the same medication, one woman may feel excessively drowsy and another woman may feel agitated and be unable to sleep at night. If a particular SSRI makes one woman sleepy, a different SSRI may give her insomnia, and she may have no side effects at all from a third one. It is impossible to predict how any individual will respond to these medications, so choosing the best SSRI for a particular patient can sometimes be a matter of trial and error. Often, physicians prescribe a "favorite" SSRI, one that they are very familiar with and have seen work well for other patients. If this SSRI causes an unacceptable level of side effects in a particular patient, they will try a different SSRI.

So if you decide to try an SSRI, keep track of your side effects. Most will disappear within a couple of weeks after your body has a chance to adapt to the drug. But if you find you have continuing problems, talk with your physician about the possibility of switching to a different medication or lowering your dosage. But no matter what side effects you experience, rest assured that they will go away completely once you stop taking the medication.

Sexual side effects deserve special mention. Studies report that between 10 and 30 percent of women who take an SSRI for depression develop sexual side effects. Clinicians who specifically ask their patients about sexual side effects think the actual rates are much higher than the reported rates, perhaps as high as 70 percent. The most commonly reported sexual symptoms are decreased interest in sexual activity (lowered libido) and difficulty reaching orgasm.

Although these types of sexual side effects have been highly publicized, they are not universal, they tend to abate over time, and they go away when the medication is stopped. Some women actually report an improvement in their sex life because they are no longer prisoners to their premenstrual symptoms and are able to reconnect with their partner emotionally. Other women notice no effect on sexual interest or function at all. Intermittent dosing, when used appropriately, appears to be less likely to cause these types of sexual side effects. Again, if you notice that the drug seems to have a negative effect on your sex life, talk with your doctor. There may be hormonal or nonhormonal medications that you can take to counteract these effects. For example, some physicians recommend taking another antidepressant medication called bupropion (Wellbutrin, Wellbutrin SR) about two hours before a planned sexual encounter. This medication is more activating and has been shown in studies to improve sexual function and increase sexual desire. Unfortunately, bupropion does not work as a treatment for PMDD, but some women find that it counteracts the sexual dampening effects of their SSRIs.

And while we're talking about sex, let's talk about pregnancy. It has been shown that half of all pregnancies are unplanned (yes, really!). This raises the question of how safe SSRIs are for the babies conceived while their mothers are taking these types of medications. There is no definitive answer, because no one does randomized placebo-controlled studies on pregnant women. We do know that these drugs cross the placental barrier into the fetal system. We know that the rate of physical abnormalities seen in babies born to women taking an SSRI for major depression is the same as the rate seen in babies not exposed to SSRIs. Much less is known about the potential for long-term developmental risks, although the data so far have been reassuring. Some infants have shown signs of irritability shortly after birth, but it disappears very soon thereafter. In animal studies, there is some evidence that brain receptor density was changed when rats were exposed to high levels of an SSRI in utero. What this means and whether it has any human correlate or clinical relevance is unknown at this time.

So what should a woman do if she finds herself pregnant or contemplating pregnancy? Unfortunately, there are no clear guidelines. If you have "pure" PMDD or PMS, your symptoms will go away during pregnancy—no cycling hormones, no symptoms. There is no reason, then, for you to continue to take SSRIs during your pregnancy. If you are taking an SSRI to treat PME, however, then talk with your physician about your personal risks for recurrence of your depression and/or anxiety and possible benefits of continuing with treatment. In general, many physicians believe that *not* treating a woman who is anxious or depressed during pregnancy can put the fetus at risk. (There is some evidence that depression itself, experienced during pregnancy, can cause the newborn to have an elevated cortisol response to stress. What the long-term consequences of this change may be remain unclear. It is clear, however, that serious psychiatric conditions must be taken seriously during pregnancy.)

Another issue concerns breastfeeding. Studies reveal that tiny amounts of the medications are excreted in breast milk, and breastfed babies whose mothers are taking SSRIs have small but measurable amounts of the drug in their blood. Short-term effects are clinically not significant for most babies, which means that there is no visible or measurable harm to the infant. Again, no one knows what the effects may be in the long term, whether there will be any positive or negative changes in a child's development due to exposure to the drug. Current data are reassuring, in that babies breastfed by mothers using SSRIs show no signs of developmental or neurologic abnormalities.

Most women have heard that they shouldn't take any medications while pregnant or breastfeeding. Although that is generally good advice, what complicates the issue for women with PMS, PME, and PMDD is that they have a greater risk for developing postpartum depression than women without premenstrual symptoms. This is especially true for women with a previous history of postpartum depression. The recurrence rate is about 70 percent. Postpartum depression is more than just the "baby blues." Imagine your worst premenstrual symptoms, then magnify them. Then imagine that those feelings don't go away for weeks or months. The depression can be so deep for some women that they cannot bond properly with their child, and they end up having a disappointing new mothering experience. Talk with your obstetrician during pregnancy about your personal risk of postpartum depression and the possible benefits of taking an SSRI shortly after delivery to prevent postpartum depression. Together, you can weigh the risks and benefits and make a decision that is healthy for you and your baby.

One final note: despite the available body of evidence, some physicians still believe that PMDD is not a "real" disorder. If you feel you would like to try an SSRI to alleviate your premenstrual symptoms, but your doctor won't discuss it with you, seek a second opinion. In some cases there may be valid reasons for not prescribing the medication, such as if you are taking another drug that doesn't mix well with SSRIs or if your symptoms diary suggests a problem other than PMDD. But women with a valid diagnosis should not be denied safe and efficacious medical help.

Making the Medication Decision

Is taking medication for your premenstrual symptoms right for you? There is no single answer that fits all women in all situations. The decision can be made only by you and your doctor, working together. You'll need to understand your options, weigh the benefits and risks, and be willing to talk openly about personal issues. Some of the factors you'll need to consider and questions you'll need to ask before arriving at a considered decision include the following:

• *Have you determined your personal pattern of premenstrual symptoms?* The key to getting the best treatment is to know whether your symptoms occur all month long to some degree and get worse premenstrually, or if they occur only after ovulation. Do you experience symptoms for more than one week of each month, or are all your symptoms confined to the week before your period? Do you have mostly emotional symptoms, or emotional plus prominent physical symptoms? By knowing this information, your doctor can make an appropriate diagnosis and understand your particular treatment needs. If you decide to take medication, this information helps your doctor know whether it might be better to recommend a continuous or intermittent dosing, and whether to start at a lower or higher dose of medication.

• *Are you taking any other medications?* Serotonin reuptake inhibitor medications interact with a wide variety of medications. You and your doctor will need to evaluate all your medications to make sure that you won't be compromising your health by adding an SSRI to your medication regimen.

• *Are you pregnant or planning to become pregnant? Are you breastfeeding? What type of birth control do you use?* Serotonin reuptake inhibitor medications are known to cross the placenta into the fetal bloodstream and to be excreted into breast milk. So far, current research suggests that babies are not harmed by the amounts of medication they receive through their mothers. But it is important to discuss these issues with your obstetrician/gynecologist and/or with your baby's pediatrician to make sure that you are comfortable with whatever potential risks and potential benefits may be associated with taking medication during your pregnancy or while breastfeeding.

continued

Making the Medication Decision (continued)

• *How dangerous are your symptoms? Have you felt suicidal? Have you had worries that you might hurt others or yourself? Have you done anything during your premenstrual phase that you later thought back on and realized was dangerous?* If so, tell your doctor. Medication should be an important part of your treatment, and your doctor needs to schedule follow-up visits to make sure your dosage is appropriate for solving the problem.

• *What are your personal feelings about these medications or medications in general?* You should feel entirely comfortable with your decision to take this medication. It is designed to make you feel better, not to scare or worry you. Try to pinpoint exactly what your worries are; then talk them over with your doctor. Ask all your questions about side effects: how other women have reacted to the medication, what you should expect the first couple of days you take it, how soon any side effects go away, if any side effects are likely to show up later, and how quickly you can stop taking the medication if you experience intolerable side effects. Some women have concerns about taking a medication that is labeled an antidepressant; other women worry that they might get "addicted" to the medication (that can't happen!). Again, discuss all your concerns with your doctor, and then make your decision.

Serotonin-Enhancing Medications

Currently, there are five medications in the class of drugs called SSRIs, and all have been tested to see how well they work to alleviate premenstrual symptoms. As of this writing, only fluoxetine (Sarafem) and sertraline (Zoloft) have received final approval for treatment of premenstrual symptoms by the FDA. This does not mean that the other drugs don't work or that physicians can't prescribe the other drugs to women with premenstrual symptoms. Approval by the FDA means that the pharmaceutical companies can advertise the approved medications as a treatment for premenstrual symptoms. For consumers, FDA approval indicates that sufficient research has been conducted to prove that the medication works as intended for that specific disorder. Often, the medical literature shows that a medication that has been approved for one indication (for example, depression) may work for another condition (such as PMDD). Doctors prescribe according to both FDA "indications" and the medical literature.

There are possible drug interactions that can occur if you take an SSRI and other medications. To be on the safe side, inform your doctor of all medications, herbal supplements, vitamins, minerals, or other alternative/complementary treatments you are using.

Some medications with potentially serious interactions require special mention. Do not take an SSRI if you are already taking a monoamine oxidase inhibitor (MAOI, such as Nardil, Parnate, or Marplan) or thioridazine (Mellaril), because serious, and possibly fatal, reactions can occur. Talk with your doctor about possible interactions if you are taking or plan to start taking any of the following medications: any cough medicine with dextromethorphan (including Robitussin, Sucrets Cough Control, and Benylin DM), certain antihistamines (Periactin and Hismanal), diuretics, statin drugs (such as Mevacor, Lipitor, and Zocor), Valium, Xanax, lithium, any other antidepressant medication, a beta-blocker for heart problems (such as Inderal, Betapace, or Lopressor), any anticonvulsant medication, any antipsychotic medication, the blood thinner warfarin (Coumadin), the migraine medication sumatriptan (Imitrex), or drugs for Parkinson disease.

Because a large percentage of women with premenstrual symptoms also suffer from migraine, it's important to mention another possible drug interaction. The common migraine medication sumatriptan (Imitrex) works to increase serotonin transmission in the brain. When sumatriptan is taken simultaneously with an SSRI, serotonin levels can, in rare circumstances, rise to dangerously high levels, causing a cluster of side effects known as "serotonin syndrome." The symptoms include muscle spasms, muscle rigidity, restlessness, tremors, shivering, extreme sweatiness, nausea, and confusion. Although generally mild, these side effects can be severe in some people. In the very worst cases, death can occur. Because most women can tolerate the combination of medications without incident, women taking an SSRI for treatment of premenstrual symptoms or depression do not need to abandon their migraine medication. Women who take both types of medications should be aware of any side effects that occur, and see their doctor immediately if they experience anything unusual. Most symptoms disappear entirely within twenty-four hours after stopping medication and receiving medical attention.

Another possible reaction to too much serotonin is a powerful "thunderclap" headache, caused by extreme vasoconstriction (narrowing of the blood vessels) in the brain. In susceptible people, such a narrowing could be enough to cause a stroke. Case studies have shown that when some patients taking an SSRI also take other common substances that have similar serotonergic effects, they can inadvertently cause serotonin levels to rise too abruptly. Substances that can augment the effects of SSRIs include other antidepressants, decongestants, diet pills, amphetamines, St. John's wort, ecstasy, cocaine, and methamphetamine. These substances should never be taken in conjunction with an SSRI. If you should experience a thunderclap headache, one that you would call your "worst-ever," seek medical attention immediately.

The five SSRI medications available are:

1. **Fluoxetine.** Because Prozac was the first SSRI approved by the FDA for the treatment of depression (in 1987), it has the longest history of use and the largest body of research in many areas. It is also FDA-approved for the treatment of obsessive-compulsive disorder and bulimia nervosa. In 2000, fluoxetine was approved by the FDA for treatment of PMDD but licensed under a new name, Sarafem.

   - *Brand names:* Prozac, Sarafem. The generic form of this drug became available in 2001.
   - *Typical dosage for premenstrual symptoms:* The recommended starting dose is 20 milligrams once a day. Women with milder symptoms sometimes use 10 milligrams. In studies comparing 10- and 20-milligram doses, both worked for premenstrual mood symptoms, but only 20-milligram doses were also shown to improve physical symptoms. Because this drug is "activating," it should be taken in the morning so it doesn't disturb sleep. It can be taken with or without food.

- *Research results:* Fluoxetine has been shown to be effective in reducing or eliminating the emotional symptoms of PMDD, especially irritability, anger, mood swings, and sadness. In addition to emotional symptoms, this medication has also been shown to relieve breast tenderness and bloating. This medication has been shown to be effective in both continuous and intermittent dosing schedules. Other studies have found that it improves social functioning, as measured by women's self-reports regarding (1) how often they avoid social commitments or cancel events, (2) ease of completing house and job routines, and (3) general sense of being able to function normally.
- *Who should not take this drug:* People taking an MAOI or Mellaril (see drug interactions discussed earlier). People with liver or kidney dysfunction, seizure disorder, diabetes, or thoughts of suicide. People with a history of manic-depressive illness (bipolar disorder).
- *Common side effects:* The most common side effects are dry mouth, anxiousness, insomnia, tiredness, nausea, weight gain or weight loss, difficulty concentrating, and sexual dysfunction. If you develop a skin rash or muscle twitches or tics while taking fluoxetine, discontinue use and see your doctor. No adverse effects have been reported when stopping this medication because of its long half-life, which means that the drug clears the body slowly, tapering off on its own.

2. **Sertraline.** This drug was first approved by the FDA for treatment of depression in 1992 and is the second-most studied SSRI. It is also FDA-approved for treating obsessive-compulsive disorder, panic disorder, and posttraumatic stress disorder. In 2002, sertraline was approved by the FDA for treatment of premenstrual symptoms.

- *Brand name:* Zoloft. No generic available.
- *Typical dosage for premenstrual symptoms:* Recommended starting dosage is 25 to 50 milligrams.
- *Research results:* Sertraline has been shown to be effective in reducing or eliminating the emotional symptoms of PMDD, espe-

cially irritability, anger, mood swings, feelings of hopelessness, and sadness. In addition to emotional symptoms, this medication has also been shown to reduce food cravings and decrease the severity of some physical symptoms. This medication has been shown to be effective in both continuous and intermittent dosing schedules. Other research has shown that sertraline improves psychosocial functioning in women with PMDD, as measured by reports of impaired productivity, interference with hobbies or social activities, or interference with relationships.

- *Who should not take this drug:* People taking an MAOI (see drug interactions discussed earlier). People with a history of liver or kidney disease, or seizure disorder. People with a history of manic-depressive illness (bipolar disorder).
- *Common side effects:* Side effects include headache, nausea, insomnia, sexual dysfunction, diarrhea, and dry mouth. When stopping this medication after taking it continuously for several months, women need to taper off gradually to give the body a chance to adapt. Abrupt discontinuation of medication may result in serotonin discontinuation symptoms, which are similar to having the flu, with nausea, dizziness, muscle aches, and even fever.

3. **Paroxetine.** This drug is not as well studied as sertraline or fluoxetine, but preliminary studies show it to be effective for women with premenstrual symptoms. It was approved by the FDA for treatment of depression in 1992 and was later also approved for treatment of social anxiety, panic disorder, generalized anxiety disorder, posttraumatic stress disorder, and obsessive-compulsive disorder. Although this medication has not been approved by the FDA for treatment of PMDD, the medical literature supports its use.

- *Brand name:* Paxil, Paxil CR. No generic available.
- *Typical dosage for premenstrual symptoms:* Most physicians prescribe a 20-milligram dosage to be taken once daily.
- *Research results:* Paroxetine has been shown to be effective in reducing or eliminating the emotional symptoms of PMDD,

especially irritability, anger, mood swings, tension/anxiety, and sadness. In addition to emotional symptoms, this medication has also been shown to relieve breast tenderness, food cravings, and bloating.

- *Who should not take this drug:* People taking an MAOI (see drug interactions discussed earlier). People with a history of mania or liver or kidney dysfunction.
- *Common side effects:* Among the common side effects are sleepiness, dry mouth, nausea, and sexual dysfunction. Paroxetine is more sedating than fluoxetine or sertraline. When stopping this medication after taking it continuously for several months, women need to taper off gradually to give the body a chance to adapt. Abrupt discontinuation of medication may result in serotonin discontinuation symptoms, which are similar to having the flu, with nausea, dizziness, muscle aches, and even fever.

4. **Citalopram.** This medication was approved by the FDA for treatment of depression in 1998 and was later also approved for treatment of panic disorder and obsessive-compulsive disorder. Although this medication has not been approved by the FDA for treatment of PMDD, the medical literature supports its use.

- *Brand name:* Celexa. No generic available.
- *Typical dosage for premenstrual symptoms:* 20 to 40 milligrams, once a day. Because this medication tends to be sedating, many women choose to take it at night.
- *Research results:* Citalopram has been shown to be effective in reducing emotional and physical symptoms of PMDD. One study found that more than two-thirds of women with PMDD who had not responded to previous SSRI treatment improved when taking citalopram. Two studies to date have found that intermittent dosing may work better than continuous dosing.
- *Who should not take this drug:* People taking an MAOI (see drug interactions discussed earlier). People with cardiovascular disease, mania, liver problems, seizure disorder, liver dysfunction, or thoughts of suicide.

- *Common side effects:* Common side effects are sleepiness, insomnia, difficulty concentrating, headache, nausea, dry mouth, and sexual dysfunction. A rare side effect is seizure. When stopping this medication after taking it continuously for several months, women need to taper off gradually to give the body a chance to adapt. Abrupt discontinuation of medication may result in serotonin discontinuation symptoms, which are similar to having the flu, with nausea, dizziness, muscle aches, and even fever.

5. **Fluvoxamine.** There have been only two studies to date that have looked at the effects of this medication on premenstrual symptoms. This medication was approved by the FDA for the treatment of obsessive-compulsive disorder in 1994. The manufacturer has not applied to the FDA for approval to treat other disorders, but the medical literature supports its use for depression and other conditions where SSRIs are commonly used.

   - *Brand name:* Luvox. No generic available.
   - *Typical dosage for premenstrual symptoms:* Typical dosage is 50 milligrams, to be taken at bedtime since this is the most sedating of the SSRIs.
   - *Research results:* There have been only two studies conducted to date using fluvoxamine for premenstrual symptoms. One study showed that the drug performed no better than a placebo; the other showed a reduction in depressed mood, irritability, anxiety, and feelings of being out of control. It is unclear whether further testing will be done using this drug to treat premenstrual symptoms.
   - *Who should not take this drug:* People taking an MAOI (see drug interactions discussed earlier). People with a history of mania, seizure disorder, liver dysfunction, or thoughts of suicide.
   - *Common side effects:* The most common side effects are fatigue, dry mouth, headache, insomnia, and nausea. When stopping this medication after taking it continuously for several months, women need to taper off gradually to give the body a chance to adapt. Abrupt discontinuation of medication may result in

serotonin discontinuation symptoms, which are similar to having the flu, with nausea, dizziness, muscle aches, and even fever.

Other serotonin reuptake inhibiting medications have been tested and used to treat premenstrual symptoms. These differ from SSRIs in that they are not selective to serotonin—they inhibit reuptake of other neurotransmitters, as well. These include clomipramine and venlafaxine.

1. **Clomipramine.** This was one of the medications first shown to be effective in treating premenstrual symptoms. This medication inhibits reuptake of both serotonin and norepinephrine and is FDA-approved for treating obsessive-compulsive disorder.

   - *Brand name:* Anafranil
   - *Typical dosage for premenstrual symptoms:* 10 to 50 milligrams per day.
   - *Research results:* Clomipramine has been shown to be effective in reducing or eliminating the emotional symptoms of PMDD, especially irritability and sadness. This medication has been shown to be effective in both continuous and intermittent dosing schedules.
   - *Who should not take this drug:* People taking an MAOI (see drug interactions discussed earlier). People with a recent history of myocardial infarction (heart attack). It should also not be taken by women at risk of becoming pregnant. (There are more data favoring the use of SSRIs when an antidepressant is indicated during pregnancy.)
   - *Common side effects:* The most common side effects are headache, insomnia, dizziness, sexual dysfunction, sleepiness, gastrointestinal distress, and dry mouth. There is a risk of heart rhythm disturbances.

2. **Venlafaxine.** This medication inhibits reuptake of both serotonin and norepinephrine and is FDA-approved for treating depression and generalized anxiety disorder. Although this medication has not been approved by the FDA for treatment of PMDD, the medical literature supports its use.

- *Brand name:* Effexor, Effexor XR
- *Typical dosage for premenstrual symptoms:* 50 to 200 milligrams per day.
- *Research results:* Venlafaxine has been shown to be effective in reducing or eliminating premenstrual symptoms, including irritability, mood swings, anxiety, sadness, ability to function, and physical symptoms.
- *Who should not take this drug:* People taking an MAOI (see drug interactions discussed earlier). People with a history of high blood pressure or seizure disorder. People with a history of manic-depressive illness (bipolar disorder).
- *Common side effects:* The most common side effects are nausea, insomnia, and dizziness. When stopping this medication after taking it continuously for several months, women need to taper off gradually to give the body a chance to adapt. Abrupt discontinuation of medication may result in serotonin discontinuation symptoms, which are similar to having the flu, with nausea, dizziness, muscle aches, and even fever.

7

Diet and Exercise

Appetite change? I shove everything in the house into my mouth. And I have to make
sure there's a lot of chocolate there. But too much chocolate might not be good, so I
have to mix it up with all this other stuff like crackers, leftovers—extra helpings.
Many meals throughout the day, but not necessarily smaller ones. I eat in a mad rage.
If I'm upset, angry, or anxious about doing something, I'll eat more then. But some-
times when I eat, it's almost like I'm in a blank daze. Either a mad rage or a blank
daze. I just have to eat; I don't know why.

—Toni

LET US IMMEDIATELY put your mind at ease: we are not going to put
you on a diet, we are not going to tell you to give up chocolate, and we
are not going to give you tips on how to curb your food cravings. In fact,
it is our considered medical opinion that if you have premenstrual cravings for chocolate or salty foods, you should eat chocolate or salty foods.
Exercise, however, is another story. Clinical experience and some studies reveal that exercise may be the best self-help method for decreasing
the severity of premenstrual symptoms. We're not talking about running
a marathon. Just a little exercise can make anyone feel better almost
immediately.

Food and Diet

Until just a few years ago, the first thing a woman with premenstrual syndrome (PMS) or premenstrual dysphoric disorder (PMDD) was told was that she had to change her eating habits. Physicians usually recommended eliminating all caffeine, chocolate, sugar, salt, and alcohol from the diet. (Imagine, this was supposed to make women feel *less* irritable!) Some physicians advocated a low-fat or vegetarian diet. Others suggested eating six small meals throughout the day, or eating every three hours, or eating only starchy foods. Some dubious alternative diet "cures" have included avoiding milk, monosodium glutamate (MSG), aspartame (NutraSweet), honey, and margarine.

None of these special diets have been shown to eliminate or reduce the severity of premenstrual symptoms among women with PMS, PMDD, or premenstrual exacerbation (PME). And yet, popular magazines keep publishing articles about the value of dietary changes. Why?

One reason is that dietary changes are easy to recommend. Most women are used to being on diets of one sort or another, so we accept the idea of dietary modification quite readily. Plus, there is no downside for the person recommending the diet. Eliminating sugar, caffeine, and salt would make nearly everyone healthier, but these measures won't significantly help alleviate severe premenstrual symptoms.

Another reason why diets are recommended so often is that they have some sound theoretical underpinnings that make dietary changes seem like a reasonable solution. Unfortunately, when scientifically tested, the diets have not been found to have any meaningful value for relieving PMDD symptoms. For example, one hypothesis is that women might benefit from eating small regular meals or cutting back on sugary foods because sweets or the digestion of large meals causes large surges of blood sugar. Later, as blood sugar levels fall, it is possible for some women to develop hypoglycemic symptoms. (Hypoglycemic symptoms, which include irritability and mood swings, are remarkably similar to premenstrual symptoms.) By keeping meals small and frequent, the body maintains a relatively steady state of blood sugar and digestion-related hormones. There have not been any studies demonstrating that these changes help women with PMS, PME, or PMDD, and there is no evidence that daily blood sugar changes affect premenstrual mood in most women. It is true, however, that skipping meals can increase irritability in just about anyone. In addition, women who have received an actual diagnosis of hypoglycemia will get worse premenstrually and, therefore, might benefit from more careful monitoring and control of their diet during their luteal phase.

Other hypotheses about the value of special diets were specific to particular ingredients. For example, caffeine was thought to be a culprit in premenstrual symptoms because it can cause jitteriness in high doses and, as a result, may increase irritability. Some studies looked at the amount of caffeinated beverages consumed by women with and without premenstrual symptoms, and found that women with PMS drank more caffeine than women without PMS. Some people took this to be a cause-and-effect relationship and assumed that the caffeine *caused* the premenstrual symptoms. Later research suggested that, in fact, the relationship was exactly reversed. Women with premenstrual symptoms, which often include sleepiness and depression, self-medicated with caffeine in an attempt to counteract their symptoms. They were trying to find a way to jolt their bodies back to "normal."

In some cases, this self-medication can worsen premenstrual symptoms. For example, if a woman experiences insomnia but also drinks coffee to alleviate depression, she risks worsening her insomnia with the additional caffeine. In addition, caffeine effects are magnified premenstrually. Just as the body reacts more strongly to stress and is more sensitive to other stimuli premenstrually, caffeine packs a greater punch for women premenstrually. But caffeine does not cause PMS, PME, or PMDD. Ceasing to drink coffee or tea will not have a significant effect on premenstrual symptoms unless you are one of the relatively few women who have premenstrual exacerbation of an underlying anxiety disorder.

A similar assumption has been made for sugar in the diet. Some studies have shown that people who are depressed eat more carbohydrates (such as potatoes, rice, pasta, and bread) and simple sugars (usually in the form of candy, cakes, and cookies) than people who are not depressed. But sugar does not cause depression. In fact, eating carbohydrates generally lifts mood. So people who are depressed might eat more sugar in order to become less depressed. Again, this would be an example of people trying to self-medicate in order to feel better. But sugar and carbohydrates themselves do not *cause* premenstrual symptoms or depression.

All this does not mean, however, that dietary changes are worthless. There are certain benefits that can be claimed, even without strict supporting research. The most important has to do with general health and well-being. Diet is one of the most important contributors to overall health. Maintaining a reasonable weight, eating a diet rich in fruits and vegetables, and limiting the amount of fats and sugars in your diet will make you an overall healthier person. That's not new information—you've been hearing that ever since you could feed yourself. What makes this information important *now* is how it might affect your premenstrual symptoms. Remember, your most physically and emotionally vulnerable time is premenstrually. If you are feeling tired and lethargic, you'll feel worse premenstrually. If you suffer from low self-esteem, it will be more of an issue premenstrually. The closer you are to a healthy weight (versus being either overweight or underweight) and the healthier your diet throughout the month, the better you'll feel. Period. Your premenstrual symptoms won't disappear, but you may regain some energy, develop a greater sense of self-confidence, and have fewer aches and pains—all of which will lessen your premenstrual distress.

Just as your physical symptoms get worse premenstrually, your reactions to foods also get worse premenstrually. This means that any foods that cause noticeable physical or mental changes will have magnified effects. For example, you might get more of a buzz from your morning coffee—and if you drink more than the usual amount of caffeine, you might find yourself feeling jittery and anxious. Similarly, alcohol's effects on the body are magnified premenstrually. If you normally feel drunk after two drinks, you might get the same level of impairment after one drink premenstrually. Once you are aware of your personal reactions and vulnerabilities to these substances, you can change your eating and drinking patterns to match your menstrual cycle timing.

Another potential benefit of monitoring and improving your diet is that it allows you to regain an overall sense of control over your health and life (but not, unfortunately, your premenstrual symptoms). There is a concept in psychology called "health locus of control." In a nutshell, what it says is this: all of us have had numerous experiences with health and wellness issues, from getting the flu to falling off a bicycle. These past experiences helped to shape your beliefs about how much control you have over your own health. A person with an internal locus of control feels that her own actions have the most impact on her health outcomes. A person with an external locus of control feels that her health is not at all in her control, that doctors, luck, or chance determine how she feels.

We know that feeling "out of control" is a major complaint among women with severe premenstrual symptoms. Premenstrually, a woman is more likely to feel overwhelmed by stress and responsibilities in her life, be more irritated than usual by normal daily events, and lose her temper more easily. After years of feeling out of control for a certain amount of time every month, it wouldn't be surprising if women with PMDD, PME, or PMS developed a more external locus of control. Indeed, studies have shown that women with premenstrual symptoms have more of an external locus of control (as determined by a special locus of control questionnaire) than women without premenstrual symptoms. Those studies also showed that the women's locus of control measures became more external in their luteal phase. It is possible that when women decide to take control of their health and wellness by altering the way they eat, they may find that the simple act of choosing to eat healthier allows them a greater sense of control in general, leading to a more internal locus of control. Although having an internal locus of control won't allow you to completely control or stop your premenstrual symptoms, it may allow you to take charge of how you react to your premenstrual changes and may influence how actively you pursue other treatment options.

Any kind of healthy change can help—you don't have to go on a starvation or deprivation diet. In fact, it's better if you don't make too many drastic changes all at once. Setting your goals or standards too high is just setting yourself up for failure, and that certainly won't help you to regain a sense of control. Most dietitians and physicians recommend starting with small, manageable changes. Choose actions that you know you can accomplish. For example, if you eat a high-fat, high-calorie, high-salt lunch at a fast-food restaurant five days a week, set a goal to cut that back to three or four days a week instead. Or continue to eat out five days a week, but choose a healthier option, such as a salad one of those days. Eventually, making these kinds of changes will seem easier, and the sense of personal accomplishment may spread to other areas of your life.

So You Really Want a Diet?

We'd like to repeat here that *there is no evidence that following a special diet helps relieve severe premenstrual symptoms.* Most women are happy to learn that they don't have to go on yet another diet. But if you want to improve your overall health, or if you want to do everything that might even remotely help relieve symptoms whether it is proven or not, there are some general dietary changes typically recommended by dietitians. If you would like to seek the help of a registered dietitian (R.D.) for more information or to discover how to incorporate these changes into your lifestyle, contact the American Dietetic Association (ADA) for a referral to a dietitian near you. (See Appendix A.)

There are three pieces of advice that go along with these recommendations. First, make these dietary changes all month long, not just when you feel symptoms. Food does not have a magic-bullet curative effect. Any changes will be felt slowly, and only after your body adapts to its new internal environment. Be patient, and focus on how healthy you'll be after a few months. Second, make changes gradually. Some women who have tried to stop eating sugar find that they experience increased moodiness and intense cravings. And a painful caffeine-withdrawal headache usually kicks in within forty-eight hours after your last cup of coffee. A slow process of gradually weaning yourself away from certain types of foods may be an easier and more tolerable way to make changes. Again, these dietary changes (should you decide to try them) are part of a lifelong process of eating well to stay healthy, not a quick fix for immediate symptoms. Third, make one change at a time. Trying to make too many changes too soon can be painful and discouraging and can feel overly restrictive.

Here's what dietitians recommend:

- **Cut down or stop drinking caffeinated coffee, tea, and soft drinks.** Caffeine can make some women jittery and nervous, and its effects are magnified premenstrually. It has been suggested that women with dense breasts (sometimes called "fibrocystic breasts") may have less breast tenderness premenstrually if they eliminate caffeine from their diets. Substitute decaffeinated coffees or teas or herbal teas.

- **Cut down or stop drinking alcohol.** Premenstrually, the effects of alcohol are magnified, so you are more likely to unintentionally overconsume. In addition,

continued

So You Really Want a Diet? (continued)

research demonstrates that alcohol has some effects on breast tissue and may contribute to breast symptoms. Alcohol also tends to lower blood sugar levels and may increase the likelihood of a hypoglycemic response.

• **Cut down or stop eating salt or salty foods.** Salt is involved in the process of maintaining your body's balance of fluid. Too much salt and your body may retain too much water. Premenstrually, this may lead to increased bloating, breast tenderness, and puffiness. The easiest way to begin decreasing the amount of salt in your diet is to stop adding table salt to your foods. The prepackaged and processed foods we eat often contain more than enough salt to meet our bodies' needs. If you stop adding salt at the table, you'll cut down on one of the biggest sources of excess salt. Also, stop buying and eating salty snack foods, such as pretzels, potato chips, and corn chips. Because so many people are concerned with salt intake for a variety of health reasons, these foods are now widely available without added salt. Other foods that contain large amounts of salt include processed meats (such as deli meats and hot dogs), most fast-food sandwiches, and many canned soups.

• **Drink plenty of water.** This is a complement to cutting back on salt. Drinking water encourages the body to excrete excess fluid, further reducing the potential for bloating or puffiness. Try to get six to eight 8-ounce glasses of water each day.

• **Stop eating, or greatly reduce your consumption of, sugar and sugary foods.** The theory is that every time you eat high-sugar foods, your body gets a virtual sugar rush—blood sugar levels rise quickly, causing the hormone insulin to be secreted to deal with the sugar load, after which blood sugar levels fall, sometimes to hypoglycemic levels. That's a bit oversimplified, but you get the picture. By eliminating sugary foods and substituting complex carbohydrates instead (foods such as whole grain breads, potatoes, and rice), your blood sugar levels remain more stable. To maintain even smoother blood sugar levels, try to eat several small meals throughout the day, rather than only two or three large meals.

• **Cut down your consumption of fats, particularly animal fats.** Fat is important in the diet, but only in moderation. Dietary fat is dense in calories, and there-

continued

So You Really Want a Diet? (continued)

fore contributes to overweight when eaten in excess. Limit your fat intake to no more than 30 percent of your diet. One easy way to do that is to read the food labels of all products you buy. Look for the total number of calories per serving and then look at the total number of *fat* calories (they will be on different lines on the labels). Take the number of fat calories and multiply it by three (to get a rough estimate of 30 percent). If that number is less than the total number of calories per serving, then that product fits in the 30 percent rule. If the number you get after multiplying is equal to or higher than the number of total calories per serving, then it should be considered a high-fat food. Other ways to cut down on fat are to reduce or elimi-nate the use of butter or margarine, eat only lean cuts of meat, avoid fried foods, and choose low-fat or no-fat dairy products.

   • **Increase consumption of fish.** Very few of us get an optimal amount of the omega-3 fatty acids found in certain types of fish. Omega-3 fatty acids are impor-tant for brain development as well as prevention and treatment of heart disease, cancer, and arthritis. Omega-3 fatty acids are found in high amounts in walnuts, soy-beans, shellfish, and certain kinds of fish, including mackerel, salmon, tuna, anchovies, trout, herring, and sardines. Although no study has found that omega-3s have an effect on premenstrual symptoms, omega-3s in fish oils have been shown to decrease depression in at least one study.

   • **Increase consumption of all kinds of fruits and vegetables.** The American Dietetic Association recommends that everyone try to eat at least five servings of fruits or vegetables each day. And more is better. Ideally, nine or ten servings would make dietitians happy, but since so few people reach even five, the higher recom-mendation is totally out of reach. Fruits and vegetables are rich in vitamins, miner-als, and other micronutrients called phytochemicals, which contribute to health in important ways that we are only just discovering. Some phytochemicals found in certain vegetables (such as sulforaphane in broccoli) have been shown to be potent cancer fighters when tested in the laboratory. Other phytochemicals act as antiox-idants to reduce cell damage in the body; still others fight cardiovascular disease. Eating fruits and vegetables is a good way to improve your overall health, now and in the long term.

Food Cravings

For many women, food cravings are just another personal sign that they are out of control. They've been brainwashed into thinking that giving in to a craving is a sign of weakness, which then only reinforces a sense of low self-esteem, which, in turn, becomes magnified premenstrually. Let us reassure you that having food cravings—and giving in to them—does not signal anything except that you are human.

Eating is never just about food. What we eat and when we eat is determined by a complex interaction of psychological, environmental, and physiologic factors. Mood, time of day, time of the month, the presence or absence of others, the color of the tablecloth, the type of music playing, a rumbling in the stomach, or a sense of being light-headed all contribute to what psychologists call our "eating behavior." Studies have even shown that women's perceptions of taste change across the menstrual cycle. When estrogen levels are high, women are more sensitive to sweet tastes, and when levels of progesterone are high, women are more sensitive to bitter tastes. Premenstrual food cravings have been analyzed from several different angles, but the outcome is always the same: cravings are real and they appear cyclically, but they are not tied to any other part of eating behavior. It doesn't matter if you are overweight or underweight, if your premenstrual symptoms are intense or mild, or if you typically diet or not. Cravings happen.

No one knows what causes the sometimes intense food cravings of PMS, PME, and PMDD, but they are real. Appetite and the amount of food eaten increases premenstrually, and cravings for sweet or salty foods are common. (Interestingly, it is rare that a woman craves both sweet and salty foods. Premenstrually, there is usually a strong preference for one or the other, but not both!) Anyone who has ever tried to stifle a food craving knows how difficult it is. Self-help diet books and women's magazines frequently offer tips on how to avoid giving in to cravings. Some of the most popular include drinking a glass of water, exercising, waiting twenty to thirty minutes to see if the craving passes, or substituting a low-fat alternative for the craved food (as if cottage cheese could ever replace chocolate). We recommend none of these. If you want to wait and see if the craving goes away, then by all means do so. But acknowledging and indulging your craving may not only make you feel better in the short run, it may actually save you from binge-eating later.

If you're like most women, you probably believe that if you give in to your premenstrual cravings, you'll gain weight. Some women fear that once they allow themselves to eat a "forbidden" food, there will be no stopping them, and they will eat their way up the scale. There are two general arguments against that. First, there is no evidence that women who fight their cravings are any thinner than women who indulge their cravings. If you eat a generally healthful diet, giving in to a premenstrual craving or two won't throw your weight out of control. Second, the very act of denying your natural eating tendencies may lead to binge eating.

Researchers at the University of Toronto, who have been studying dieting behavior for more than a decade, have discovered that women who "restrain" their eating (diet) are prone to overeat significantly once they go off the diet. Restrained eating is an unnatural behavior. Women who carefully control what they eat are fighting their physiologic, psychological, and social instincts—and success hangs by a very thin thread. If the thread (and the diet) is broken, most dieters eat much larger quantities of food than they would have if they hadn't been dieting in the first place. Physiologically, it may be an atavistic response to the fear of starvation, our bodies' natural tendency to want to store up food (in the form of body fat) before the next bout of starvation. Psychologically, it's the equivalent of saying, "I've already overeaten, so what the heck, I might as well overeat even more." Denying a craving may have a similar effect. Many women report that if they give in to a premenstrual craving, they actually eat very little of the craved food. But if they try to substitute other, lower-calorie foods or delay gratifying their craving until it can no longer be resisted, they tend to overeat dramatically once they finally give in.

NOTE: As with every other disease or disorder, women with eating disorders also get worse premenstrually. Women who compulsively overeat will eat even more premenstrually; women who binge and purge may do so with greater frequency premenstrually. If you are concerned about the amount of food you consume premenstrually, or if you find yourself purging, talk with your physician. You may have premenstrual exacerbation of an eating disorder. Once the underlying eating disorder is diagnosed, proper treatment can help control monthly eating cycles.

Chocolate

As the single most common craving, chocolate deserves special mention. Although no one would go so far as to call it a health food, there's more to chocolate than mere taste satisfaction. Chocolate contains minerals necessary for good health, such as copper, magnesium, iron, and zinc. Chocolate also contains other natural compounds—flavonoids, catechins, and polyphenols—which act as antioxidants in the body to help cells resist damage caused by other substances called free radicals. It has been suggested that these healthful compounds in chocolate may help contribute to heart health by decreasing the damage done by low-density lipoprotein (LDL) cholesterol.

Most important to women with premenstrual symptoms is that chocolate contains compounds that can increase levels of neurotransmitters, including the all-important serotonin. Chocolate contains phenylethylamine (which improves mood), methylxanthines (which act like stimulants), and *N*-acylethanolamines (which can chemically alter the functioning of serotonin and other neurochemicals, and help to create a sense of well-being). Further, it has been suggested that chocolate increases serotonin production in the brain. Even the American Dietetic Association acknowledges that chocolate cravings are common, and that rather than deny this powerful force, women can find ways to incorporate chocolate in moderation into their healthful diet.

Exercise

For many women, exercise is the last thing they want to do when they're experiencing the worst of their premenstrual symptoms. Put on tights when you're feeling bloated? Run or do aerobics when your breasts hurt every time you bounce? Risk meeting and having to talk with someone during your neighborhood walk? None of it sounds appealing. But exercise may be the single best thing you can do to feel better—immediately and in the long term. Physicians who treat women with premenstrual symptoms report that just about every woman feels better after starting even a modest program of regular exercise.

Scientific studies have shown that any type of physical exercise can help improve mood, decrease anxiety, and reduce stress reactions. One review of the medical literature reported that more than 85 percent of relevant studies found that exercise improved mood to some degree. Studies looking at many different types of people in different situations have found that exercise is related to reductions in levels of anxiety, stress, depression, tension, anger, and fatigue. Women who exercise have also been reported to feel happier on the days they exercise, and they appear to be less bothered by minor irritations. This effect is not "all in your head." Even the body's natural autonomic reactions to stress are different in people who exercise. For example, numerous studies show that people who exercise have a lower heart rate and lower blood pressure after being in a stressful situation than people who don't exercise.

Outside of scientific studies, clinical observations reinforce how powerful the effects of exercise can be. First, PMDD is rarely seen in professional athletes. Second, athletes who break training often find themselves experiencing symptoms for the first time in their lives. For example, a marathon runner who breaks her ankle and is unable to train for several months may experience her first-ever bout of premenstrual symptoms while she is inactive and recovering.

Although no one knows for sure how exercise exerts these effects, there are several theories. First, it is known that exercise is related to a rise in levels of endorphins in the blood. Although no actual link has been made between endorphin level and mood, it seems logical that increasing the amount of natural "feel good" chemicals in your body might make you happier. Second, some researchers believe that exercising is distracting, and a distracted mind doesn't fret or worry as much. This type of distraction might be enough to break a cycle of worry and depression temporarily, leading to a more positive mood. Third, it has been suggested that the positive feelings are a result of having tackled and completed a difficult task (exercising). Fourth, one study found that exercise increased the amount of phenylacetic acid in the urine, which is an indicator of body levels of phenylethylamine. This is the same mood-enhancing compound found in chocolate.

Finally, the positive effects of exercise may be due to a more global effect of physical activity. Think of all that happens during exercise: your heart rate increases, blood flow through your whole body increases, muscles work, metabolism increases, body temperature rises, endorphin levels rise, and so on. Psychologically, you feel in control and happy about doing something positive for yourself. In all probability, the effect from all of these factors, working separately or together, may never be teased apart sufficiently to allow them to be scientifically tested. But observational studies make it clear that exercise helps—no matter how.

Regardless of the mechanisms involved, most scientists agree that exercise lifts mood. Although there have been just a handful of preliminary studies on the effects of exercise on premenstrual symptoms, they found similar positive effects. One study found that normally sedentary women who took part in a six-month running training program experienced decreased breast symptoms as well as lower levels of water retention and personal stress. Normally active women who increased their level of exercise also experienced less depression. Other studies have found that as little as three months of regular exercise improved many premenstrual symptoms, including depressed mood.

To get the full stress-reducing, mood-enhancing benefits of exercise, you'll need to follow a few guidelines.

- *Don't* **push yourself too hard when you exercise.** Bet you weren't expecting that recommendation! Although high-intensity workouts will help improve cardiovascular health, they seem to be of no greater benefit than low-intensity workouts in improving mood or premenstrual symptoms. And scientists have discovered that women do best when they exercise at a level that is individually comfortable for them. High-intensity workouts can even make mood *worse* unless you are already exercising at a high-intensity level. From a commonsense standpoint that seems logical. Exercise should be an enjoyable part of your daily routine, not a painful chore. Mood enhancement is optimal when women are allowed to choose the type of exercise they do, and then do it at an intensity with which they are comfortable.

- **Choose an exercise activity you enjoy.** Choose something you find fun (or at least tolerable), something you'll be able to engage in regularly. Walking, running, swimming, hiking, and cycling are good general exercises because, although you may need special equipment, you don't need to depend on another person in order to participate regularly. Add in other types of exercise if you have the interest, capability, and access to facilities or partners. What counts as exercise? Racquetball, squash, tennis, skiing, mountain climbing, rollerblading, aerobics, dance, and anything else you can think of that requires you to move. Although most research has been done with these types of aerobic exercises, some studies show that nonaerobic exercises may also work, but to a lesser degree. Nonaerobic exercises—such as doing yoga or working out with dumbbells, weights, and circuit machines at a gym—have been shown to reduce premenstrual symptom severity in at least one study. But aerobic exercises were superior in terms of overall symptom improvement and relieving depressed mood.

- *Don't* **worry about your initial fitness level.** Your level of fitness has nothing to do with the mood-enhancing benefits of exercise. Even people who never exercised before feel better after beginning a moderate exercise program. Granted, you'll become more fit once you start exercising, but fitness is not a prerequisite.

- **Exercise at least thirty minutes to begin with.** Many previously sedentary people who begin an exercise program hate it. It feels different from sitting on the couch, that's for certain. Muscles work that may not have worked for a while, and the activity may seem unnatural. Studies have shown that while levels of anxiety may begin to decrease as early as ten minutes after beginning exercise, it isn't until after about thirty minutes that people begin to enjoy the exercise and can feel measurable mood improvements. No one is sure why this happens. It may be because that's when the body's feel-good chemicals, such as endorphins, start to kick in, or it might have to do with a sense of accomplishment. If you make a commitment to stick with your chosen activity for at least thirty minutes, you may be pleasantly surprised to find how much better you feel.

- **Be patient with the results.** Although people tend to feel better immediately after exercising, the true benefits in terms of overall mood improvement take at least five weeks to take effect. That means you'll go through at least one, possibly two, menstrual cycles before you'll feel a greater sense of calm premenstrually.

8

Nutritional Supplements

For a while I was taking everything—calcium, vitamin E, vitamin C, zinc, a multivitamin, and I can't even remember what else. Really, I just remember feeling nauseous and bloated after taking them, and it cost a fortune. Now I only take calcium, but I wish I could remember to take it more often.

—Caren

NUTRITIONAL SUPPLEMENTS are often touted as a cure-all by health food vendors and supplement manufacturers, but this is another case where the hype is greater than the results. Some, such as calcium, really seem to work and are a valuable addition to any woman's diet. Others have less research to recommend them, and still others are downright dangerous. In the hands of a careful and informed consumer, however, the right supplements can help relieve some premenstrual symptoms.

It's hard to argue against taking nutritional supplements. After all, most of us grew up with candy-flavored chewable vitamins, and we are used to thinking of them as harmless additions to a less-than-optimal diet. So when we see dozens of special supplements made "just for women" lining the shelves of supermarkets and health food stores, it is perfectly natural to assume that they must contain some unique combination of necessary vitamins and minerals that we really ought to be taking. That's exactly what the manufacturers want you to think. Don't fall for it.

When it comes to relieving premenstrual symptoms, the results of scientific tests on vitamins, minerals, and other nutritional supplements have been underwhelming, to say the least. That's really not surprising when you consider that the medical literature suggests that our monthly discomfort is due to the effects of changing hormone levels, neurotransmitters, social and psychological factors, and special in-born biological sensitivities. Vitamins and minerals play a negligible role in these areas. Still, that doesn't stop supplement manufacturers from creating dozens of special formulas to relieve premenstrual symptoms and claiming that they will vanquish all signs of premenstrual syndrome (PMS). At best, these "special" formulas are not much different from a chewable daily vitamin made for children, although the PMS supplements are often more expensive and contain considerably lower amounts of vitamins and minerals. At worst, the PMS supplements may contain potentially toxic doses of vitamin B_6.

In addition, the treatment value of supplements has to be weighed against their cost. Depending on the brand and supplier, combination supplements can be very expensive. If you consider that insurance plans often cover much of the cost of prescription medications, supplements claiming to help with PMS symptoms can be more expensive per month than a prescription for a selective serotonin reuptake inhibitor (SSRI). It is not unusual to find these types of supplements selling for $20 to $40 per bottle or more, with average costs of $0.66 to $1.85 daily, when used as recommended.

There are some supplements worth trying, but they don't require purchasing special combination formulas. And some supplements carry hidden dangers. For example, tryptophan and 5-hydroxytryptophan (5-HTP) may contain toxic impurities that may cause permanent disability or even death. If you decide you would like to try taking nutritional supplements, there are a few safety notes to be aware of:

- **Do not take more than the amounts recommended here.** Too much of a good thing may result in side effects such as nausea, constipation, or even irreversible nerve damage (as is seen with vitamin B_6 toxicity).

- **Do not rely on the dosage amounts recommended on package labels.** We have seen dosage recommendations three or more times higher than what is considered generally safe.

- **Purchase name-brand supplements, and buy them from reputable dealers.** Currently, supplement manufacturers do not need to register with the U.S. Food and Drug Administration (FDA) or get FDA approval before making and selling supplements. This means that virtually anyone can create a product and begin selling it. The quality and purity of the products you buy depend on the overall quality of the company making them. Look for names you trust.

- **Do not buy any product over the Internet unless you are already familiar with the manufacturer and specific supplement.** Many times, Internet sales sites don't include even basic information, such as the quantity of the nutrient in each pill you are purchasing or how many pills are in a bottle.

- **If you decide to purchase over the Internet and want to be assured that you are getting what you order, make sure the site has received Verified Internet Pharmacy Practice Sites (VIPPS) certification.** The blue VIPPS oval is usually found at the bottom of the site's home page. This seal of approval from the National Boards of Pharmacy assures that the Internet site has been evaluated by an outside agency and can be considered reputable. With certified sites, you can rest assured that the product you purchase is the product you'll receive. Some disreputable sites have been known to substitute lesser products for name-brand products but sell them in the name-brand bottle! Not all noncertified sites are deceptive, but a VIPPS certification guarantees that the site is legitimate.

- **Don't bother with any of the special formulas that specifically claim to help with premenstrual symptoms.** Some contain vitamins in quantities too high to be safe. Others contain smaller amounts of vitamins and minerals than even a child's multivitamin. Still others claim to include herbs that might help relieve premenstrual symptoms. As we will discuss in Chapter 9, many popular herbs have been shown not to work. Plus, the purity and quality of herbal products are not regulated in the United States, which means that the amounts listed on the product labels in these special formulas are likely to be inaccurate. If you want to try herbal medicines *and* vitamins and minerals, buy each separately in the dosages and standardizations recommended in this book.

- **Don't waste your money on unproved products.** Any vitamin, mineral, or other nutritional supplement not listed here has not been shown to have any relevance to PMS and premenstrual dysphoric disorder (PMDD). For example, we've seen some specialty PMS supplements that contain high doses of vitamin C. Although vitamin C is important for health in general, there is no reason to believe that it plays any role in relieving premenstrual symptoms.

Although further research is needed before we can say definitively if, how, or why a particular supplement works for PMDD symptoms, the following is an overview of what is known so far.

What Works

Only calcium has had consistent statistical success in relieving premenstrual symptoms. This means that during scientific studies, women who were treated with calcium supplements had greater levels of symptom relief than women who were given a placebo. Unfortunately, statistical success isn't always related to clinical success. Most women with premenstrual symptoms severe enough to lead them to seek medical care often find that supplements don't completely relieve their symptoms but only decrease symptoms by about half. If you decide to give supplements a try, hang in there for at least three menstrual cycles because the effects of supplements will be slow and subtle. This is not a quick fix.

Calcium

- *Dosage:* Take a total of 900 to 1,200 milligrams per day, in a divided dose. (That means don't take it all at the same time. For example, you can take 300 milligrams three or four times a day, or 500 milligrams twice a day.) The divided dose is necessary because your body can absorb only about 500 milligrams of calcium at a time; any more than that will simply be eliminated. Take with meals.

- *Evidence:* Way back in 1930, a scientific study found that levels of calcium in the bloodstream were lower in women during the week before their menstrual periods compared with the week after their periods. Other researchers noted that the symptoms of PMS and PMDD are similar to symptoms experienced by people with abnormally low levels of calcium (hypocalcemia). These findings gave scientists a place to start their investigations.

  All studies that have been conducted with calcium show that it has at least some usefulness in relieving premenstrual symptoms, including negative affect, water retention, and food cravings. However, the placebo effect tends to be very large in these studies. For example, in the largest and best-designed study to date, women who took 1,200 milligrams of calcium per day had their premenstrual symptoms reduced by 48 percent, but women who took a placebo (an inactive substance) had their symptoms reduced by 30 percent. Although calcium caused a significantly greater reduction in symptoms than the placebo, the actual difference in relief between the two conditions was quite small.

  We do recommend that women try taking calcium. Aside from any reduction in premenstrual symptoms, calcium is necessary to protect bone density as we age. There is some evidence that having a premenstrual disorder is related to lower bone mass. No one knows why or how premenstrual symptoms and bone loss are related, but calcium may be a link. Unfortunately, most women don't get enough calcium in their diets, and because most of us develop lactose intolerance as we grow older, adding significant amounts of dietary calcium may not be possible. By taking calcium supplements now for your premenstrual symptoms, you may also be helping to preserve your long-term bone health.

- *What to buy:* Any brand will work, so choose the form, flavor, and price you are comfortable with. Many calcium supplements also contain vitamin D. This is fine but not necessary. Although vitamin D is needed to help the body use calcium properly, we create vitamin D in our bodies with just a few minutes of natural sunlight every day.

Although most studies of the effects of calcium on premenstrual symptoms have used a form of calcium called calcium carbonate, that form may not be right for everyone. If you tend to have digestive problems—such as an easily upset stomach, constipation, bloating, or irritable bowel syndrome—take a different form called calcium citrate. Calcium citrate causes fewer gastrointestinal problems and creates less gas.

An inexpensive and convenient product that delivers all the calcium you need is Tums E-X and Tums "Calcium for Life" PMS tablets. These flavored, chewable tablets each contain 300 milligrams of calcium carbonate and are available in most grocery stores. Both Tums products should cost the same, but check prices and choose the one that costs less.

Another good choice (mainly because it is enjoyable to eat and therefore more easily remembered) is the Viactiv brand of soft chewable calcium supplements. These are more expensive but taste like candy—available in milk chocolate, mochaccino, orange cream, and caramel.

- *Cautions:* Calcium supplements are generally safe. Do not take calcium supplements in the form of bonemeal or dolomite, because these products may contain lead. Calcium supplements may reduce the effectiveness of certain medications, including the tetracycline antibiotics and the anticonvulsant medication phenytoin (Dilantin). Do not take calcium supplements within three hours of taking either of these medications. Talk with your doctor about whether calcium supplements are right for you if you have a problem with your parathyroid gland or have experienced kidney stones or kidney disease. Although side effects are very rare, discontinue taking calcium supplements if you experience severe constipation, nausea, large urine output, or unusual fatigue.

What Might Work

For the following nutrients, some studies suggest that they help relieve premenstrual symptoms, but other studies suggest that they don't. Again, any beneficial effects are likely to be subtle.

Magnesium

- *Dosage:* Take a total of 320 to 500 milligrams each day, in a divided dose. Take with meals. Researchers conducting studies of magnesium instructed women to take the supplements only during their luteal phase (beginning on Day 15 of their menstrual cycles and ending on the day menstrual bleeding began), but you can take them all month if you wish. Some women find it easier to take supplements every day rather than have to mark the calendar to remind themselves.

- *Evidence:* Similar to calcium, the level of magnesium in a woman's bloodstream changes over the course of her menstrual cycle. The few studies of the effectiveness of magnesium in reducing premenstrual symptoms have yielded mixed results that don't give a clear picture of the value of this mineral. A study published in 1991 found that 360 milligrams of magnesium (given in three doses of 120 milligrams each) reduced reported levels of negative affect, water retention, and overall menstrual distress. The reduction was most dramatic after four months of taking magnesium. Another study using only 200 milligrams of magnesium found that the supplements reduced water retention but no other symptoms. The same researchers later investigated the effectiveness of a combination of 200 milligrams of magnesium and 50 milligrams of vitamin B_6 (see the following section for more information on vitamin B_6). After one month of treatment with this combination, women reported lower levels of anxiety. Neither magnesium nor vitamin B_6 individually had any effect on premenstrual symptoms in this study. It is not known whether higher doses of magnesium, as were used in the 1991 study, would change the outcome.

Because so few studies have been done and because the data don't point to any definitive recommendation, our best advice is that it can't hurt to give magnesium a try, but we can't guarantee that it will work. It seems to take two to four months for the effects to kick in, so be patient.

- *What to buy:* Any brand and form will work.

- *Cautions:* Magnesium supplements may reduce the effectiveness of tetracycline antibiotics. Don't take magnesium within three hours of taking tetracycline medications. Talk with your doctor about whether magnesium supplements are right for you if you have heart disease or kidney problems. Although side effects are very rare, discontinue taking magnesium supplements if you experience severe diarrhea, nausea or vomiting, red or flushed skin, dizziness, confusion, difficulty breathing, or slow heartbeat.

Vitamin B6

- *Dosage:* Take *no more than* 50 to 100 milligrams each day. Take with meals.

- *Evidence:* Vitamin B_6 has been demonstrated to bind to receptors that normally bind with estrogen, progesterone, and other hormones. This may explain why researchers have been so interested in exploring its use in relieving premenstrual symptoms. A 1999 review of studies of the efficacy of vitamin B_6 found that most of the studies were of poor quality. Of the studies reviewed, only about half showed that vitamin B_6 supplements were more effective than placebos at reducing premenstrual symptoms. The successful studies reported reduced levels of depression, breast tenderness, and irritability.

Because the research results have been so mixed, taking vitamin B_6 may not be worth the effort and cost. If you keep daily doses to 100 milligrams or lower, it can't hurt to try, but there is no guarantee that it will work.

- *What to buy:* Any brand and form will work. Vitamin B$_6$ is also known as pyridoxine.

- *Cautions:* Unlike most other vitamins and minerals, it is possible to overdose on vitamin B$_6$. At doses as low as 200 milligrams per day, women have developed peripheral neuropathies—nerve damage that causes tingling in the hands and/or feet. This nerve damage is often permanent. Vitamin B$_6$ supplements may keep the medication levodopa (Larodopa) from working properly. If you are taking levodopa, talk with your physician before taking vitamin B$_6$. Discontinue taking vitamin B$_6$ supplements and see your physician if you experience any tingling or numbness in your hands, fingers, feet, or toes.

Vitamin E

- *Dosage:* Take 400 IU (international units) each day. Take with meals.

- *Evidence:* To date, only one full study has looked at the effect of vitamin E on premenstrual symptoms. It showed that 400 IU of vitamin E supplements (in the *d*-alpha tocopherol form) were more effective than placebos at reducing physical and emotional premenstrual symptoms. It is difficult to understand why vitamin E might have an effect, however. Levels of vitamin E in the bloodstream do not fluctuate throughout the month, and vitamin E has no significant effect on concentrations of hormones in the bloodstream.

  Because there has been so little research on the effects of vitamin E, it is difficult to make a reasoned recommendation. Vitamin E is very safe, and most people don't get enough vitamin E in their diets. Because vitamin E may be valuable in preventing some types of cardiovascular diseases, you may get added health benefits beyond any reduction in premenstrual symptoms. It certainly can't hurt to try, but there is no guarantee that it will work.

- *What to buy:* Any brand and form should work, but buy *d*-alpha tocopherol if it is available. (Vitamin E is also known as alpha tocopherol.)

- *Cautions:* Vitamin E supplements are generally very safe. Even very large doses are well tolerated. No side effects are associated with doses of 400 IU daily.

Omega-3 Fatty Acids

- *Dosage:* Take 3,000 to 6,000 milligrams each day (that's equivalent to 3 to 6 grams). Take in divided doses, with meals. Depending on the type of supplement you choose, you may see quantities for two different substances listed on the label: EPA (eicosapentaenoic acid) and DHA (docosahexaenoic acid). These are just the two major types of fatty acids that make up omega-3s. Add the two numbers and you'll get the total quantity.

- *Evidence:* Omega-3 fatty acids are essential nutrients, meaning that they are necessary for good health but that they are not made in the body. We have to get all our omega-3 fatty acids from diet or supplements. The one study to date that looked specifically at the effects of essential fatty acids in treating PMS showed that the fatty acids had no effects. However, there are some intriguing studies that suggest that omega-3s in the form of fish oils may be valuable in treating mild depression.

  Omega-3 fatty acids have not been shown to help relieve or reduce most physical and emotional premenstrual symptoms. If your major premenstrual symptom is depression, or if you have PME with mild depression throughout the month, you may find some relief after taking omega-3 fatty acids. Even then, there is no guarantee that fish oil will work.

- *What to buy:* The best form of this supplement to buy is fish oil capsules. They are more stable than the other types of omega-3 fatty acids. Some may need to be refrigerated—check the label for instructions. Do *not* buy cod liver oil, because it contains high amounts of vitamin A, which can be toxic in large doses. Like herbal products, fish oil capsules are not under FDA regulation. This means that manufacturers are not required to prove quality or reliability of their products. It is possible that the amount of fatty acids in each capsule is less than what has been promised on the label. Buy only respected name brands.

- *Cautions:* Fish oil supplements are generally safe. Although side effects are rare, discontinue use if you experience nausea, diarrhea, belching, or a bad taste in your mouth. Omega-3 fatty acids reduce the "stickiness" of blood platelets, which means that they act as a blood thinner. Talk with your doctor before taking omega-3 fatty acids if you have bleeding problems or if you are already taking a blood thinner, such as warfarin (Coumadin). Like other types of fat, omega-3 fatty acids are relatively high in calories. Read the package label to learn how many extra calories the supplements will add to your diet.

Potentially Dangerous Supplements

There are a few supplements taken by some women worldwide that we cannot recommend because of their potential serious effects on the body.

Tryptophan

Tryptophan is a naturally occurring amino acid that is a precursor of serotonin, which means that your body uses it to create serotonin. In scientific studies, tryptophan supplements have been shown to be moderately helpful in decreasing premenstrual mood symptoms as well as mild depression and insomnia.

In late 1989, several people developed a rare blood disease called eosinophilia-myalgia syndrome (EMS), which causes intense muscle pain and long-term muscle weakness, profound fatigue, muscle and joint pain, memory loss, and other signs of nerve and muscle damage. By the end of 1991, more than 1,500 people in the United States were diagnosed with EMS, and 37 had died of the disease. In 95 percent of cases, the cause of the disease was traced to tryptophan supplements produced by one manufacturer, Showa Denko K.K. of Japan. After additional investigation, scientists determined that impurities (now called "peak X") in the product might have contributed in some way to the development of EMS.

Since then, scientists have been working to find the exact cause of tryptophan-related EMS. Although peak X was initially thought to be responsible for nearly all the cases, the FDA reports that animal studies have since shown that some rats fed tryptophan *without* impurities also developed EMS-type disorders.

The current position of the FDA is that the true cause of EMS in relation to tryptophan supplements is unknown. Scientists now believe that the development of the disease may be due to a combination of substances in the supplements (contaminants or the active ingredient), individual susceptibility, and perhaps even environmental triggers. In a 2001 information paper, the FDA stated that it still couldn't determine if tryptophan supplements are safe.

Although the FDA does not prohibit the marketing of tryptophan in the United States, government regulations put the burden of proof of safety with the manufacturer—and so far no manufacturer has decided to risk the liability. In addition, the FDA bans the importation of tryptophan (except for certain medically necessary uses). This means that tryptophan supplements are unavailable in the United States to the average consumer. Some European countries have also banned or limited access to tryptophan.

In the 1990s, another substance called 5-hydroxytryptophan (5-HTP) began being sold in supplement form. In the body, tryptophan is converted first to 5-HTP and then to serotonin, so it was hypothesized that 5-HTP should work at least as well as tryptophan in relieving mood symptoms. That looked to be true, but the peak X family of contaminants has also been detected in some 5-HTP supplements.

Because EMS is a potentially lethal disease that has left hundreds of people with chronic pain, and because scientists cannot yet claim that tryptophan and 5-HTP are safe and free of contaminants, we cannot recommend trying these supplements. Serotonin reuptake inhibitor medications (see Chapter 6) perform the same functions, but with more success and a regulated purity of product.

Dehydroepiandrosterone (DHEA)

Dehydroepiandrosterone is a hormone secreted by the adrenal glands. Although some manufacturers claim that DHEA can help relieve depression, there is no research that shows that it is at all helpful for women with premenstrual symptoms. In fact, one study conducted by researchers in Sweden found that blood levels of DHEA and other androgens are higher in women with PMS or PMDD at various times of the month compared with women without premenstrual symptoms. This would suggest that taking additional DHEA would only make premenstrual symptoms worse. One study looked at the effects of DHEA on women with perimenopausal symptoms, including moodiness, dysphoria, poor memory, and a lack of a general sense of well-being. DHEA did not improve any of those symptoms.

Melatonin

Melatonin is another hormone that is sometimes taken in supplement form. Because melatonin has been used as a treatment for jet lag, some women assume that it might also help them with the fatigue associated with premenstrual disorders. There have been questions about the safety of melatonin supplements, but the biggest reason it is not recommended for women with PMDD, PME, or PMS is that melatonin supplements have been known to increase depressive symptoms in some people.

We cannot recommend the use of DHEA, melatonin, or any other over-the-counter hormone product. Although they are sold as supplements, hormones are powerful, biologically active substances. Research has not shown that there is any benefit to taking these over-the-counter supplements, and there may be some serious repercussions, such as suppression of other hormones naturally produced in the body. Hormones are responsible for your good health, but under certain conditions, they can also do harm. It's best not to use any hormone-related product without the advice of a physician.

9

Complementary Treatments

My doctor tried a holistic approach as well. She told me to take evening primrose oil. I have no idea whether it works or not. I take it every day just because I never want to feel the kind of depression I felt before. I try to stave that off any way I can. When I started becoming this "freak" around this time of the month, I tried everything. Anything anyone would suggest to me, I tried.

—MARISA

IF YOU'VE EVER brewed a cup of chamomile tea to help you sleep, or massaged your temples to relieve a headache, then you've already used two of the most common types of complementary medicine—herbal remedy and acupressure. In the broadest sense, complementary or alternative treatments include any health maintenance or disease treatment methods that fall outside the usual scope of standard medical practice.

There are more than a hundred different modalities and subcategories of complementary treatment. The most popular are use of herbs, acupuncture, acupressure, meditation, traditional Chinese medicine, chiropractic manipulation, and massage. Before modern medicine became a science, these types of complementary therapies were all that was available to treat the sick. Some, such as acupuncture and traditional Chinese medicine, have been used by Asian cultures for thousands of years. Until penicillin made its medical debut in the 1940s, physicians routinely recommended folk remedies to treat infections. In a home health guide published in 1901, John C. Gunn, M.D., devoted dozens of pages to the use of plants for treating illnesses, including instructions on how to recognize, collect, and prepare various barks, roots, and seeds.

Did these methods work? It's hard to say. Back then the value of these types of treatments wasn't determined by evidence-based research studies; instead, family doctors observed how their patients responded and assumed that the treatment made the difference.

Today, in spite of increasingly complex medical treatments, or perhaps because of the complexity of conventional medical care, people are more interested than ever before in complementary medicine. Whether people are looking for additions to their conventional medical treatment, or looking for alternatives to medical care, we spend billions of dollars every year on complementary treatments. And doctors are increasingly being called upon to answer questions about complementary and alternative medicine (or CAM)—questions about the effectiveness of specific folk remedies, or how some herbs might interact with prescribed medications, or how certain practices might contribute to wellness. In some cases, the answers are known. But in most cases, there has not been enough research, and science simply cannot provide those answers at this time.

General Information About Complementary Medicine

For any kind of treatment, complementary or otherwise, no one can say how well it works until it is tested scientifically. Without carefully controlled scientific studies, normal healing may be mistaken for treatment effectiveness. For example, let's say you put a special herbal salve on a wound and cover it with a bandage for three days. If the wound is mostly healed when you take the bandage off, did the salve help the healing, or would the body have healed on its own even without the salve? Without a scientific study comparing the healing times of identical cuts that were treated with and without the herbal salve, there's no way to know the value of the herbs.

Sometimes the claims of CAM cannot be supported. In carefully controlled scientific studies, CAM treatments often work no better than placebo or sham (pretend) treatments. Other times, however, this type of rigorous research supports the use of CAM. A recent study found that chicken soup, perhaps the oldest of all folk remedies for the common cold, contains a mild anti-inflammatory agent that may help reduce nasal symptoms. If a treatment works reliably and effectively in scientific studies, then you are assured it has some value.

Research is currently being conducted to determine how well various CAM practices work for specific ailments. The majority of our scientific understanding of complementary medicine thus far comes from European research. European scientists began doing clinical research with herbs and other CAM modalities years ago, but researchers in the United States are just getting started. In 1998, in order to convey its serious intention to investigate CAM, Congress established the National Center for Complementary and Alternative Medicine (NCCAM) at the National Institutes of Health (NIH). Its goal is to use scientific methods to investigate the safety and efficacy of the most popular alternative treatments, and they've already begun funding studies in university centers across the country.

Quality assurance is another area in which European progress has outpaced that of the United States. In Europe, there are standardized formulations of herbal medicines, which assure that the contents of the bottle match what is advertised on the label in terms of quantity and strength. Currently in the United States there are no guidelines and no protections for the consumer. The United States also has no standardization policy, and no federal agency oversees the quality of herbal supplements. As a result, it has been discovered that the quality and quantity of packaged herbs in this country varies greatly from manufacturer to manufacturer, bottle to bottle, and pill to pill. When scientists tested what was actually contained in the capsules sold as herbal supplements, they found that different capsules *in the same bottle* often contained different amounts of the herb. In some cases, capsules contained only filler, with no herb at all. It has also been shown that potentially harmful contaminants are common.

Right now, pork rind processing has higher standards of consistency and quality than does production of CAM supplements—and pork rinds don't claim to have psychoactive properties or medicinal ingredients. Until there are regulations regarding the quality and standardization of CAM products in the United States, as well as an agency to oversee compliance with those regulations, the reliability and value of CAM will be called into question.

There are some commonsense precautions you can take to protect yourself when using complementary treatments.

- Don't stop taking prescription medications, and don't stop seeing your regular doctor. Standard medicine is still the best option for treating any illness.
- Do some research or talk with your doctor before trying an expensive complementary treatment. Don't throw good money away on an unproven treatment.
- If the alternative medicine sounds too good to be true, it probably is. There is no such thing as a miracle cure.
- Don't assume that just because a complementary treatment is called "natural" that it is automatically safer than prescription medication. If the alternative medicine is strong enough to cure a disease or ease symptoms, then it is strong enough to cause side effects, some of which may be severe.
- Don't take more than the recommended amount of any supplement. Some people believe that if a little is good, more is better. Too much of an active herb, however, can be dangerous and have consequences similar to taking an overdose of a prescribed medication.
- Talk with your doctor before trying any complementary medicine that involves eating, drinking, or otherwise taking anything into your body. Some herbs can affect how well your prescription medication works. Always tell your doctor everything you are taking.
- Noninvasive treatments, such as massage, progressive relaxation, visualization, or yoga are generally safe and may increase general wellness by reducing stress. Feel free to try them if you think they might make you feel better.
- When purchasing herbal supplements, look for the words *standardized extract* on the label. Although this is no guarantee of quality (in the United States), it at least tells you that the manufacturer is aware that consumers are looking for specific active ingredients, and the product is more likely to conform to standardizations set internationally.
- Don't expect detailed treatment information about complementary medicines from manufacturers or medical literature. Studies thus far

have been only preliminary. Very little is known about the mechanisms of action, optimal dosing, concentrations, or frequency of treatment. Until multiple studies are completed, any recommendations given here or by complementary medicine practitioners are only guidelines.

What Seems to Work for Some Premenstrual Symptoms

Based on some preliminary scientific research, each of the following types of treatment has been shown to have a benefit in relieving at least some premenstrual symptoms. It is important to note, however, that when studies of complementary therapies are rigorously reviewed, most of the effects are less than dramatic. Many studies are poorly designed, and those that are well designed often fail to show much benefit.

Chasteberry

Also known as the extract of the fruit of *Vitex agnus castus.*

- *Improves:* Mood swings, irritability, anger, headache, breast symptoms.

- *Recommended dosage:* One 20-milligram tablet once a day. Look for *Vitex agnus castus* fruit extract Ze 440 tablets.

- *Relevant studies:* One study demonstrating the efficacy of chasteberry extract was published in the *British Medical Journal* in 2001. Nearly 170 women with premenstrual dysphoric disorder (PMDD), diagnosed according to the criteria in the *Diagnostic and Statistical Manual of Mental Disorders*, third edition, were enrolled in the study. Half were given a placebo, and half were given one 20-milligram tablet of *Vitex agnus castus* fruit extract Ze 440 daily. Premenstrual symptoms from before treatment were compared to symptoms at the end of three menstrual cycles after treatment, with ratings completed by the research physicians and the women themselves. The results showed that a little over half the women who received chasteberry tablets had significant improvement in all their premenstrual symptoms except bloating. There were no side effects associated with this treatment.

This study confirms the results of several other smaller studies, which also showed that chasteberry is effective in eliminating or decreasing the severity of many premenstrual symptoms. In general, most studies show about a 50 percent improvement in premenstrual symptoms while women were taking chasteberry extract, with symptoms returning shortly after discontinuing treatment.

- *Possible action:* The chasteberry contains iridoids and flavonoids, natural chemicals that may act to reduce anxiety and inflammation. It may also work by reducing levels of prolactin, a hormone that may contribute to menstrual irregularity. Chasteberry may have some progesteronelike effects, because some forms of progesterone have been found in the flowers and leaves of this herb.

- *Cautions:* Discontinue use if rash develops. It may decrease libido, although this has not been proved. Other possible side effects include gastrointestinal distress and headache.

St. John's Wort

Also known as *Hypericum perforatum.*

- *Improves:* Depressed mood, anxiety, confusion, crying, feeling out of control, and other premenstrual mood symptoms.

- *Recommended dosage:* One 300-milligram tablet of hypericum extract taken once a day. Look for brands that are standardized to 900 micrograms (0.3 percent) hypericin. Studies of the effects of St. John's wort on people with pure depression (not premenstrual depression) have used up to 900 milligrams of hypericum per day—three times the dose used in studies treating premenstrual syndrome. More studies will be needed to determine the optimal dosage. If you want to try St. John's wort, start with the lower dose of 300 milligrams, and try it for two months. If your symptoms don't improve after two cycles, try 600 milligrams for another two cycles. Never exceed 900 milligrams, because there have been reports of toxicity in some people who took greater amounts.

- *Relevant studies:* St. John's wort is among the most studied herbs. It has been demonstrated in several clinical trials to reduce mild to moderate depression to about the same degree as low doses of antidepressant medications, but it does not seem to perform any better than placebo for severe depression. For premenstrual symptoms, one small study found that treatment with St. John's wort decreased symptoms by half in the majority of women.

- *Possible action:* It is believed that the active substances in St. John's wort are the natural chemicals hyperforin, polycyclic phenols, hypericin, and pseudohypericin. These are thought to relieve depression by inhibiting the reuptake of serotonin in the brain (similar to the selective serotonin reuptake inhibitor [SSRI] medications).

- *Cautions:* It has been reported that at least two women in Europe who were taking both oral contraceptives and St. John's wort became unexpectedly pregnant. Although these reports are rare, it is possible that St. John's wort weakens the effects of the oral contraceptive. To avoid pregnancy while taking St. John's wort, you may want to consider using a different (or additional) form of birth control, such as a condom or diaphragm.

  If taken in high doses or over long periods of time, St. John's wort can cause photosensitivity, which will cause a skin rash in response to direct sunlight. Discontinue use if this occurs. Other possible side effects include dry mouth, dizziness, gastrointestinal distress, and fatigue. Because of possible drug interactions or additive effects, do not take St. John's wort if you are also taking fluoxetine (Prozac, Sarafem), sertraline (Zoloft), paroxetine (Paxil), fluvoxamine (Luvox), citalopram (Celexa), or any other antidepressant medications.

Ginkgo

Also known as *Ginkgo biloba.*

- *Improves:* Breast symptoms. May improve ability to concentrate by increasing blood flow to the brain. Has been suggested, without definitive proof, that it may reduce the effects of SSRI medications on sexual function.

- *Recommended dosage:* Typical doses are 120 to 160 milligrams per day. These can be taken as one 40-milligram tablet taken three times a day or one 80-milligram tablet taken twice a day. Look for the standardized *Ginkgo biloba* extract EGb 761 or a brand that is standardized to 24 percent flavone glycosides. Women have shown improvement in breast symptoms when ginkgo was taken starting from Day 16 of one cycle until Day 5 of the next cycle (basically, starting just after ovulation and stopping the last day of menstrual bleeding).

- *Relevant studies:* Ginkgo has been studied most for the treatment of blood-flow disorders, including dementia and peripheral arterial disease. There has been one major study, conducted in France, that studied the effects of ginkgo or a placebo in 165 women with premenstrual syndrome (PMS). After evaluation by a physician and the review of self-reports by the women themselves, the study showed that after two cycles of treatment, breast symptoms were significantly reduced in the women who took ginkgo.

- *Possible action:* Ginkgo contains a variety of natural chemicals unique to this herb, including ginkgetin, ginkgolic acid, and ginkgolides. It contains a relatively large amount of flavonoids, which have anti-inflammatory properties. Ginkgo acts as an anticoagulant and produces changes that allow blood vessels to dilate (or enlarge). The overall effect is improved blood flow.

- *Cautions:* High doses may cause nausea, vomiting, diarrhea, restlessness, or insomnia. Discontinue use if you experience side effects.

Because ginkgo acts as a blood thinner, if you are taking an anticoagulant medication, such as warfarin (Coumadin), talk with your doctor about possible interactions before taking ginkgo. These effects can also be seen in the easy bruising that has occurred in people taking both ginkgo and aspirin (another potential blood thinner) or ginkgo and vitamin E. If you regularly take vitamin E or aspirin, be cautious and talk with your doctor about potential interactions. Although studies have shown breast symptoms to be reduced, ginkgo may increase irritability and may therefore be an inappropriate treatment for women with irritability as a major premenstrual symptom.

What Might Work for Premenstrual Symptoms

Research results have been mixed or inconclusive regarding the abilities of the following types of treatment to relieve premenstrual symptoms.

Black Cohosh

Also known as *Cimicifuga racemosa*. This treatment is usually used for symptoms associated with menopause, but one study has suggested that it may be generally effective in reducing anxiety, tension, and depression. Analysis of one Asian species suggests that black cohosh may act as a mild serotonin reuptake inhibitor. Because this herb has not been studied in clinical trials, there are no proven recommended dosages. However, the commonly suggested dosage is 20 milligrams, twice daily. Possible side effects include gastrointestinal distress, headache, weight gain, and dizziness.

Reflexology

Reflexology is a pressure technique in which specific areas on the feet, hands, and/or ears are "activated" by pressure. According to practitioners of this modality, different zones on the hands, feet, or ears correspond to different systems of the body. Pressing on those spots is thought to activate the distant body part. The general benefits of reflexology are similar to those of massage—relaxation, stress reduction, and enhanced circulation. What makes reflexology worthy of note is one study that found that women with mild premenstrual symptoms got some relief when they received foot, ear, and hand reflexology performed by a trained reflexologist once a week for eight weeks, at thirty minutes per session. These women had significantly more relief than women who received a false, or "sham," reflexology treatment. Although more study needs to be done before this modality can be definitely recommended, trying it will do you no harm.

Acupuncture

Acupuncture involves the skilled placement of hair-thin needles in the skin along the so-called energy meridians that are part of Chinese medical beliefs. Although acupuncture has been touted as a treatment for premenstrual symptoms, no scientific research has been done to verify this claim. There is some support, however, for the value of acupuncture in treating mild depression. A recent study found that extended use of acupuncture (ten or more visits) resulted in mood improvement in many patients with mild depression and reduced anxiety symptoms in patients with generalized anxiety disorders. Electroacupuncture, in which a mild electric current stimulates the embedded needles, seems to be superior to traditional acupuncture in alleviating depression. An even newer method, computer-controlled electroacupuncture, is currently being tested. This last method takes the guesswork (and the art) out of the procedure because voltage, amplitude, frequency, and duration of the stimulus are precisely controlled by a computer. Some preliminary results show that computer-controlled electroacupuncture is superior to both traditional acupuncture and regular electroacupuncture. Not all studies have shown positive results with acupuncture treatment of depression, however.

Acupuncture appears to be a safe procedure when performed by trained and experienced acupuncturists. We have reservations about recommending this treatment because of the mixed results of scientific studies, the lack of data for premenstrual symptoms specifically, and the difficulty involved in locating a properly trained and experienced professional. If, however, you feel that you have located a trustworthy acupuncturist (one who is trained, experienced, and licensed, and who uses disposable needles), it doesn't appear that there are any significant harmful side effects of acupuncture.

Relaxation

It is possible that relaxation may help relieve some premenstrual symptoms. Because one of the theories of premenstrual disorders is that women have a sensitivity and greater response to stress, relaxation may help reduce stress levels. In one study of a particular type of relaxation called the "relaxation response," a group of women practiced the relaxation response for fifteen to twenty minutes twice a day for three months (see the following sidebar for more details). To control for the effects of simply having some quiet

---

The Relaxation Response

Who doesn't need more relaxation? But true relaxation is more than just sitting in a chair flipping through a magazine, as pleasant as that might be. The "relaxation response" was first described by Dr. Herbert Benson in 1974 and has been a staple of stress relief ever since. It combines progressive relaxation with a form of focused meditation as a way of calming physiologic responses typically associated with tension and stress. Benefits come with continued practice. Ideally, you should practice this twice a day for fifteen or twenty minutes each time.

To begin to practice the relaxation response, sit comfortably with your eyes closed in a quiet room. Relax all your muscles as thoroughly and deeply as possible. Do this by focusing on each part of your body individually, from your face down to your toes. Consciously feel the tension in each body part, and then allow the tension to melt away, leaving the muscle relaxed. When you've relaxed your muscles, begin to relax your mind. Breathe in through your nose and out through your mouth. Be aware of your breath as you inhale. Then, as you exhale, repeat the word *one* silently to yourself. (This isn't a counting exercise. You will silently say "one" at each exhale.) This keeps you lightly focused on the out-breath. If distracting thoughts enter your mind, notice them, but don't allow your mind to stick to them. Go back to focusing on your breathing. Don't allow yourself to become concerned with whether you are doing it "correctly" or whether you're getting the right relaxation response. No one is there to judge you. The relaxation will come in time. Focus on your breathing, on releasing stray thoughts before they become worries, and on keeping your muscles relaxed.

---

time, there were two other groups in the study: one group was instructed to read for fifteen to twenty minutes twice a day for three months, and the other was instructed simply to chart their symptoms. After three months, women who practiced the relaxation response had a 58 percent improvement in their symptoms, compared with about a 27 percent improvement for the reading group and a 17 percent improvement for the charting group. Anyone can learn the relaxation response or other relaxation techniques in just a few minutes. Even if it doesn't help, it certainly can't hurt, and it can be a good general stress reliever.

What Probably Does Not Work for Premenstrual Symptoms

Some treatments that are highly publicized and marketed as valid treatments for PMS really don't work. What tends to happen is that a poorly designed research study finds a small positive response to a particular treatment. Even though the outcomes may be weak or inaccurate, media outlets that scan for interesting articles may publish the results in newspapers or report them as news on television. And manufacturers are quick to use any kind of scientific backing to try to sell more product by referring to the research in advertising or on product labels. Soon the modest results of a bad research study are circulated like a rumor and eventually become part of "general knowledge."

Oil of Evening Primrose

Despite its popularity and reputation as a treatment for PMS, oil of evening primrose does not seem to work to relieve premenstrual symptoms. A review of available research conducted by scientists from Belfast found that of seven studies conducted, only two were well designed and controlled for other factors that might affect the outcome of the study. Those two studies showed that treatment with oil of evening primrose had no greater benefit than placebo in relieving premenstrual symptoms.

Massage

Massage also does not seem to help premenstrual symptoms. One study that looked at the effect of massage on short- and long-term symptom reduction found that anxiety, sadness, and pain were reduced immediately after massage but that the effects did not last. Massage can be restful and relaxing and may be beneficial in reducing acute stress levels. If you enjoy massage, feel free to add it to your general health regimen, but don't expect it to provide premenstrual relief.

Homeopathy

One of the treatments most difficult to test is homeopathy. The treatment in homeopathy is based on "like cures like," such that if you want to cure diarrhea, for example, you would give the patient a small amount of a substance that causes diarrhea. According to homeopathy, the smaller the amount of that substance, the greater the healing. For the most "powerful" homeopathic remedies, the amounts are so dilute that when the medicine is scientifically analyzed, no trace of the active substance can be found. Although homeopathy has a rather large popular following, there is no scientific or medical principle that can justify its claims. To date, there has been one small study that looked at the effects of homeopathic medicine in controlling menstrual distress. Although positive results were claimed, the measures of success were much lower than those used in standard studies. Even then, the results were slight, bordering on insignificant. Most medical practitioners advise spending your money elsewhere until more definitive and robust effects can be seen.

Chiropractic Manipulation

Although chiropractic manipulation can be of benefit for some muscular problems, it has not been demonstrated to be of any help in relieving premenstrual symptoms. One study looked at the benefit of a true chiropractic treatment compared with a false, or "sham," treatment. The results were that whichever treatment was received first—real treatment or sham treatment—relieved symptoms to the same degree. This means chiropractic treatment was of no special benefit to women with PMS.

Dong Quai

Some women ask about the possible benefits of dong quai for treating premenstrual symptoms. This Chinese herbal supplement has been touted as a treatment for menstrual problems (such as cramping or pain) and symptoms associated with menopause. To date, there have been no studies looking at the benefits of dong quai for treating premenstrual symptoms, and recent studies have shown that it is of no greater benefit than placebo for relieving menopausal symptoms. This herb does contain potent anticoagulants that can make it dangerous for some women, and its general safety has yet to be properly evaluated. It cannot be recommended at this time.

Under Evaluation

Kava, also known as Kava kava, has been successfully used to treat mild anxiety and restlessness. In well-designed, randomized, double-blind control studies, kava was shown to significantly decrease anxiety. These results were seen sometimes as soon as one week after beginning treatment but could take four to eight weeks of treatment. In a review of all studies published through June 1998, scientists found that kava was shown to be a safe and effective treatment for anxiety.

Unfortunately, that "safe" rating has since been called into question. In 2001, scientists in Europe reported that kava supplements were suspected to be responsible for more than two dozen cases of liver toxicity. Switzerland and France banned sales of kava. Other countries called for voluntary withdrawal of the product by manufacturers. In March 2002, the U.S. Food and Drug Administration (FDA) issued a consumer advisory warning of these potential risks. The herb is still under review. It is unknown whether the liver toxicity cases were due to the kava alone or to drug interactions, simultaneous alcohol use, or some contaminant in the supplements. Drinking alcohol while taking kava will increase the potential for toxicity. It is known to have interactive effects with many medications, including benzodiazepines (such as Ativan, Klonopin, Librium, Valium, Xanax, or others), levodopa (Larodopa), or other sedative or sleep-inducing agents. Long-term use of high doses of kava can cause flaky, dry skin; hair loss; and some loss of hearing. *Because of the potential for toxicity, we cannot recommend this herb for treatment of premenstrual symptoms at this time.*

10

Light and Sleep Therapies

*My husband often jokes and says that I am "solar-powered." I feel so much more ener-
gized in the spring and summer. Winter is a nightmare. I'm depressed, tired, and
totally unmotivated for months. And, as always, everything's worse around my period.*

—Caren

Most of us meet our daily schedules by using a series of timers that track
important hours and minutes. We wake to alarm clocks, punch a time clock
at work, change classes at school after a bell, watch the news at 11:00 P.M.,
and go to bed by midnight (but not before setting the alarm clock to start
the whole thing all over again the next day). Most of the time, life runs
smoothly and you barely have to think about the schedule. But what happens if you forget to set the alarm clock? If you wake up late, your whole
day can seem out of sync as you run to catch up with your usual routine.
If you arrive late for work, you may have to work through lunch, which
means you'll be hungry for dinner earlier. So much hinges on that one little alarm.

What works in your hectic, scheduled life also works in your body with
the help of an internal regulator known as a "body clock," or circadian
rhythm. Our bodies function according to a series of internal timers that
control myriad physiologic activities, including cellular metabolism, hormone production and release, and our sleep-wake cycle. Scientists hypoth-
esize that this internal clock is set and reset by (or "entrained" to) the

external environment, so our body schedules are related to nature's schedules. This includes waking up when the sun comes up, having high physiologic activity during the day, and falling asleep when it is dark. All living creatures have some type of internal clock or rhythm, although they can be set differently. For example, nocturnal animals have a body clock that tells them to wake when it is dark and sleep when the sun rises.

Every cell in our bodies has a circadian rhythm. When scientists remove cells and keep them alive in a Petri dish, the cells still follow a cyclical pattern of activity, although they slowly drift out of sync with the body over time. It is hypothesized that the body has a "master clock" that regulates all the smaller internal clocks. This is similar to the way we depend on Greenwich Mean Time as the official time all around the world, so we know how to reset our watches and clocks when they gain or lose minutes. But in the body, even the master clock is continually reset to keep it in tune with the environment.

As you might guess, given the importance of body rhythms in signaling the sleep-wake cycle, the most powerful factor known to be able to reset the circadian clock is light. Any kind of light will do—sunlight, reading light, indoor fluorescent light, or even the light emitted by a television in an otherwise darkened room. Stay up reading to a bright light for a couple of nights and you'll reset your circadian clock. Cover the windows in your bedroom with dark shades so that the morning light can't get through and you'll reset your circadian clock. Get on an airplane and travel several time zones away and you'll reset your circadian clock (and experience the effects of body clock dysregulation in the form of jet lag).

PMDD and the Circadian Clock

For most people most of the time, the circadian clock ticks away without any difficulty or problems. Hormones are released at the appropriate time and in the right amounts, the body's metabolism works well, and physiologic states (such as body temperature and brain waves during sleep) follow a consistent pattern. But people with certain illnesses or conditions have significant and measurable changes in these types of physiologic patterns.

People with seasonal affective disorder (SAD) are a prime example. In the fall and winter months, when SAD is most commonly experienced, people with SAD develop symptoms such as depression, carbohydrate cravings, a greater need to sleep, an inability to concentrate or focus, and increased anxiety. As devastating as these symptoms are from October through March, they virtually disappear during the spring and summer months. Why? As the seasons change, so do the strength and duration of the sunlight outdoors. It has been suggested that people suffering from SAD have a greater sensitivity to these changes in light, and they experience a heightened physiologic reaction. Other mood disorders, including major depression, also have been shown to be related to circadian rhythm dysregulation.

So where does premenstrual dysphoric disorder (PMDD) fit in?

As with other mood disorders, PMDD is thought to be affected by circadian rhythm changes. And because menstruation itself keeps a monthly cyclical rhythm, some researchers have hypothesized that PMDD may be the result of some monthly dysregulation in the body's internal clock. It was a logical step, then, for researchers to investigate how women with PMDD differ from women without PMDD in terms of the physiologic activities that are regulated by the circadian clock. They found important differences in several areas.

1. **Melatonin.** This naturally occurring hormone is strongly affected by light and is believed to be one of the main regulators of the body's sleep-wake cycle. Production of melatonin kicks into high gear when it gets dark, with blood levels ten times higher at night than during the day. Light is a cue for the body to shut down production of melatonin, an effect so dramatic that even turning on a lamp in the middle of the night will virtually halt production until the light is turned off again. Research shows that women with premenstrual symptoms have overall lower nighttime levels of melatonin, and their melatonin secretion shuts off earlier in the morning than it does in women without premenstrual symptoms.

   On a clinical note, this does not mean that adding melatonin will reverse PMDD changes. In fact, over-the-counter melatonin supplements are not recommended for women with premenstrual symptoms because they are likely to cause depressive symptoms.

2. **Prolactin.** Prolactin is a hormone that works with other hormones in the body to stimulate the development of female breasts and production of milk after childbirth, but all women have low levels of circulating prolactin in their bloodstreams. On a daily basis, normal secretion of prolactin also follows a circadian rhythm, with peak amounts found in the blood in the early morning hours, just after midnight. Research shows that women with PMDD have higher peak levels of prolactin than women without PMDD. The clinical significance of this difference has not been extensively explored.

3. **Cortisol.** Cortisol is a naturally occurring immune-regulating hormone that is secreted by the body in a predictable circadian pattern, with the highest levels occurring in the early morning and the lowest levels occurring at night, around bedtime. Research shows that during the late luteal phase of the menstrual cycle, women with PMDD reach their peak cortisol levels at different times of the night than women without PMDD. The overall amount of cortisol secreted, however, does not differ. Clinically, cortisol differences also have been noted in women with depression or chronic stress.

4. **Sleep electroencephalography (EEG).** When we sleep, our brain waves follow a distinct pattern. When sleeping, we pass through five stages of sleep about every ninety minutes: stage I (light sleep); stages II, III, and IV (deep sleep); and REM (rapid eye movement), or dream sleep. Research shows that women with premenstrual symptoms have longer stage II sleep and shorter amounts of REM sleep than women without premenstrual symptoms. Many medications also alter sleep stages (for example, REM sleep occurs earlier and perhaps more frequently in persons using certain antidepressant drugs).

5. **Body temperature.** Although we've been taught that "normal" body temperature is 98.6 degrees Fahrenheit, our actual body temperature fluctuates during a twenty-four-hour period. Our highest body tem-

perature usually occurs in the evening, then falls to its lowest point while we sleep. Research shows that women with premenstrual symptoms hit their lowest body temperature earlier and have overall higher nighttime body temperatures than women without premenstrual symptoms. The clinical implications of this finding are unclear at this time.

Similar research has been conducted with people who have seasonal affective disorder or major depression. Interestingly, these conditions also show circadian rhythm disruptions, but not always in the same directions as the disruptions found in women with PMDD. For example, compared to women without mood disorders, women with PMDD have an earlier shutoff of melatonin secretion, whereas women with seasonal affective disorder have a later shutoff. The fact that PMDD (without an underlying mood disorder) has its own set of definable and measurable physiologic changes suggests that PMDD is a distinct disorder, not merely depression masquerading as a premenstrual mood change.

So what do all these different factors and observations mean? Taken together, they paint a portrait of PMDD as a disorder that is, indeed, related to circadian clock changes, although the exact cause-and-effect relationship is not yet clear. Circadian rhythm expert Dr. Barbara Parry of the University of California, San Diego, and her colleagues believe that women with PMDD may have a disturbance in the regulating mechanism of their circadian clock, which causes their bodies' physiologic timing to differ from that of women without PMDD. Indeed, when women with and without PMDD are exposed to morning light during the follicular and luteal phases of their menstrual cycles, women with PMDD have a reduced and *reversed* melatonin response—but only during their luteal phase. While women without PMDD had a decrease in melatonin after exposure to light, women with PMDD had an increase in melatonin after the same exposure to light when they were in their luteal phase. This suggests that there is some dysfunction that occurs in the circadian clock or its link to the environment that occurs only during the symptomatic time of the month in women with PMDD.

Truth be told, the significance of this type of circadian clock dysregulation hasn't been firmly established, and the mechanism by which it is related to mood is unknown. Do the circadian changes themselves somehow affect mood, or are they merely an interesting side effect of other bodily changes? As of now, no one can say for certain. But some intriguing research suggests that resetting the circadian clocks of women with PMDD may help reduce the severity of some symptoms. And it may be as easy as flipping on a light switch or setting an alarm clock.

Light and Sleep Research

Researchers have been studying circadian rhythms unrelated to premenstrual symptoms for decades. The cumulative results have taught us that the internal circadian clock can be reset by numerous factors and that the most potent factor is the pattern of light and dark in the environment. For example, we get jet lag because our bodies are tuned into the light/dark patterns of our particular place on the globe. Traveling across time zones changes those familiar patterns. For each time zone we cross, our bodies become one hour out of sync. If we cross enough time zones, the difference between what our bodies expect (in terms of predictable patterns of sunrise and sunset) and what the new location's pattern of daylight is throws our bodies into a state of hormonal confusion. That is, in a nutshell, what jet lag is. Symptoms of jet lag include sleep disruption, fatigue, difficulty concentrating, and headaches. Eventually we get used to the different light/dark patterns of our new environment, signaling that the body clock has been reset.

Sleep deprivation also appears to have an effect on the circadian rhythm, but no one knows exactly why. One hypothesis is that sleep deprivation affects the timing of cortisol secretion, which may, in turn, affect the circadian clock. Other research indicates that the difference may be related to melatonin since melatonin levels increase after sleep deprivation. Melatonin affects the circadian clock; therefore, by changing the quantities of melatonin, sleep deprivation may affect the circadian clock.

Some studies have shown that women with premenstrual symptoms who are treated with bright light therapy can have a significant improvement in mood. Bright light therapy consists of sitting in front of a full-spectrum bright light of a predetermined intensity for about thirty minutes each day for one to two weeks before a period is due. In general, studies that have looked at the effects of light therapy on women with premenstrual symptoms have found the following:

- Women with PMDD have a response to bright light that is different from the response of women without PMDD. For most women, being exposed to bright light in the morning during the luteal phase of their menstrual cycle will make their melatonin cycle occur earlier in the night. Women with PMDD either experience no change or have their melatonin cycle later in the night—just the opposite of what is found in women without PMDD.
- Women with PMDD have lower melatonin levels than women without PMDD. When treated with bright light therapy, women with PMDD report improvements in their moods, but melatonin levels remain lower.
- Treatment with bright light therapy in the evening (usually between 7:00 and 9:00 P.M.) seems to work best for improving mood in women with PMDD, although not all studies' results are consistent.

Studies that have looked at the effects of sleep deprivation on women with premenstrual symptoms have found the following:

- Women with PMDD report improvements in mood after a single night of sleep deprivation. The effects on mood are not usually seen the very next day but manifest after a night of "recovery" sleep.
- Sleep deprivation affects the release of circadian-related hormones. Late-night partial sleep deprivation caused cortisol peaks two hours earlier in women with PMDD but not in women without PMDD. And the higher levels of prolactin usually found in women with PMDD were lowered after late-night partial sleep deprivation.
- Although both early and late-night types of partial sleep deprivation, and even total sleep deprivation for one night, have been shown in scientific studies to improve mood, late-night partial sleep deprivation seems to work best—although the total effect is quite short term.

Using Bright Light and Sleep Deprivation Therapies

Although research has shown that bright light and sleep therapies can help improve mood in some women with premenstrual symptoms, the effects are quite inconsistent. There have been difficulties devising appropriate placebo treatments to test the real effects of bright light and sleep deprivation. With some of the studies on bright light therapy, women responded as strongly to the placebo as to the full-spectrum light treatment, suggesting that bright light therapy itself for premenstrual symptoms may be nothing more than a placebo response. Even if bright light and sleep therapies work, it is also uncertain how much of the effect is due to relief of an underlying mood disorder. Both treatments have been shown to more consistently improve mood in people who are depressed than they do in women without premenstrual symptoms, so it could be that these mild therapies are helping to relieve a low-level depression instead of relieving premenstrual symptoms.

In studies that have shown the success of bright light or sleep therapies, the results are for improvement of depressive symptoms only. Studies have not directly addressed irritability, mood swings, or physical symptoms. If your major symptoms include depression, sadness, or teariness, it certainly can't hurt to try these treatment options.

Bright Light Therapy

Bright light therapy is most beneficial for women with premenstrual symptoms who also suffer from seasonal affective disorder, or the "winter blues." If you notice that your premenstrual symptoms get worse in the winter months or if you've been deprived of sunlight (such as if there is a long period of dark, overcast skies), then bright light therapy may help improve your mood.

There are some women who should not use bright light therapy. Avoid this therapy if you have bipolar disorder, if you have migraine or frequent headaches, if you have a skin disorder or use skin care products that are affected by certain wavelengths of light, or if you are susceptible to or suffer from eye conditions, especially cataracts or retinal disorders. All these disorders could theoretically be made worse by bright light therapy.

To try bright light therapy, you'll need a full-spectrum light of at least 2,500 lux (a measure of brightness). Some studies reporting success have used 10,000 lux lights. Prepackaged "light boxes" are available commercially, or you can make one from supplies you can buy at any home improvement store. Light boxes contain several full-spectrum lightbulbs (as many as it takes to get the full lux required), the kind used to grow plants from seedlings. You'll also need a diffusing screen to reduce glare. Two of the most reputable and respected light box companies are The SunBox Company (1-800-LITE-YOU, 1-800-548-3968; www.sunboxco.com) and Enviro-Med (1-800-222-DAWN, 1-800-222-3296; www.bio-light.com). Many other companies also sell high-quality light boxes. You can find them online by doing a search on your Internet search engine with the key words *full spectrum light boxes.*

Here's what you do: For the two weeks before your period (your entire luteal phase), make time every evening between 7:00 and 9:00 P.M. to sit in front of the bright light for thirty minutes. Because light diffuses with distance, you'll have to sit close to the light box. The exact distance will vary depending on the strength of the light, but generally the light should be no farther than two feet away from your eyes. Arrange the box in front of you, either straight ahead or slightly above, so that the light hits your eyes. Do not look directly at the light. You should start to feel an improvement in your mood after a few days.

Other studies have shown that when treating mild depression or seasonal affective disorder, light therapy is best used first thing in the morning, right after you get out of bed. If you find you don't get any relief from the nighttime light, try using the light in the morning for a few days. It won't make your premenstrual symptoms worse, and it may help relieve some mild depression.

Side effects of using bright light therapy are mild and usually disappear after a few days. Some people who use high-intensity light boxes have reported feeling "jumpy" or "wired" and have experienced headaches, nausea, or eye irritation. Discontinue light therapy if you experience any of these side effects.

Sleep Deprivation Therapy

Women with premenstrual depression may feel some improvement from sleep deprivation therapy. Do not try sleep deprivation on days when you cannot afford to feel tired and sleepy.

Here's what you do: For one night, go to bed so that you can be asleep by 9:00 P.M., and set the alarm clock for 1:00 A.M. When the alarm goes off, get up and start your day. Stay up until your normal bedtime the next night, then get a full night's sleep. Many women feel an improvement in mood the day after sleep deprivation, but others won't feel any difference until after that night of full sleep.

"The Right Stuff"

Here's what it takes to be a subject in a PMDD/circadian clock experiment. Women who allow themselves to be studied for circadian clock dysregulation are the unsung heroines of modern research. The process is long, arduous, and highly inconvenient.

Although the particulars vary from study to study, the research usually spans at least two months so that the measurements (blood hormone levels, brain wave patterns, body temperature, etc.) can be taken through two or more menstrual cycles. The study may require daily or weekly participation, but the women must be available at various stages of the month for rather rigorous testing. A typical study could require any or all of the following:

- **Urine analysis.** Each woman's urine is analyzed to determine which phase of her menstrual cycle she is in. Because women with PMDD suffer during the luteal phase, participation will always be required at that time of the month, but measurements may also be taken at other times of the month.
- **More urine analysis.** This screens the women for prescription or illicit drug use.
- **Mood ratings.** Paper-and-pencil questionnaires that ask a woman to rate her mood may be required as often as twice a day, and an interview may be conducted once a week for outside evaluation of mood or depression ratings.
- **Blood tests.** These tests provide baseline measures of the hormones that will be studied and make sure that each woman is otherwise healthy.

---

continued

"The Right Stuff" (continued)

- **Laboratory sleepover.** Because the measurements need to be taken at night, the women spend the night at the research facility. "Check-in" can be as early as 4:30 P.M. and "check-out" at about 9:00 A.M.

- **Catheters, electrodes, or probes.** Samples for the study need to be collected throughout the night, so researchers are very clever at collecting them without disturbing the women volunteers. For blood sampling, an intravenous catheter is inserted into an appropriate blood vessel, then the tubing is passed through an opening in the wall to an adjoining room. Blood is drawn from the catheter tube every half hour by a professional in the adjacent room. For studies of brain waves, electrodes are applied to the head, with readings taken throughout the night. For studies of body temperature, women insert vaginal or rectal temperature probes and leave them in for twenty-four hours.

- **Fashion statements.** If the research requires bright light treatment, the women may be asked to wear dark goggles when they go outside to avoid excess sun exposure that could throw off the study results.

11

Psychological Therapies

Sometimes after snapping, I'll have to sit down and apologize to the kids. I'll tell them, "Remember there's this week I told you about, before I get my period—that week is now. I didn't mean to yell at you." I'm just trying to give them an explanation, instead of them thinking Mom is just being crazy.

—Toni

PREMENSTRUAL DISORDERS are based in biology. Even though scientists are still researching the exact physiologic mechanisms involved, premenstrual dysphoric disorder (PMDD), premenstrual exacerbation (PME), and premenstrual syndrome (PMS) are distinctly linked to hormone shifts. Medications that stop hormonal cycling also stop premenstrual symptoms. Medications that influence brain chemistry also influence premenstrual symptoms. And women with unpredictable, irregular menstrual cycles get symptoms only premenstrually, whether that means getting symptoms every four weeks, six weeks, or eight weeks. For these women, their premenstrual symptoms are often the only clue that they need to stock up on sanitary products.

What this means is that psychological treatments and support groups have a limited impact on premenstrual symptom severity. However, these types of treatments can have an effect on the *experience* of premenstrual symptoms. Many women say that they psychologically feel better when they understand what the disorder is, that it is beyond their control, and that they are not losing their minds. When women talk openly about their disorder with their husbands, partners, or friends, they don't have to expend quite so much energy covering up their physical pain and emotional turmoil. Talking with other women who have similar symptoms can make a woman feel less isolated or stigmatized.

These subtle types of experiential changes are difficult to test scientifically or measure statistically. Still, scientists are finding ways to judge the effectiveness of various types of psychological therapies, and there have been some promising results.

Cognitive Therapies

Cognitive behavioral therapy (CBT) and insight-oriented psychotherapy are what most of us think of when we talk about seeing a psychiatrist or psychologist. These treatments are based on the principle that our thoughts— our cognitions—are related to our behavior and our emotions. The purpose of CBT or insight-oriented psychotherapy is to change behavior and/or improve emotions by changing the way we think. That isn't as simple as it sounds. Our thoughts are a product of all our life experiences and habitual ways of responding to the world. Eventually, we end up on a kind of emotional and behavioral automatic pilot. That's what we mean when we jokingly say that a person we find annoying knows how to "press our buttons." Something that person does engages our emotional automatic pilot so we can't help but respond the same way over and over again. One way to disconnect the power supply to our behavioral "buttons" so that we can break the cycle of automatic responses is to recognize what precipitates our undesired behavior and why we respond in certain ways.

The experience of having PMDD is not merely like having someone press our buttons. It's more like having our buttons get stuck in the "on" position for a few days every month. We may not be able to turn off the biological aspects of the disorder, but it may be possible for us (and those around us) to learn how to respond differently to irritations during that time of the month. Unfortunately, just thinking things through isn't enough to solve the problem. Women with PMDD routinely report that they know their behavior is irrational and that what they are saying is hurtful, and yet they feel powerless to stop themselves. During this biologically vulnerable time, irritability trumps insight time after time.

Of the two types of therapy (CBT and insight-oriented psychotherapy), CBT seems to hold more promise for treatment of the experience of premenstrual symptoms. In insight-oriented psychotherapy, a therapist will talk with you about the history of your problem, when it began, and what factors in your life might have been involved in setting up the kinds of reactions you have now. The goal is to help you realize the possible origins of your thoughts, emotions, and behaviors. The theory is that until you have this type of insight into your problem, until you see the big picture of how your current thoughts and behaviors fit into the full scope of your life, it is impossible to make positive, lasting changes. But most women who seek help for their premenstrual symptoms know exactly when the symptoms started, and insight alone doesn't seem to change the symptoms or their experience of them.

In CBT, a therapist will talk with you to explore fully the nature of your problem and the types of responses and behaviors you find most troubling. The therapist will attempt to help you identify distorted thinking or beliefs, then assist you in finding new ways of looking at the world. There are several different techniques that can be used, but one of the most common is a process called "cognitive restructuring." This process allows women with premenstrual symptoms to recognize that thoughts such as "I'm totally out of control" or "I'm a worthless human being" are not only inaccurate, but they can be harmful to self-esteem and may lead to undesirable behaviors. By replacing those thoughts with more accurate and rational thoughts, such as "I *feel* out of control but that's only because my hormones are changing again. I've dealt with this before, so I know I can handle it now," women can substantially alter their patterns of thinking. Once thought patterns are revised or restructured, it becomes possible to change the way we respond in the face of such thoughts. After enough practice, it becomes easier and easier to recognize distorted thoughts, and replacing them with more accurate and considered thought patterns becomes automatic.

The next step is to recognize potentially destructive behavior patterns and replace them with more acceptable behavior patterns. For example, some women who say they feel out of control can be taught stress reduction, relaxation, and assertiveness techniques to give them the tools to calm themselves down and feel more in control of themselves regardless of what is going on in their environment. It may not be easy, but there are ways to stop autopilot types of behavior and replace them with more constructive (or at least less destructive) types of behavior.

It's important to understand that gaining insight about the problem won't change the symptoms. You won't *feel* different, but therapy may help you change the way you act in response to the way you feel. As a very simple example, consider a woman who thinks she is on the verge of going insane because she feels irrational and out of control premenstrually. That's a frightening thought, and her fear may play a part in her emotional responses. Fear can change our biochemistry, create a surge of nonreproductive hormones, which may in turn create additional mood symptoms. With education and cognitive therapy, she may start to feel more comfortable with the explanation that premenstrual symptoms are due to her biology and are not a sign of mental imbalance. With the fear taken out of the equation, she can recognize the sequence of thoughts that precipitate her symptoms and plan new ways of responding to the situations when they arise.

Each woman has her own set of thoughts, feelings, emotions, and behaviors, and a good therapist will tailor a program that fits the needs of the individual. There is no single proper "method" for CBT. It's not like following a recipe, with step-by-step instructions, although many specific cognitive behavioral therapies have a manual or workbook that can be used during treatment. There will usually be instruction about the therapy process itself and education about how one can build a sense of oneself that is, indeed, capable of making behavioral changes. Other types of training may include coping skills training (how to deal in a more positive way to life stress), assertiveness training (how to make one's needs known without aggression), relaxation training, and stress management training. These treatments, given individually or in a group, can help women gain confidence in their ability to deal with stress and life situations and give them the tools to change the response when their buttons are pushed.

Some preliminary research shows that CBT may be helpful for premenstrual symptoms. One study conducted in Australia enrolled women with self-reported severe premenstrual symptoms in group CBT. The therapy included cognitive restructuring, exercises to help build self-efficacy, relaxation training, assertiveness training, and information about stress, diet, and exercise as means of controlling premenstrual reactions. As controls (to make sure the results weren't simply due to the placebo response), another group of women took a movement class and a third group of women were put on a waiting list. All women were tested for menstrual distress, depression, anxiety, and irrationality before and after six weeks of either CBT, movement class, or being placed on a wait list. They were tested again nine months later. After six weeks, the results showed that women who had CBT had significant reductions in the severity of their premenstrual symptoms and significant decreases in their scores for irrational thinking. The other groups had no significant improvements. Improvement following CBT was still measurable when evaluated nine months later.

In another study, women either received CBT or were put on a waiting list. The twelve-week course of treatment was conducted with each woman individually. Discussions focused on the factors that were most troubling and likely to set off a bad reaction, how she dealt with those factors, and what attitudes might be creating negative behaviors. Each woman was instructed to try out new behaviors as homework, and specific incidents were discussed, dissected, and used as starting points to talk about relationships, stress, and other life factors that might contribute to her difficult reactions to the biological changes premenstrually. Results of this study showed that the women who received CBT felt significantly less depressed and had fewer emotional and physical premenstrual symptoms. The beneficial effects were still there four months later, when the follow-up measures were taken.

In an interesting aside, the authors of the previous study noted that women arrived with considerable knowledge about PMS and had tried several other treatments beforehand. They understood the medical nature of their symptoms. They also reported being uneasy about seeking psychological treatment for fear of being told that the symptoms were "all in their heads" and of the stigma of having a psychological problem. In the study, the women were reassured. This raises the question, however, of how women in the "real world" perceive psychological treatments. The best way to view psychological treatments is as another of the tools available to women who want to learn ways to cope with their symptoms.

How to Choose a Therapist

Choosing a good therapist requires a combination of objective and subjective judgments. You need to find someone qualified, but then you need to make sure that there is a good "fit" between your personalities.

First, you need to decide which type of therapist you would like to see: a counselor, a social worker, a psychologist, or a psychiatrist. A counselor may have a master's degree (M.S. or M.A.) or a doctorate (Ph.D. or Psy.D.) in counseling psychology. A social worker will have a master's degree in social work (M.S.W.). Both counselors and social workers will have had specialized training in counseling people through difficult life circumstances. They should be certified or licensed. They are often trained in a particular specialty, such as marriage counseling or bereavement counseling, but they can deal with a broad range of issues. They usually are the least expensive, compared with psychiatrists and psychologists. A list of counselors in your area can be obtained by contacting the National Board for Certified Counselors referral service, and a list of social workers can be obtained by contacting the National Association of Social Workers (see Appendix A).

Psychologists usually hold a doctorate degree (Ph.D. or Psy.D.) in clinical psychology and need to be licensed in the state in which they practice. Like counselors, they also can specialize in dealing with certain types of problems but generally deal with a broad range of life issues. Their fees are usually higher than those of counselors. To find a psychologist in your area, call the American Psychological Association and ask for a referral to a psychologist who specializes in premenstrual disorders (see Appendix A for contact information).

Psychiatrists are medical doctors (M.D.s) who specialize in treating disorders of the mind. Along with their medical training, they also study psychotherapeutic techniques. Because psychiatrists are qualified to prescribe medication, they have a broader range of treatment options available than counselors or psychologists. To find a psychiatrist in your area, ask your primary care physician or other trusted health care professional for a recommendation, or contact your local chapter of the American Psychiatric Association (see Appendix A for contact information).

Once you have the name of one or more therapists, call the offices of the ones you are interested in and find out more about their practices. Questions you might ask include:

continued

How to Choose a Therapist (continued)

- *Are you certified or licensed to practice in this state?* There are some therapists who are practicing legally but are not certified or licensed. Licensing and certification processes are in place to make sure that the therapist you choose has been properly trained and understands therapeutic guidelines and ethics.

- *What are your areas of specialty? Have you treated other women with premenstrual disorders?* You'll want someone who has experience with your type of problem.

- *What types of therapies do you offer?* This will give you a brief idea of what to expect.

- *Will my treatment be covered by my insurance? If not, what are your fees?* Choose a therapist you can afford. Depending on your particular situation, you may need a single visit or multiple visits over time, as judged appropriate by you and your therapist.

- *What hours are available for treatment?* Some therapists offer evening or weekend hours; some don't. Make sure you can fit the therapy sessions in your schedule.

Once you find someone who seems to fit all your needs, make an appointment. Now comes the subjective part of the choice. You should feel comfortable and at ease with your therapist because you'll need to form a positive, trusting, and supportive partnership with your therapist. It is possible that, despite all your work choosing a therapist, you may find that you and your therapist don't "click." In that case, talk about the problem with the therapist to see if the issues can be resolved. If not, you may need to look for a new therapist.

Cognitive behavioral therapy, usually conducted by psychiatrists or psychologists, appears to be a valuable treatment option and can be used either alone or in conjunction with other treatments. If you are considering some form of psychological therapy, a good therapist will put your mind at ease at your first meeting. You will not be judged or labeled "crazy." You will be supported, calmed, educated, and listened to.

Couples Therapy

"Help me fix this, or my partner will leave me." That statement is commonly heard by professionals who treat women with severe premenstrual symptoms. Embedded in that sentence is a clue to the type of help that might be most valuable for the situation. Anytime the words *my partner, my husband, my lover,* or *my boyfriend* appear in the complaint or plea for help, it is a sign that couples therapy should be considered as a psychological treatment option.

Although there are no head-to-head scientific comparisons, psychiatrists, psychologists, and social workers recognize that couples therapy seems to work better than individual therapy for premenstrual distress. Logically, this makes sense. After all, a woman's premenstrual symptoms, as personally distressing as they are, can also have an effect on relationships and families. Words spoken in anger premenstrually may still be hurtful after the irritability subsides. There are always echoes and ramifications, the exact nature of which are determined by the very personal dynamics within each relationship.

What are some of the possible responses by family members to behavior changes that occur premenstrually? You undoubtedly have already experienced many of them. They can include fear, concern, guilt, anger, frustration, helplessness, combativeness, and withdrawal. Each of these reactions creates another set of reactions in the women, which can lead to more fear and difficulty coping with premenstrual symptoms in the future, which in turn creates more outside reactions, and so on. It can be a vicious cycle of emotions feeding on emotions, with the intensity gradually increasing over the years. Interpersonal stresses are created and built up. Emotional wounds can scar a relationship. Trust and intimacy are sometimes broken.

That is why couples working together can have greater success stabilizing their relationships. Couples therapy, which can be done by psychiatrists, psychologists, social workers, and other professional counselors, involves many of the same treatment goals and methods described for other psychological treatments. In that setting, the therapist will help partners see a new way of conceptualizing the biological vulnerability of women premenstrually and to figure out management strategies that can help keep negative emotions from escalating. When both halves of the team are playing the same game, so to speak, the rules are clearer and it is much easier to reach the ultimate goal.

Since there is no male equivalent to premenstrual changes, many men just don't understand the mood swings and how to avoid creating turbulence, so they become passive in the face of premenstrual symptoms. One study that looked at how families coped with intense premenstrual symptoms found that husbands were more likely than their wives to believe that the problem would go away if they just waited long enough. In a way, they are right. The symptoms do go away, at least for part of the month (and symptoms would go away entirely if they waited until menopause). Unfortunately, this waxing and waning of symptoms creates an expectation that the symptoms could be controllable all of the time. An educated partner knows what to expect and how to respond most effectively. Issues regarding the effects of premenstrual symptoms on the marriage or partnership, children, or friendships can also be addressed in these sessions.

Support Groups

There are many different kinds of support groups. Some are run by a trained professional, such as a nurse or a therapist; others are entirely run by the members; still others aren't actual groups at all but conversation "rooms" on the Internet. Each has value, depending on what you are looking for.

A professionally run group is most valuable for information-based support. In these groups, a professional is available to answer questions, correct misperceptions, and lead the group in an objective manner. Groups run by the members (also called peer groups) are best for emotion-based support. The leader is also a member of the group, so everyone present has similar experiences and can relate to one another on an empathetic level. The purpose of peer groups is to validate the experience of having the condition, sharing experiences that assist in dealing with the condition and sometimes just plain venting. Information presented at peer groups runs the risk of being less medically sound, however well intended. Internet support groups have the benefit of being available anytime, day or night (provided someone else is logged on). They allow total anonymity. The risk is that the people in the chat rooms may not be who they claim to be. There are many examples of a salesman logging on as a woman and claiming that "she" tried this wonderful product (which he sells) and that everyone else should try it, too. Internet support groups should never be used to gather information, but they can be helpful for women who need a place to vent emotions and connect with others anonymously.

It seems that women with premenstrual symptoms have naturally discovered that talking is a way of coping with their disorder. At least one study has shown that women with premenstrual symptoms tend to use self-disclosure (talking about one's self) as a coping mechanism. Another study showed that women with PMDD tend to use catharsis (venting) to cope with problems more often premenstrually than postmenstrually. Social support, however, is another issue. Research results are mixed, with some studies showing increased use of social support by women with premenstrual symptoms and others showing decreased use of social support. These disparate findings are not that surprising, considering that women may *want* to talk as a way of venting, but the disorder itself may make a woman less inclined to go out and gather with others when she is feeling the worst of her symptoms.

Research designed to test the effectiveness of support groups has given conflicting reports as well, with some showing no benefit and some showing a significant improvement in symptoms. Conflicting results among studies are especially difficult to interpret because some of the "support" groups actually included treatment interventions such as changing diet, exercising, and increasing vitamin intake, all of which may have contributed to symptom improvement.

If you feel the need to commune and talk about your premenstrual symptoms with other women who share similar experiences, by all means find or start a support group. But the current scientific evidence makes it impossible to recommend it as a proven and valuable treatment option.

Stress Reduction

One of the hypotheses about the cause of premenstrual disorders is that some women have a dysregulation of the natural stress response, with the result that their bodies overreact to stressors that other people find manageable. Indeed, some studies show that women with premenstrual symptoms tend to have (or perceive that they have) more life stress premenstrually than women without premenstrual symptoms, but these results are not found consistently. And measuring the amount of stress in a woman's life doesn't necessarily help predict how severe her premenstrual symptoms will be.

Still, common sense suggests that if women with premenstrual disorders have an inborn sensitivity that makes them react more intensely to stress, then symptoms should decrease if stress is reduced or managed better. Unfortunately, there has not been enough stress-specific research to determine whether stress reduction techniques actually work. Stress reduction and coping methods are taught in cognitive behavioral therapy, but stress reduction as a self-help treatment has not been investigated. Relaxation may help (see Chapter 9), but personal stress management is an unknown.

Our recommendation: try anything that helps you reduce your personal level of stress—short of abusing medications, illicit drugs, or alcohol. Although the following techniques haven't been shown specifically to help premenstrual symptoms, they are standards in stress reduction.

Deep Breathing

Not many of us breathe properly—fully, deeply, from the diaphragm. When breathing, we inhale oxygen-rich air and exhale carbon dioxide waste. Oxygen is essential for life. It travels in the blood and feeds every part of our bodies. The more fully, slowly, and deeply we breathe, the more oxygen we circulate. Many of us breathe from the chest. These quick, shallow breaths are associated with anxiety attacks, fear, and distress. And when people are under stress, their chests can tighten (which makes breathing even harder), or they can unknowingly hold their breath. Breathing slowly and deeply from the diaphragm pulls air deep into the lungs. This process helps to short-circuit stress and anxiety. It relaxes the chest, keeps oxygen circulating, distracts us from distressing thoughts, and helps us feel more relaxed. The results can be felt almost immediately. Continued practice can have long-term benefits, because as deep breathing becomes second nature, we are less likely to automatically tense up when facing stress.

Here's what you do: Stand or sit with your back straight. Put one hand on your diaphragm, located about where your stomach is, just below your ribs. Breathe in slowly by expanding your diaphragm. If you do this correctly, your hand should move outward as you breathe in. Then exhale fully by contracting your diaphragm (the feeling is similar to what you do when you suck in your stomach). Some people may find it difficult to breathe this way, and it may take some time before breathing from your diaphragm feels at all natural. Once you've practiced this enough to know that you are doing it correctly, begin to inhale to a slow count of four, then exhale to a slow count of four. *In . . . two . . . three . . . four. . . . Out . . . two . . . three . . . four.* Continue breathing slowly and deeply for two minutes to start; then increase the time as you feel comfortable. The best part about deep breathing for stress relief is that you can do this anywhere, anytime—in a business meeting, or in your car, or whenever you need to stop a rising feeling of anxiety or tension.

Prioritizing and Scheduling

There's no getting around it, our lives are stressful. And when you're feeling premenstrual symptoms, you'll feel the stress more. As obvious as it sounds, a good way to de-stress your body is to de-stress your life. Of the hundred things you feel you must do today, how many are really necessary and how many do you do out of guilt, a misplaced sense of obligation, habit, or a need to be "superwoman"? How many do you really have to do? How many do you actually enjoy doing? By prioritizing the things you do in your life and then setting up a realistic schedule, you can cut down on many of the daily hassles that help build a stress load.

Here's what you do: Make a list of all your tasks, obligations, routines, and activities. Include everything you can think of, from making breakfast to commuting to taking the kids to dance class—anything you do in an average week. Evaluate each item and determine exactly how necessary it is, how much you enjoy it, and what priority it takes. Place a "1" next to items that are a high priority for you in terms of the fulfillment they bring or how important they are to your life. Place a "2" or a "3" next to lower-ranked items. For each item you ranked "3," find ways to eliminate it. Consolidate tasks, ask others for help, or simply stop doing it. For each item you eliminate, you decrease a little stress and regain a little time. You also regain some sense of having control over your day and your life.

Thought Stopping

This one sounds easy, doesn't it? If it were as easy as it sounds, none of us would obsess over irrational fears or worry continuously. We all have a constant internal monologue, those thoughts that pass with lightning speed through our heads. But sometimes we get stuck on a thought, and it blows up out of proportion, creating stress, worry, anxiety, or fear. This is a common symptom in women with premenstrual disorders. Thought stopping is a psychological technique that has been around for decades. It involves cutting off an obsessive or unwanted thought, being aware of its obsessive nature, replacing it with a positive or distracting thought, and moving on. Simple? Wait till you try it.

Here's what you do: When you recognize a destructive or obsessive thought, you must consciously break into that thought. Different people have different ways of doing it. Some say the word *STOP* out loud (when they are alone). Others imagine a big red stop sign. Others pinch the back of their hands, or shake their heads as if to shake the thought out, or clap their hands. It should be something that you can do easily that is a clear signal that you have broken the thought chain. (Early on, you'll need these types of strong distracters. Eventually, with practice, you'll be able to stop a thought just by recognizing that you are having destructive or obsessive thoughts and then just thinking about stopping.) You may need to repeat this several times if the obsessive thoughts start back up. As an example, imagine that you are struggling in a crowded airport and beginning to obsess and worry. As your tension rises, you recognize your destructive ruminations and say, "STOP." Once the thought is stopped, try replacing it with another thought, such as "I love that my job allows me to travel," or "I know I can handle this minor irritation," or "This is a beautiful day." The thought should be positive and relevant to your situation. If you combine this practice with deep breathing, the effect will be even stronger.

12

Other Medical Treatments

There wasn't a lot of laughing. It wouldn't have been what I would call a happy home. No, it was my goal to get away from the kids as much as possible at night. I would go and retreat. I just wanted to be away, just be by myself and sometimes just do nothing. Now, since I've been treated, I can laugh a whole lot more with my husband and the kids. These little, teasing, fun things can happen. Before it was "Don't come near me." Now, I can actually say, "Wow, look, we have a happy home again."

—Toni

ALTHOUGH THE medical treatment of choice for intense premenstrual symptoms is a selective serotonin reuptake inhibitor (SSRI, see Chapter 6), there are some women who need to seek other medical options. Some women are particularly sensitive to SSRI side effects and cannot tolerate the medication. And as good as SSRIs are for relieving premenstrual symptoms, they don't work for every woman. SSRI treatment delivers safe and effective relief to about 80 percent of women who try it. That means there are still 20 percent for whom the SSRI medications have little or no effect.

If you want medical treatment for your premenstrual symptoms and SSRIs have not worked for you, there are other options to pursue. Some, such as spironolactone, tend to have a focused effect on specific symptoms. Others, such as medical or surgical ovulation suppression, can be highly effective but are truly treatments of last resort. You'll need to discuss these options with your physician to determine which might be right for you.

Pain Relievers

The most common treatment for premenstrual pain—typically headaches, cramps, or backaches—is a nonsteroidal anti-inflammatory drug (NSAID). Some short-acting NSAIDs are available without a prescription (these include such familiar names as Advil, Motrin IB, Nuprin, Orudis KT, Aleve, and even plain old aspirin). Others are longer acting and are available only with a prescription, such as Anaprox, Motrin, Naprosyn, Ponstel, and Orudis.

There have not been many studies using NSAIDs for premenstrual symptom relief, but the few that have been done showed promising results. Two studies that looked at the use of naproxen sodium (the active ingredient found in Aleve and Anaprox) showed that this NSAID was better at preventing menstrual migraine than placebo and was successful at decreasing overall premenstrual and menstrual pain. Studies that looked at mefenamic acid (Ponstel) showed that this NSAID reduced headache, pain, fatigue, and mood swings.

Because we are used to thinking about pain relievers as over-the-counter medications, it is tempting to underestimate the potency of NSAIDs. Although most people can tolerate these medications well, possible side effects include heart dysrhythmias, stomach or intestinal bleeding, pancreatitis, kidney problems, or difficulty breathing. People who have had an allergic reaction to aspirin should *not* take NSAIDs.

Diuretics

Diuretics are medications that help the body get rid of excess water. These medications are most helpful for women who retain a lot of water premenstrually, causing significant weight gain. But a few studies have demonstrated that the diuretic spironolactone (Aldactone) not only relieves bloating but may even help relieve other premenstrual symptoms, including irritability, depression, breast tenderness, and food cravings.

The most noticeable effect of diuretics is the increase in urination that occurs in the first two to three weeks after beginning the medication. (This is how the body gets rid of excess water.) Because of this effect, it is recommended that you take the medication at a time when it is most convenient for you. If you take the medication at night, you may have difficulty sleeping because of all the bathroom runs you'll have to make. Mornings are usually best, but if you have a job that doesn't allow you regular or frequent bathroom breaks, you may want to wait until you get home to take the medication.

Spironolactone and other diuretics are generally safe. The most common possible side effects include diarrhea, nausea or vomiting, dizziness, and rash. Women with severe kidney disease should not take diuretics.

Antianxiety Medications

The research data are mixed with regard to whether antianxiety medications, also called anxiolytics, help alleviate premenstrual symptoms. The anxiolytic most often recommended for premenstrual symptoms is alprazolam (Xanax). Alprazolam is one of a class of drugs called benzodiazepines. Their general function is to slow down the nervous system, which facilitates relaxation, reduces anxiety, and tones down emotional behavior. Researchers have had differing results using alprazolam to treat premenstrual symptoms. Some studies show no difference in premenstrual mood or depression scores between women who take alprazolam and women who take a placebo, and some show that alprazolam impairs women's ability to perform certain tasks. Other studies show that women taking alprazolam have improved mood and mental function. But even these good results are limited. In one study conducted by Dr. Ellen Freeman of the University of Pennsylvania School of Medicine and her colleagues, only 37 percent of women taking alprazolam during the luteal phase of their menstrual cycles had at least a 50 percent reduction in symptoms. Still, relief is relief. Women who cannot tolerate SSRIs may respond well to alprazolam.

There are drawbacks to using alprazolam for the treatment of premenstrual symptoms. Perhaps most important to women who experience fatigue and food cravings is that benzodiazepines, including alprazolam, are sedative (they make you sleepy) and they increase appetite. Women who take alprazolam tend to eat about 10 to 25 percent more premenstrually than they did before taking the medication. So although some symptoms may (or may not) improve while taking alprazolam, tiredness and cravings will likely get worse.

Another potential problem is that benzodiazepines can cause mental or physical dependence when used over a long period of time. Although at least one study has shown that alprazolam taken only in the luteal phase of the menstrual cycle does not cause withdrawal symptoms when the medication is stopped, long-term use of intermittent benzodiazepine use has not been studied. Women with a history of drug abuse or dependency should not take benzodiazepines, because they are more likely to become dependent.

Another anxiolytic that has been tested for use in treating premenstrual symptoms is buspirone (BuSpar). This medication is not a benzodiazepine but belongs to a different class of drugs called azaspirodecanediones. The difference is in the types of brain receptors affected. Unlike alprazolam, buspirone does not cause muscle relaxation or sedation. Like other anxiolytics, buspirone reduces tension and anxiety, and there is evidence that it increases appetite.

The few studies that have been conducted using buspirone showed that this medication is mildly effective in reducing premenstrual irritability and provided a general sense of improvement in fatigue and mood symptoms premenstrually. Unfortunately, buspirone has to be used continuously because it takes three to four weeks of continuous use to establish its pharmacologic effect. The most common side effects are dizziness and nausea. Some researchers suggest that because side effects are minimal, this might be a viable—albeit less effective—option for women who cannot tolerate SSRIs.

Other Antidepressants

Selective serotonin reuptake inhibitors are just one type of antidepressant. They work best for premenstrual symptoms because of their direct and specific action, which increases the amount of serotonin in the brain. Other antidepressants have effects on different neurotransmitters, such as dopamine and norepinephrine.

Although none of the other antidepressants work as well as SSRIs for premenstrual symptoms, there may be some use for bupropion (Wellbutrin,

Wellbutrin SR). In a study comparing the SSRI fluoxetine, bupropion, and placebo for their ability to relieve premenstrual symptoms, fluoxetine was the best, but bupropion offered some mild improvement. Clinically, however, it does not appear to have much effect on irritability, so it has limited use for the majority of premenstrual women. Another common use for bupropion has been improving sexual function. It can be a useful add-on therapy for women who experience sexual dysfunction as a side effect of taking SSRIs. Some physicians prescribe bupropion to women and recommend that they take the medication two hours before lovemaking to counteract some of the libido dampening effects of the SSRI. Although this medication is usually well tolerated, it should not be taken by people who have a history of seizures or eating disorders. Common possible side effects include agitation, insomnia, nausea, or vomiting.

A few researchers have looked at another antidepressant, nefazodone (Serzone), as a treatment for premenstrual symptoms. This medication increases the amounts of both serotonin and norepinephrine in the brain. Some preliminary studies have shown that it can relieve premenstrual depressive symptoms. Additionally, clinical evidence suggests that nefazodone seems to work well for women with premenstrual exacerbation of major depression. This medication is well tolerated. Common possible side effects include dizziness, light-headedness, sleepiness, nausea, and gastrointestinal upset. In 2002, the U.S. Food and Drug Administration (FDA) required that a warning be put on nefazodone labels stating that rare cases of liver failure leading to transplant and/or death in patients have been reported.

Another commonly used antidepressant, venlafaxine (Effexor, Effexor XR), has been shown to be effective for premenstrual symptoms in some research trials. (See Chapter 6.)

Progesterone, Estrogen, and Oral Contraceptives

Because premenstrual symptoms are related to the changing levels of estrogen and progesterone, those hormones were among the first to be tested as a possible treatment. The idea that progesterone withdrawal during the luteal phase triggers symptoms has generated considerable research into the value of progesterone as a treatment. Although some early researchers reported positive results, more recent studies with a more objective design find that progesterone—natural or artificial—is no better than placebo at controlling premenstrual symptoms and, for many women, will actually worsen them. A 2001 review and meta-analysis of the medical literature found that progesterone is of no value in treating premenstrual disorders. Unfortunately, some physicians continue to prescribe progesterone to their patients with premenstrual symptoms based on the earlier flawed studies. If your physician recommends progesterone, seek a second opinion.

Estrogen has a different research history. The mechanics of a typical menstrual cycle show that estrogen levels rise in the early part of the luteal phase, and then fall precipitously in the late luteal phase. This drop in estrogen levels corresponds to the part of the menstrual cycle when most women experience their worst premenstrual symptoms. Estrogen's role in the body is greater than just reproduction. Animal studies suggest that estrogen helps increase levels of serotonin in the brain. That means that it may be a natural antidepressant. Psychiatrists have begun treating perimenopausal women who experience depression with estrogen in addition to antidepressants. In addition, women who experience premenstrual migraine are sometimes treated prophylactically with estrogen, usually via an estrogen patch. A woman would start using estrogen before her first predicted migraine and continue for three to six days until estrogen levels in the body naturally began to rise again. The most commonly reported side effects of estrogen treatment are nausea, headache, and breast tenderness.

Oral contraceptives have interested researchers because these contraceptives combine forms of estrogen and progesterone in a way that suppresses ovulation. Interestingly, research provides no clear answer about whether oral contraceptives make premenstrual symptoms better or worse. Well-controlled studies show that oral contraceptives can reduce breast pain and bloating, but not mood symptoms. In fact, some women find that oral contraceptives make their depression worse. However, in 2001, researchers discovered that a new oral contraceptive that replaced the usual progestin part of the pill with a spironolactone-like progestin (marketed under the brand name Yasmin) showed promise in reducing premenstrual symptoms.

Other Medications You May Hear About

In the search for an effective medication to treat the worst premenstrual symptoms, many drugs have been tested. Some showed initial success but were later found to be ineffective when more rigorous research criteria were implemented. Some of these medications are still being tested, but they are currently not considered safe, effective, or desirable for most women. They have other medical uses, some very valuable, but they should not be used to treat premenstrual dysphoric disorder (PMDD), premenstrual exacerbation (PME), or premenstrual syndrome (PMS). If your doctor suggests any of these medications, seek a second opinion.

- **Bromocriptine (Parlodel).** This medication, usually used to treat symptoms of Parkinson disease, blocks the release of prolactin from the pituitary gland. Although studies show that bromocriptine significantly decreases breast pain, it does not relieve premenstrual symptoms. Common possible side effects include dizziness, headache, nausea, or vomiting. Rarely, this medication can also cause much more serious side effects, including stroke, seizure, or heart attack.

- **Tamoxifen (Nolvadex).** This is a complex medication with modes of action that are not entirely understood yet. It is most often used as an additional (adjunct) therapy for women with breast cancer because it competes with estrogen for receptor sites in breast tissue. Some physicians recommend this medication to women for treatment of breast pain, and it seems to be effective for that purpose. Studies show that after about three months of treatment with tamoxifen, more than 70 percent of women have total relief and the remaining women have partial relief. With long-term treatment (twelve months or longer), some women start to feel pain again. However, the long-term consequences of the medication in healthy women are not known, and the side effects are unpleasant. Common possible side effects include hot flashes, headache, light-headedness, nausea or vomiting, bloating, depression, and menstrual irregularity. Tamoxifen can cause precancerous changes in the uterus.

- **Danazol (Danocrine).** This drug works by depressing the production and secretion of follicle-stimulating hormone (FSH) and luteinizing hormone (LH), which

continued

Other Medications You May Hear About (continued)

keeps the ovaries from producing a mature egg and ultimately keeps levels of estrogen and progesterone low. Although some studies have shown that danazol may
help relieve many premenstrual symptoms, those findings are not universal. And the
side effects of danazol are difficult to tolerate. Danazol is an androgen, the primary
male hormone. Because of this, side effects include weight gain, facial hair, acne, a
deepening of the voice, and depression.

The most common possible side effects of oral contraceptives include nausea, breast tenderness, headache, and weight gain. Women who have a history of stroke or blood clots should not take oral contraceptives. Women
smokers over age thirty-five should not take oral contraceptives because of
increased risk of heart attack.

Ovulation Suppression

As the name suggests, ovulation suppression is the stopping of the menstrual
cycle by preventing the ovaries from maturing and releasing eggs, thereby
eliminating the cyclic rhythm of hormone production and eliminating cyclic
mood symptoms. This can be done chemically with medication, or by surgery (discussed in the next section). The main problem with stopping ovulation and hormone production is that estrogen levels fall into the
postmenopausal range, and women begin to experience hot flashes, sleep
disturbances, mood changes, and loss of bone density. Adding back estrogen will protect against menopausal symptoms and osteoporosis. Because
estrogen taken without progesterone can cause precancerous changes in the
uterine lining, add-back progesterone may also be considered if a woman
still has her uterus. Unfortunately, add-back progesterone causes recurrence
of mood symptoms.

The most common medications used for ovulation suppression are
gonadotropin-releasing hormone (GnRH) agonists, such as leuprolide

(Lupron) and goserelin (Zoladex). In the normal menstrual cycle, GnRH is the hormone that starts the whole cascade of hormone communication that results in a new menstrual cycle. A GnRH agonist blocks GnRH from doing its job, so there is no more ovulation and the typical menstrual cycle is halted. Studies show that GnRH agonists work well at controlling premenstrual symptoms. Up to 75 percent of women who are treated with a GnRH agonist experience reductions in irritability, tension, depression, tiredness, mood swings, and breast tenderness. With the add-back hormones, some symptoms reappear, but there is still significant relief.

Use of GnRH agonists is experimental and currently is not approved as a treatment for premenstrual symptoms. It is used for women whose premenstrual symptoms cannot be relieved by any other medication and for women contemplating surgery. Be aware that GnRH agonists cannot be taken orally but must be given by injection or nasal spray. Possible side effects are those associated with the GnRH agonist, such as hot flashes, breast tenderness, decreased libido, and headaches, as well as those associated with estrogen and progesterone, such as depression, nausea, and weight gain.

Surgery

The treatment of last resort is surgery to remove the ovaries (oophorectomy). Surgery is not recommended lightly, and it is not appropriate for most women. But for some women, surgery can save their lives. Women with treatment-resistant depression *plus* premenstrual exacerbation of symptoms are the primary candidates for surgery. These women have major depression that does not get better after taking antidepressants. Premenstrually, their deep depression worsens. If a woman with depression makes multiple suicide attempts, it is not unusual to find that all the attempts were made premenstrually. With surgery, she will still have depression, but her mood will be leveled out, free of premenstrual exacerbation. It may be just enough of an improvement to keep her from trying to harm herself again.

Similarly, some women with diabetes cannot control their blood sugar levels premenstrually and have repeated episodes of ketoacidosis, the build-up of ketones in the body that can result in coma and death if not treated. After surgery, there will no longer be PME of diabetes complications, and blood sugar control will be on a more even keel.

On the other hand, women with premenstrual migraine are not good candidates for surgery. For reasons no one understands, the effects of natural and artificial menopause are different when it comes to migraines. Women with premenstrual migraines who go through natural menopause tend to get better, but women with premenstrual migraines who have surgical procedures that cause an abrupt early menopause tend to get worse.

If surgery is considered as an option, your physician can first treat you with medications that chemically turn off your ovaries using GnRH agonists, such as leuprolide. This mimics the effects of surgery, but the effect is reversible by stopping the GnRH agonist. It is, basically, a trial run to see whether surgery is the right option for you. This type of therapy—chemical ovulation suppression with estrogen add-back—is generally tried for six months. During those six months, your physician will look for three indications that surgery is a good option for you.

1. *Can you tolerate estrogen?* Estrogen protects women from osteoporosis, heart disease, colon cancer, and other conditions associated with aging. But estrogen can cause side effects, including fluid retention, mood changes, and breast tenderness. In some women, these side effects can be so severe that they are better off dealing with premenstrual symptoms or the side effects of other medications.

2. *Did you get better?* Some women with PME may have an underlying disorder that remains severe even after ovulation suppression, or they just don't respond as well as would be hoped. If chemical ovulation suppression doesn't help, neither will surgery.

3. *Did the cure persist throughout the six months?* There is a strong placebo effect that can occur with this treatment. It would not be unusual to find that, for some women, symptoms go away for one or two months but then reappear. Again, this is a signal that surgery will not be a permanent cure and should not be performed.

If you have a good response to the chemical ovulation suppression, and if you can tolerate the estrogen you'll have to take to stay healthy, then you may be a good candidate for surgery. If a woman with severe psychiatric symptoms that worsen premenstrually has a good response to GnRH plus estrogen therapy, it is more practical to remove both the ovaries and the uterus, although it is the ovarian hormones that are the problem. The reason is that if you leave the uterus in and you are using just estrogen therapy, you are at risk for uterine cancer. To counter precancerous changes, you have to use progesterone, which may precipitate the same types of symptoms you were trying to fix.

The surgery itself is relatively easy, as surgeries go. Details such as the type of anesthesia used or the location of the incision will be worked out in consultation among you, your surgeon, and your psychiatric provider.

13

PMDD Game Plan

Before, I didn't feel sexy. I didn't feel good about myself. I didn't even want him to touch me. Now, I feel better about myself. I feel more affectionate. And I can enjoy the extra hugs, the extra kisses I get from him, too. Things are so different since my symptoms went away. I don't know how we managed before.

—Toni

As with any other disorder, the best treatment strategy for a woman with premenstrual dysphoric disorder (PMDD), premenstrual exacerbation (PME), or severe premenstrual syndrome (PMS) is a combination of basic steps and individualized choices. As we said at the beginning of this book, different women can have different responses to the same treatment options. There is no single approach that will make every woman feel better every time. But there is a starting place and a series of recommended steps that can help each woman find the treatment that works best for her.

Step 1: Begin a Symptoms Diary

Start keeping a symptoms diary immediately. A symptoms diary is the single best way to get an accurate view of your symptoms across time. It will give you a clear picture of exactly which symptoms are most troubling, when they occur, and when they disappear. It will provide you and your physician with the type of information needed to make a diagnosis of PMDD,

PMS, or PME. (See Chapter 3 for more information about the symptoms diary. Blank diary pages are available in Appendix B.)

Once you begin treatment, whether it is medication or some of the self-help methods discussed in this book, continue to keep the symptoms diary until your symptoms are under control. This allows you to see exactly how effective the treatment is. For example, you'll be able to discern between treatments that offer long-lasting relief and those that work mainly because of the "placebo effect" (see the sidebar that follows). No matter which treatment you try, chances are you'll feel better for a little while. With a symptoms diary, you can monitor your well-being and determine how well the treatment works for you over time. Once you have a stable symptom-management strategy that is working for you, you no longer need to keep track of your symptoms. But if, at some later point, your symptoms seem to be coming back, start keeping the diary again. Many women think that keeping the diary may be tedious, but once they start tracking their symptoms, they find that their diary is an indispensable tool for accurately monitoring their physical and emotional condition.

As you keep the diary, try to mark the sheet at about the same time every day. Many women choose nighttime, just before bed, so that they can review their symptoms from that current day. Others choose morning, so that they can think back more objectively to the previous day's symptoms. Keeping track of symptoms at the same time every day allows you to get into a routine that will make it more difficult to forget and also keeps any effects of memory changes during the day consistent throughout the month.

On the symptoms diary, you are asked to monitor how you feel every day and then judge the intensity of your symptoms. There is no absolute definition for each intensity level. The ratings are, by definition, subjective. For example, you cannot compare your intensity of breast tenderness with your friend's intensity of breast tenderness. The perception and experience of each symptom will differ for each person. Every day, mark how the symptom feels *to you* on that day. If you have no symptoms, leave the intensity boxes for that day and symptom blank (but check the box under the date to show that you visited the diary that day). If you feel mild or low-intensity symptoms, fill in the bottom box. If you feel moderate or medium-intensity symptoms, fill in both the bottom and middle boxes.

The Placebo Effect

The mind-body connection is a powerful thing. As we've discussed previously, the way we physically feel at any given moment is determined by much more than simple anatomical functions. We are more than just machines made of flesh. Every thought that passes through the brain and every movement we make causes some sort of biochemical reaction that has an effect somewhere in the body. For example, some people can literally be "worried sick" and may end up having gastrointestinal upset over nothing more than out-of-control thoughts in their heads.

The same thing happens with medical treatments. The "placebo effect" occurs when patients are given a false treatment but show signs of improvement anyway. Simply being treated makes people feel better, even when that "treatment" is nothing more than a sugar pill. There is no medical reason why their symptoms should get better, and yet they do. Research has shown that, on average, 30 percent of improvement after any treatment is due to the placebo effect. The effect is so powerful that when researchers design studies, they include a "placebo group," which receives an inactive treatment that is similar to the actual treatment being studied. If a new drug is being studied, some patients receive the real medication, while those in the control group receive a pill that looks identical but contains an inactive substance, such as sugar. If a new surgery is being studied, some patients undergo the true surgical procedure. Those in the control group may go under anesthesia and have their skin cut and sutured so that it looks like they had surgery, but they don't undergo the actual surgical procedure. (Don't worry, all participants in these studies are informed ahead of time that both these options exist, and they give their consent to be randomly assigned to either the active treatment group or the placebo group. No one is ever given placebo treatment without prior consent.)

Studies show that people in the placebo groups often get better, at least a little, and at least for a short while. In these "placebo-controlled" studies, the true effect of the treatment being tested can only be determined by statistically comparing the improvement of the patients in the active treatment group with the improvement of the patients in the placebo group. If the active treatment group doesn't improve by considerably more than the placebo group, then the treatment is said to have no value beyond the placebo effect.

continued

The Placebo Effect (continued)

No one knows exactly why the placebo effect occurs. It could be that people get better because they feel cared for, and that allows them to relax in a way that either improves symptoms or makes symptoms less noticeable. It could be that there is some healing power in being optimistic about a treatment, that being hopeful has physiologic effects. Whatever the reason for the placebo effect, one thing is certain: it doesn't last. The exact length of time it lasts depends on the individual, the disorder being treated, and the type of placebo, but the positive effects rarely last longer than three months.

And if your symptoms are severe or of high intensity, fill in all three boxes. (Similar to a reading on a thermometer, the higher your intensity, the more boxes will be filled in.) What you'll end up with is a gauge that will graphically show when your most severe symptoms occur.

Many women also find that it helps to have their husband or partner keep a symptoms diary of the things they see. Women with premenstrual symptoms may be unaware of changes in their behavior that are obvious to the people who live with them. (For example, your partner may notice that you sleep less well for a couple of nights before your symptoms start.) Also, by having an outside view of your symptoms, you'll have a chance to compare how well your observations match those of others, and you'll also have another objective measure of whether the symptom management strategies you try are working effectively.

Step 2: Make a Doctor's Appointment

Make an appointment with a physician you trust, someone you are comfortable with and with whom you can discuss anything. It can be your OB/GYN, family doctor, or a psychiatrist. All are capable of diagnosing PMDD and recommending appropriate treatment options.

Make the appointment for sometime after you have at least one month of symptoms charted on your symptoms diary. Having the completed diary pages will allow your doctor to see your pattern of symptoms and provides a place to begin discussing treatment recommendations. NOTE: If you feel suicidal or have severe depressive or anxious symptoms, contact your doctor immediately.

Some women are more comfortable trying to solve the problem on their own before making an appointment to see a doctor. Really, the optimal strategy is to have the support of your doctor while you are trying various treatment strategies. Just because you see a physician doesn't mean you have to take medication. Your doctor can guide you through the process of making decisions about which treatments to try, provide advice about herbal therapies and nutritional supplements, and give you a reassuring place to turn if symptoms get worse. But if you are set on exhausting all other options before seeking medical help, continue to keep a symptoms diary throughout the process so you know how the self-help treatments are working. Give yourself three months, then reevaluate how you feel. If your symptoms have not improved, see your doctor.

Step 3: Start Lifestyle Changes

Immediately, even before you see your doctor, begin a regular program of exercise. This is the single best self-help treatment there is for premenstrual symptoms. If you've never exercised before, start light. You don't have to be an Olympic-grade athlete to reap the symptom-relieving benefits of exercise. Choose activities you like, and do them for at least thirty minutes a day, three to four days each week. Exercise at an intensity level that is comfortable for you. (See Chapter 7.)

We also recommend that every woman take calcium supplements, 900 to 1,200 milligrams each day, no more than 500 milligrams at a time. Because magnesium may help reduce premenstrual symptoms, and because it works in conjunction with calcium in regulating some body systems, adding 320 to 500 milligrams of magnesium each day may help as well. (See Chapter 8.)

On Combining Treatments

When women experience improvements in their premenstrual symptoms, it can sometimes be difficult to separate out which treatment is the one that made the difference. Scientific studies tend to look at discrete, individual treatments, but real life is not so tidy. Women often use several treatments simultaneously in an effort to make themselves feel as good as possible as quickly as possible. And there is nothing wrong with this approach. Premenstrual disorders are complex, people are complex, and symptoms are complex. It should come as no surprise that optimal treatment may involve combined therapies.

A few studies have looked at the effects of a more global approach to treatment. One study that took place in Hong Kong enrolled girls, ages fourteen to eighteen, into one of two groups: one received education about PMS and the other group received no special classes. The education group learned much of the same information in this book, including information about the female anatomy and physiology of menstruation, the myths and misconceptions about menstruation, what PMS is and its possible causes, the impact of PMS symptoms on women's lives, the relationship of stress to PMS, progressive relaxation, stress reduction, recommended dietary changes, and the benefits of regular exercise. Although the researchers did not measure what changes the girls made in their behaviors or lifestyles because of the education classes, the girls who learned about PMS had significant decreases in reported levels of premenstrual anxiety, cravings, and bloating. The girls who had no education reported no differences in premenstrual symptoms.

Another study evaluated the benefit of a combined program of professional guidance and peer group support on premenstrual symptoms. The program required more than just talking about symptoms and emotions. It involved several different facets of treatment, including monitoring of symptoms, stress reduction training, a specific diet regimen, vitamin supplementation, exercise, time management training, communication skills training, and problem-solving skills training. The women were required to complete weekly homework exercises based on what they learned. The researcher reported that this type of multiple-treatment program reduced premenstrual symptoms by 75 to 85 percent. The improvement was seen as early as three months after beginning the program and continued throughout the eighteen-month follow-up period. In addition to providing premenstrual symp-

continued

On Combining Treatments (continued)

tom relief, the women in the program also reported overall less depression and distress, which the researcher attributed to a greater sense of well-being and self-esteem in those women.

The overall lesson is that learning about premenstrual disorders and taking basic steps to improve health and well-being have a beneficial effect on premenstrual symptoms, or at least the perception of premenstrual symptoms. Doing just about anything that has global health benefits is likely to make you feel better. Stress reduction will make you feel better overall, as will keeping a healthy diet and exercising regularly. Each additional thing you do will make you feel that much better. It may not be enough to make all your symptoms disappear, but you will feel better—not just premenstrually, but every day of the month. And if you decide to take medication, try to maintain your healthy lifestyle changes as part of your combined therapy. Medications can seem like "magic bullets" or easy-to-swallow cures, but lasting good health, self-esteem, and well-being depend on a variety of long-term, health-promoting behaviors.

Step 4: Add Other Noninvasive Treatments if Desired

While you are feeling motivated, take advantage of the time before your doctor's appointment to learn stress reduction techniques (see Chapter 11), practice the relaxation response (see Chapter 9), add dietary changes (see Chapter 7), or talk with a therapist (see Chapter 11). These treatments cannot hurt, may help, and can certainly improve your overall health. Some studies have shown that a combination of nonmedical treatments can help improve symptoms for some women.

We don't recommend taking any herbal remedies or nutritional supplements (other than calcium and magnesium) without the advice and counsel of a physician. There are too many possible drug interactions that can occur. If you want to try these treatments, do so only after discussing them with your doctor.

Step 5: Discuss Your Symptoms and Concerns with Your Doctor

When it's time for your doctor's appointment, discuss all your symptoms openly and honestly. The doctor is there to help you, not judge you. Bring all your completed symptoms diary pages. After reading this book, you probably have an idea of different treatment options you'd like to try, whether they are strictly lifestyle changes, complementary medicines, prescription medicines, cognitive or couples therapy, or some combination. Tell your doctor what your treatment preferences are, discuss any treatments you've already begun, and then ask what his or her recommendations would be. The two of you, in partnership, should be able to make a medical decision that is both satisfying and medically sound.

Ask your physician what the procedure is if you have questions during your next bout with premenstrual symptoms. For example, if you are given a prescription for medication but it doesn't control your intense premenstrual symptoms, you may need to contact your doctor before your next scheduled appointment to see if you need a different medication or if you need to increase the dosage premenstrually. Some physicians have special telephone consultation hours, others have a nurse or physician's assistant on hand to answer phone calls, and others might prefer those kinds of questions by E-mail. By knowing in advance the best ways to get information, you'll be more likely to feel comfortable contacting the office when you're feeling your worst.

Step 6: Decide Whether You Want to Take Medication

If you have severe premenstrual symptoms, it is likely that your physician will give you the option of taking a medication to help relieve your symptoms. The choice of taking or not taking medication is totally up to you. And you can change your mind at any time. But that doesn't mean you have to make the decision alone. If you have concerns, use your doctor as a sounding board. Ask the hard questions. No one can tell you exactly how a medication will work for you, nor can anyone predict what side effects you'll feel. Those vary by individual. But your doctor should be able to provide you with information about how most women respond to the medication, what their side effects are, and what the success or failure rate has been. Then—in partnership with your doctor—weigh the pros and cons, the risks and benefits, and make the best decision for you. If you decide against taking medication, ask your doctor for guidance about which other treatments you might try. If you decide to take medication, you can always stop if you decide later that it's not for you. Any side effects that might appear while taking the drug will disappear once you stop taking it.

For mild premenstrual symptoms, physicians may offer more conservative treatment. They may suggest lifestyle changes, stress reduction, vitamin supplements, or psychological therapy. If weight gain or edema are major symptoms, they may recommend a prescription diuretic called spironolactone (Aldactone), which helps the body rid itself of excess fluid and has also been shown to help reduce the severity of other premenstrual symptoms.

For moderate symptoms associated with PMDD, physicians may offer an intermittent selective serotonin reuptake inhibitor (SSRI), to be taken during the whole luteal phase. If symptoms don't improve after two cycles, the dose may be increased, or you may need to change to continuous dosing (taking the medication throughout the month). For severe PMDD or PME, continuous dosing with an SSRI is likely to be recommended. (See Chapter 6.)

Step 7: When You Are Ready, Talk with Your Loved Ones About Premenstrual Disorders

Different women have different reactions to receiving a diagnosis of a premenstrual disorder and to discussing it with others. Some women are relieved to finally understand why they've been feeling so bad for so many years, and they are eager to tell others what they've learned. For some women, however, discussing menstrual cycle issues is embarrassing. Whether and how much you decide to talk about your premenstrual symptoms depends on how you feel, what your personal relationships are like, and how much of an effect your premenstrual symptoms may have had on those relationships.

There is no right or wrong choice about talking about these issues. The choice is yours. Chances are the people close to you have already noticed that you seem different at certain times of the month, but they may not have made the connection to your menstrual cycle. Or, they may have made the connection but are wary of bringing it to your attention. By discussing your premenstrual symptoms, you give them the opportunity to be supportive in any treatment you decide to pursue and you let them know that you are taking steps to alleviate your personal distress and any strain your symptoms have put on your relationships. If you are uncertain how to begin the conversation, we have provided a summary of what the loved ones of women with premenstrual disorders need to know in Chapter 14.

Step 8: Reevaluate Your Symptoms and Treatment at Critical Change Points

The special sensitivities that make women at risk for premenstrual symptoms also make them more susceptible to symptoms during other life transitions that involve changing hormone levels.

Pregnancy is protective for premenstrual symptoms because hormone levels stay steadily high throughout pregnancy, so the hormone fluctuations linked with premenstrual symptoms are absent. For this reason, many women find that their worst symptoms, including menstrual migraine, improve during pregnancy. It is not unusual to hear pregnant women with a history of severe PMS say that they feel better during pregnancy than at any other time in their lives. However, women with premenstrual symptoms are hit especially hard after delivery. Postpartum is a biologically critical time for all women, but the crash of hormones from their nine-month steadily high level is likely to trigger extreme symptoms in women with PMDD or PME.

The transition to menopause also creates problems for women with premenstrual symptoms. This is not true with menopause itself, or what is sometimes called postmenopause. After your hormones stop cycling, your symptoms will disappear. It's the transition to menopause, the perimenopause, that is tough, because during the perimenopause period hormone levels not only fluctuate, they are also irregular. One study conducted by researchers in Australia found that during the menopausal transition, women with premenstrual symptoms experienced more dysphoric symptoms than women without premenstrual symptoms.

The best way to deal with these transitions is to have an open dialogue with your physician before and during these periods. If you are already being treated with an antidepressant medication, it may be necessary to alter the dose of your medication. If you are heading toward one of these "milestones" and are not being treated, you may want to consider medical treatment, at least to get you through the tough hormonal time. This is especially important during the postpartum phase, when prophylactic medications will allow a good mother-child bonding experience in those important first months.

Step 9: Follow Up for Difficult-to-Control Symptoms

Follow up with your doctor regularly. Even if you've tried all the basic treatments and nothing has worked, don't give up. Medications work slightly differently for every individual. If you've tried one medication that didn't work, you may have success if you switch to a different medication. For extremely difficult to control symptoms, hormonal therapies may be helpful. It is also possible to take advantage of cutting-edge research by enrolling in a clinical trial.

Clinical trials are scientific studies designed to test new treatments. Before a drug can be approved as a treatment for a particular disorder, a series of studies must show that the drug is safe for humans, that it actually works, and at what dosage it works best. There are three phases of clinical trials:

- In Phase 1 clinical trials, scientists investigate how much of a drug (or treatment) should be given, how often, in what form, and whether it causes safety concerns. If it proves to be safe, Phase 2 trials can begin.

- In Phase 2 clinical trials, scientists investigate whether the drug (or treatment) actually works to treat the disease or symptoms for which it is being tested. Sometimes successful Phase 2 clinical trials are enough to allow a new medication or treatment to be approved for use by the U.S. Food and Drug Administration (FDA).
- In Phase 3 clinical trials, scientists compare the new drug (or treatment) with the current standard of care to see which treatment is better.

You can find clinical trials that are testing new treatments for just about any disorder, including premenstrual disorders. To find a clinical trial that is currently recruiting women with premenstrual disorders, talk with your physician, or search one of the clinical trials databases now available online, including www.ClinicalTrials.gov and CenterWatch Clinical Trials Listing Service (see Appendix A for more information).

Step 10: Be Kind to Yourself

We've said this before, but it is worth repeating. Premenstrual symptoms are not your fault. You didn't do anything to cause them, and they are not a sign of personal failure. It is not self-indulgent to want to feel better; it is a medical imperative. Give yourself the space and time to breathe and relax. Modify your schedule as much as possible to avoid or reduce stress premenstrually and give yourself permission to seek out the treatments that work best for you.

14

What You Should Know if Someone You Love Has PMDD, PME, or Severe PMS

I tell my boyfriend, "When I get like this, ignore me." That's the best way to say it. I could say, be understanding. But you know what, I don't even understand it. It really is something beyond my control. My own guilt over the way I act and my exasperation could be more easily lifted off my shoulders if it was more easily ignored. Don't make me feel like more of a freak than I already do.

—Marisa

This chapter provides a summary of information about premenstrual disorders, as well as some advice about how to understand and respond to a woman with PMDD, PME, or PMS. You can use it as a reference for yourself, or share it with your partner, family, or friends.

If you've never experienced them, trying to understand premenstrual disorders can be a challenge. But rest assured they are real and command attention. And usually they affect more than just the woman who suffers from them. Premenstrual disorders are biologically based disorders that cause some women to experience potentially severe mood and physical symptoms for a certain period of time every month. If the symptoms are relatively mild but still problematic, the disorder is called premenstrual syndrome (PMS). If the symptoms are severe, interfere with a woman's ability to function properly, and cause strain in interpersonal relationships, the disorder is called premenstrual dysphoric disorder (PMDD). If there is another underlying disorder, and its symptoms get worse premenstrually, the disorder is called premenstrual exacerbation (PME).

No one knows exactly what causes some women to experience severe premenstrual symptoms while other women have virtually no symptoms at all. One popular theory is that women with premenstrual disorders have a sensitivity to the fluctuating hormone levels that occur every month. This sensitivity is related to a number of other physiologic occurrences, including a change in the amount of serotonin—the chemical messenger in the brain that helps keep mood stable. Lower levels of serotonin in the brain cause animals to become more aggressive, and scientists believe it causes humans to become more irritable, angry, and depressed, as well. Women with premenstrual symptoms seem to have lower levels of serotonin, or have some dysfunction in their serotonin system that affects the amount of serotonin available in the brain.

The symptoms of premenstrual disorders include irritability, anger, depression, mood swings, anxiety, fatigue, food cravings, a sense of being out of control, breast tenderness, weight gain, bloating, and headaches. There may be a tendency to withdraw from social interactions, be argumentative, and have more frequent emotional outbursts. These symptoms are not imaginary, and they cannot be controlled by willpower or personal strength. They are triggered by the changing hormone levels and are as uncontrollable as allergic reactions. The disorder is real, and the symptoms are highly distressing.

There are a variety of treatments available for women with premenstrual disorders. Exercise, vitamin supplements, and stress reduction are likely to help. Some herbal supplements or other complementary therapies may also help reduce the severity of some symptoms. The newest treatments are antidepressant medications, which can have dramatic results. In addition, psychological counseling and couples therapy can help women and their partners learn how to deal with premenstrual symptoms. Regardless of which therapy or combination of therapies is tried, it is recommended that women with premenstrual disorders see a physician to monitor their symptoms, make the proper diagnosis, and help them make the best treatment decisions.

There are things you can do to make life easier for yourself and the woman in your life with premenstrual symptoms.

- **Ask her what she needs to help her get through her worst premenstrual time.** Some women want to be ignored or left alone. Others need more reassurance and signs of affection. Let her needs be your guide.
- **Ask her how she wants you to respond to emotional outbursts (but don't ask this *during* an outburst).** Women have compared their raw premenstrual emotions to having a deep sunburn—everything hurts and everything is irritating. Their responses feel out of their control. If you yell back, that will definitely make things worse. If you walk away, it may make things worse. If you hug her, it may also make things worse. It all depends on the individual. Talk about it during a quiet time, and she'll tell you the best way to respond.
- **Try to reduce stress around her premenstrual time.** Again, talk in advance about some of the things she finds most stressful when she's feeling the worst symptoms. For example, if making meals is stressful, try to find ways to reduce that stress—arrange to order in or eat out more often during that time, take on more responsibility for the cooking, or help her make frozen meals in advance that can be easily defrosted. If she simply needs some time alone, help her arrange for quiet time.
- **Offer support for any treatments she tries.** Premenstrual disorders are difficult, and the symptoms don't always respond quickly. Some treatments may take months before any difference is noticed. If she decides to try medication, she may have a rapid response if it is the right medication for her. Otherwise, there may be a period of adjustment while the proper drug and dosage are determined.

Along with those helpful suggestions, women with premenstrual disorders invariably have advice about what you should *not* do:

- **Don't blame all emotions or fights on her premenstrual disorder diagnosis.** Even after the disorder is being successfully treated, there may still be emotional outbursts, fights, and interpersonal conflicts—

but they won't have anything to do with PMS, PME, or PMDD. Being treated doesn't take away one's emotions. Phrases like, "So, is this your PMS again?" will only aggravate the situation, whether it is PMS or not.

- **Don't take premenstrual blowups personally.** Until the disorder is treated, women feel out of control of their emotions and their actions premenstrually. They can say hurtful things, and they usually regret it later. If you take any verbal attacks personally and respond immediately, you'll only escalate a bad situation. Wait until a quiet moment, discuss how the things she said made you feel, and try to resolve the situation outside the emotional flurry of PMDD, PME, or PMS.
- **Don't make PMS jokes when she is premenstrual.** You might think they are funny and that they fit the situation, but most women won't find them funny when they are feeling their worst symptoms.
- **Don't "parent" her or try to control her food choices.** Women with premenstrual symptoms may have some seemingly out-of-control behavior, but they are still adults. They are especially capable of making their own decisions about what and when to eat. Many times, women report intense food cravings around the time of their menstrual periods. There is nothing wrong with eating a craved food, and no one should be made to feel guilty about food choices.

The woman in your life is not "crazy" or on the verge of "going insane." Watching someone you love suffer through the symptoms of a premenstrual disorder can be frightening. But as frightening or out of control as it *looks*, it *feels* even worse. It's important to remember that help is available, and more stable emotions are possible. The best way to help is to remain supportive and understanding, and to encourage her as she explores treatment options.

APPENDIX A

Resources

The American College of Obstetricians and Gynecologists (ACOG)
409 12th St. SW
P.O. Box 96920
Washington, DC 20090-6920
Telephone: 202-638-5577
www.acog.com

The public can search this website for information pertaining to women's health, including premenstrual symptoms and mood disorders. Website also has a feature to help you find an ACOG-affiliated OB/GYN anywhere in the world.

American Counseling Association
5999 Stevenson Ave.
Alexandria, VA 22304-3300
Telephone: 800-347-6647 or 703-823-9800
www.counseling.org

The association provides free access to some articles about specific issues important to consumers, answers common questions about counseling, and offers guidance on how to find a professional counselor.

American Dietetic Association (ADA)
216 W. Jackson Blvd.
Chicago, IL 60606-6995
Telephone: 312-899-0040
www.eatright.com

This association's website can provide answers to all your diet and nutrition questions. Search for ADA-affiliated dietitians by state.

American Psychiatric Association (APA)
1400 K St. NW
Washington, DC 20005
Telephone: 888-357-7924
Fax: 202-682-6850
www.psych.org

Public information section has information fact sheets about a variety of psychiatric issues and disorders, as well as information on insurance issues, psychiatric medications, and more. Under "How to Choose a Psychiatrist," the APA Referral section includes contact information for local APA chapters in the United States and Canada.

American Psychological Association (APA)
750 First St. NE
Washington, DC 20002-4242
Telephone: 800-374-2721 or 202-336-5510
TDD/TTY: 202-336-6123
www.apa.org

This organization offers a "Consumer Help Center" with information on how to find help for life's problems. The APA offers a "Find a Psychologist" referral service (800-964-2000) that can put you in touch with a qualified psychologist in your area.

CenterWatch Clinical Trials Listing Service
www.centerwatch.com

This site lists clinical trials, drugs currently being tested, and information about clinical trials. Offers a patient notification service that will notify you whenever an appropriate trial becomes available.

ClinicalTrials.gov
www.clinicaltrials.gov

A service of the National Institutes of Health, this website links patients to medical research, including a section on understanding clinical trials. You can enter a specific search term, or look under "Mood Disorders" for current list of PMS, PMDD, and PME clinical trials.

National Association for Premenstrual Syndrome (NAPS)
7 Swift's Court, High Street
Seal, Kent
United Kingdom TN15 0EG
Telephone: 0-1732-760011
Helpline: 0-1732-760012
www.pms.org.uk

This is a medical charity (nonprofit organization) that provides information, advice, and support to women affected by PMS, their partners, and families. Information packets are available for a cost. Internet site offers message boards and chat rooms. There is a team of specialists who respond to sufferers online at help@pms.org.uk.

National Association of Social Workers (NASW)
750 First St. NE, Suite 700
Washington, DC 20002-4241
Telephone: 202-408-8600 or 800-638-8799
www.naswdc.org

The National Association of Social Workers provides an online referral service.

National Board for Certified Counselors (NBCC)
Telephone: 336-547-0607
www.nbcc.org
E-mail: counselorlist@nbcc.org

This organization provides information about counseling and offers a referral service by telephone or online (in the United States) or by E-mail (international).

**National Center for Complementary and Alternative Medicine
  (NCCAM)**
P.O. Box 8218
Silver Spring, MD 20907-8218
Telephone/TTY: 888-644-6226
Fax: 301-495-4957
www.nccam.nih.gov

This center provides fact sheets, information packages, and publications to enhance public understanding about complementary and alternative medicine research supported by the National Institutes of Health. NCCAM public information is currently free of charge; however, due to printing and duplication costs, only a limited number of copies can be requested. Information specialists can answer inquiries in English or Spanish.

National Health Information Center
P.O. Box 1133
Washington, DC 20013-1133
Telephone: 800-336-4797 or 301-565-4167
Fax: 301-984-4256
www.health.gov/nhic

The National Health Information Center helps the public and health professionals locate health information through identification of health information resources, an information and referral system, and publications. Uses a database containing descriptions of health-related organizations to refer inquirers to the most appropriate resources. Does not diagnose medical conditions or give medical advice.

National Institute of Mental Health (NIMH)
NIMH Public Inquiries
6001 Executive Blvd., Rm. 8184, MSC 9663
Bethesda, MD 20892-9663
Telephone: 301-443-4513
TTY: 301-443-8431
Fax: 301-443-4279
www.nimh.nih.gov

The public can search this website for information about women's mental health issues, including PMS and other mood disorders.

National Women's Health Information Center
8850 Arlington Blvd., Suite 300
Fairfax, VA 22310
Telephone: 800-994-WOMAN (800-994-9662)
TDD: 888-220-5446
www.4woman.gov

This is a U.S.-based national health information and referral center for women. Website has a searchable database of information about most medical topics, including PMDD and PMS. Free "Healthy Women Today" newsletter is available by E-mail or on the website. The website is available in English or Spanish.

U.S. Food and Drug Administration (FDA)
Office of Consumer Affairs
5600 Fishers Lane
Rockville, MD 20857
Telephone: 888-INFO-FDA (888-463-6332)
Fax: 301-443-9767
www.fda.gov

This governmental organization provides information about foods, drugs, cosmetics, and medical devices. Searchable database allows you to find information about medications and about the government's role in monitoring herbal and nutritional supplements.

APPENDIX B

Symptoms Diary Sheets

THESE SYMPTOMS DIARY SHEETS are provided to help you track your symptoms and rate their severity. By looking at the pattern of your symptoms across the month, your doctor can make an appropriate diagnosis and choose the best treatment plan for you.

Here you'll find instructions for filling in the sheets, along with a sample of what a completed sheet might look like. This is just a sample. Your own completed diary sheet may look very different. The key to getting the best treatment is having an accurate assessment of your personal symptoms, so try to fill in your symptoms ratings every day, at the same time each day. This way, you'll be recording your symptoms while they are still being felt, instead of having to rely on your memory.

Immediately following the sample are several months of blank diary sheets. They can be torn out, copied, or completed directly in the book. (We recommend leaving at least one blank that can be copied as needed in the future.)

Instructions: Begin recording your symptoms today, using the column corresponding to the day of the month on the calendar. For example, if today is the 11th of June, start in the column labeled "11." For each day you visit the calendar, put a check mark in the box above the date to show that you visited the diary that day, even if you had no symptoms. For each of the symptoms on the left side of the diary page, fill in the level of that symptom that you experience each day in the boxes labeled "low," "med," or "high." If you have no symptoms, leave all boxes empty. If you have a low level of that symptom, fill in just the "low" box. If you have a medium level of that symptom, fill in the "low" and "med" boxes. Fill in all three boxes if you have a high level of that symptom.

Circle the date that corresponds to the first day of your menstrual period this month. Start a new diary page with each new calendar month.

Symptoms Diary for the month of: MAY

Diary visited today?	√	✓	✓	✓	✓	✓	✓	✓	✓	✓	✓	✓	✓	✓	✓	✓	✓	✓	✓	✓	✓	✓	✓	✓	✓	✓	✓	✓	✓	✓
Day of the calendar month		1	2	3	4	5	6	7	8	9	10	11	12	13	14	15	16	17	⑱	19	20	21	22	23	24	25	26	27	28	29	30	31

Depressed mood sad, blue, hopeless, feeling worthless	high / med / low	low:1																high 17-18; med; low (15-18)														
Anxiety tense, keyed up, jittery, restless, on edge	high / med / low																															
Mood swings suddenly sad, overly sensitive, cries easily	high / med / low													high–low 13–18																		
Anger irritability, increased interpersonal conflict	high / med / low																															
Decreased interest in usual activities	high / med / low													high–low 13–16																		
Difficulty concentrating forgetfulness, confusion	high / med / low																															
Fatigue lack of energy, lethargy, apathy	high / med / low	low:1												high–low 13–16																		
Appetite changes overeating, food cravings, binge eating	high / med / low																	high–med 17–18														
Sleep changes oversleeping, insomnia, broken sleep, napping	high / med / low																															
Feeling out of control or overwhelmed	high / med / low																high–low 16–18															
Physical symptoms headaches, breast pain, bloating, weight gain	high / med / low																	high–low 17–18														
Lifestyle impact strains relationships, interferes with activities	high / med / low																high–low 16–18															

Previously diagnosed disorders (e.g., depression, anxiety, eating disorder, IBS, diabetes, asthma)

| Write in your disorder: | high / med / low | | | | | | | | | | | | | | | | | | | | | | | | | | | | | | | |

Other symptoms (e.g., menstrual cramps, acne, constipation, hot flashes, change in sex drive)

| Write in your symptom: **BAD CRAMPS** | high / med / low | | | | | | | | | | | | | | | | | | med (18) | | | | | | | | | | | | | |

Symptoms Diary for the month of:

		1	2	3	4	5	6	7	8	9	10	11	12	13	14	15	16	17	18	19	20	21	22	23	24	25	26	27	28	29	30	31
Diary visited today?	√																															
Day of the calendar month																																
Depressed mood sad, blue, hopeless, feeling worthless	high																															
	med																															
	low																															
Anxiety tense, keyed up, jittery, restless, on edge	high																															
	med																															
	low																															
Mood swings suddenly sad, overly sensitive, cries easily	high																															
	med																															
	low																															
Anger irritability, increased interpersonal conflict	high																															
	med																															
	low																															
Decreased interest in usual activities	high																															
	med																															
	low																															
Difficulty concentrating forgetfulness, confusion	high																															
	med																															
	low																															
Fatigue lack of energy, lethargy, apathy	high																															
	med																															
	low																															
Appetite changes overeating, food cravings, binge eating	high																															
	med																															
	low																															
Sleep changes oversleeping, insomnia, broken sleep, napping	high																															
	med																															
	low																															
Feeling out of control or overwhelmed	high																															
	med																															
	low																															
Physical symptoms headaches, breast pain, bloating, weight gain	high																															
	med																															
	low																															
Lifestyle impact strains relationships, interferes with activities	high																															
	med																															
	low																															

Previously diagnosed disorders (e.g., depression, anxiety, eating disorder, IBS, diabetes, asthma)

Write in your disorder:	high																															
	med																															
	low																															

Other symptoms (e.g., menstrual cramps, acne, constipation, hot flashes, change in sex drive)

Write in your symptom:	high																															
	med																															
	low																															

Symptoms Diary for the month of:

		1	2	3	4	5	6	7	8	9	10	11	12	13	14	15	16	17	18	19	20	21	22	23	24	25	26	27	28	29	30	31
Diary visited today?	√																															
Day of the calendar month		1	2	3	4	5	6	7	8	9	10	11	12	13	14	15	16	17	18	19	20	21	22	23	24	25	26	27	28	29	30	31
Depressed mood sad, blue, hopeless, feeling worthless	high																															
	med																															
	low																															
Anxiety tense, keyed up, jittery, restless, on edge	high																															
	med																															
	low																															
Mood swings suddenly sad, overly sensitive, cries easily	high																															
	med																															
	low																															
Anger irritability, increased interpersonal conflict	high																															
	med																															
	low																															
Decreased interest in usual activities	high																															
	med																															
	low																															
Difficulty concentrating forgetfulness, confusion	high																															
	med																															
	low																															
Fatigue lack of energy, lethargy, apathy	high																															
	med																															
	low																															
Appetite changes overeating, food cravings, binge eating	high																															
	med																															
	low																															
Sleep changes oversleeping, insomnia, broken sleep, napping	high																															
	med																															
	low																															
Feeling out of control or overwhelmed	high																															
	med																															
	low																															
Physical symptoms headaches, breast pain, bloating, weight gain	high																															
	med																															
	low																															
Lifestyle impact strains relationships, interferes with activities	high																															
	med																															
	low																															

Previously diagnosed disorders (e.g., depression, anxiety, eating disorder, IBS, diabetes, asthma)

Write in your disorder:	high																															
	med																															
	low																															

Other symptoms (e.g., menstrual cramps, acne, constipation, hot flashes, change in sex drive)

Write in your symptom:	high																															
	med																															
	low																															

Symptoms Diary for the month of:

Diary visited today?	√																														
Day of the calendar month		1	2	3	4	5	6	7	8	9	10	11	12	13	14	15	16	17	18	19	20	21	22	23	24	25	26	27	28	29	30	31

Depressed mood
sad, blue, hopeless, feeling worthless — high / med / low

Anxiety
tense, keyed up, jittery, restless, on edge — high / med / low

Mood swings
suddenly sad, overly sensitive, cries easily — high / med / low

Anger
irritability, increased interpersonal conflict — high / med / low

Decreased interest in usual activities — high / med / low

Difficulty concentrating
forgetfulness, confusion — high / med / low

Fatigue
lack of energy, lethargy, apathy — high / med / low

Appetite changes
overeating, food cravings, binge eating — high / med / low

Sleep changes
oversleeping, insomnia, broken sleep, napping — high / med / low

Feeling out of control or overwhelmed — high / med / low

Physical symptoms
headaches, breast pain, bloating, weight gain — high / med / low

Lifestyle impact
strains relationships, interferes with activities — high / med / low

Previously diagnosed disorders (e.g., depression, anxiety, eating disorder, IBS, diabetes, asthma)

Write in your disorder: — high / med / low

Other symptoms (e.g., menstrual cramps, acne, constipation, hot flashes, change in sex drive)

Write in your symptom: — high / med / low

Symptoms Diary for the month of:

Diary visited today?	√																															
Day of the calendar month		1	2	3	4	5	6	7	8	9	10	11	12	13	14	15	16	17	18	19	20	21	22	23	24	25	26	27	28	29	30	31

Depressed mood sad, blue, hopeless, feeling worthless	high / med / low	
Anxiety tense, keyed up, jittery, restless, on edge	high / med / low	
Mood swings suddenly sad, overly sensitive, cries easily	high / med / low	
Anger irritability, increased interpersonal conflict	high / med / low	
Decreased interest in usual activities	high / med / low	
Difficulty concentrating forgetfulness, confusion	high / med / low	
Fatigue lack of energy, lethargy, apathy	high / med / low	
Appetite changes overeating, food cravings, binge eating	high / med / low	
Sleep changes oversleeping, insomnia, broken sleep, napping	high / med / low	
Feeling out of control or overwhelmed	high / med / low	
Physical symptoms headaches, breast pain, bloating, weight gain	high / med / low	
Lifestyle impact strains relationships, interferes with activities	high / med / low	

Previously diagnosed disorders (e.g., depression, anxiety, eating disorder, IBS, diabetes, asthma)

Write in your disorder:	high / med / low	

Other symptoms (e.g., menstrual cramps, acne, constipation, hot flashes, change in sex drive)

Write in your symptom:	high / med / low	

Symptoms Diary for the month of:

		1	2	3	4	5	6	7	8	9	10	11	12	13	14	15	16	17	18	19	20	21	22	23	24	25	26	27	28	29	30	31
Diary visited today?	√																															
Day of the calendar month																																
Depressed mood sad, blue, hopeless, feeling worthless	high																															
	med																															
	low																															
Anxiety tense, keyed up, jittery, restless, on edge	high																															
	med																															
	low																															
Mood swings suddenly sad, overly sensitive, cries easily	high																															
	med																															
	low																															
Anger irritability, increased interpersonal conflict	high																															
	med																															
	low																															
Decreased interest in usual activities	high																															
	med																															
	low																															
Difficulty concentrating forgetfulness, confusion	high																															
	med																															
	low																															
Fatigue lack of energy, lethargy, apathy	high																															
	med																															
	low																															
Appetite changes overeating, food cravings, binge eating	high																															
	med																															
	low																															
Sleep changes oversleeping, insomnia, broken sleep, napping	high																															
	med																															
	low																															
Feeling out of control or overwhelmed	high																															
	med																															
	low																															
Physical symptoms headaches, breast pain, bloating, weight gain	high																															
	med																															
	low																															
Lifestyle impact strains relationships, interferes with activities	high																															
	med																															
	low																															

Previously diagnosed disorders (e.g., depression, anxiety, eating disorder, IBS, diabetes, asthma)

Write in your disorder:	high																															
	med																															
	low																															

Other symptoms (e.g., menstrual cramps, acne, constipation, hot flashes, change in sex drive)

Write in your symptom:	high																															
	med																															
	low																															

References

Chapter 1 Is PMDD Real?

Adenaike OC, Abidoye RO. A study of the incidence of the premenstrual syndrome in a group of Nigerian women. *Public Health.* 1987;101:49–58.

Banerjee N, Roy KK, Takkar D. Premenstrual dysphoric disorder—a study from India. *Int J Fertil.* 2000;45(4):342–344.

Brauer LH, Rukstalis MR, de Wit H. Acute subjective responses to paroxetine in normal volunteers. *Drug Alcohol Depend.* 1995;39(3):223–230.

Chandra PS, Chaturvedi SK. Cultural variations of premenstrual experience. *Int J Soc Psychiatry.* 1989;35(4):343–349.

Endicott J, Amsterdam J, Eriksson E, et al. Is premenstrual dysphoric disorder a distinct clinical entity? *J Womens Health Gend Based Med.* 1999;8(5):663–679.

Frank RT. The hormonal causes of premenstrual tension. *Arch Neurol Psychiatry.* 1931;26:1053–1057.

Freed SC. The treatment of premenstrual distress, with special consideration of the androgens. *JAMA.* 1945;127(7):377–379.

Gelfin Y, Gorfine M, Lerer B. Effect of clinical doses of fluoxetine on psychological variables in healthy volunteers. *Am J Psychiatry.* 1998;155(2):290–292.

Greenblatt RB. Syndrome of major menstrual molimina with hypermenorrhea alleviated by testosterone propionate. *JAMA.* 1940;115(2):120–121.

Greene R, Dalton K. The premenstrual syndrome. *BMJ.* 1953;1:1007–1014.

Greenhill JP, Freed SC. The electrolyte therapy of premenstrual distress. *JAMA.* 1941:117(7):504–506.

Hippocrates. On virgins; translated and referenced in: *Women's Life in Greece and Rome—a Sourcebook in Translation,* 2nd ed. MR Lefkowitz & MB Fant. Baltimore, MD: Johns Hopkins University Press; 1992.

Israel SL. Premenstrual tension. *JAMA.* 1938;110(21):1721–1723.

Janiger O, Riffenburg R, Kersh R. Cross-cultural study of premenstrual symptoms. *Psychosomatics.* 1972;13(4):226–235.

Kessel B. Premenstrual syndrome: advances in diagnosis and treatment. *Obstet Gynecol Clin North Am.* 2000;27(3):625–639.

Monagle L, Dan A, Krogh V, et al. Perimenstrual symptom prevalence rates: an Italian-American comparison. *Am J Epidemiol.* 1993;138(12):1070–1081.

Monteleone P, Luisi S, Tonetti A, et al. Allopregnanolone concentrations and premenstrual syndrome. *Eur J Endocrinol.* 2000;142:269–273.

Morton JH. Premenstrual tension. *Am J Obstet Gyn.* 1950;60(2):343–352.

Parry BL, Berga SL, Mostebi N, et al. Plasma melatonin circadian rhythms during the menstrual cycle and after light therapy in premenstrual dysphoric disorder and normal control subjects. *J Biol Rhythms.* 1997;12:47–64.

Parry BL, Javeed S, Laughlin GA, et al. Cortisol circadian rhythms during the menstrual cycle and with sleep deprivation in premenstrual dysphoric disorder and normal control subjects. *Biol Psychiatry.* 2000;48(9):920–931.

Rapkin AJ, Edelmuth E, Chang LC, et al. Whole-blood serotonin in premenstrual syndrome. *Obstet Gynecol.* 1987;70(4):533–537.

Severino SK, Moline ML. *Premenstrual Syndrome: A Clinician's Guide.* New York: Guildford Press; 1989.

Stieglitz EJ, Kimble ST. Premenstrual intoxication. *Am J Med Sci.* 1949;218:616–623.

Stolberg M. The monthly malady: a history of premenstrual suffering. *Med Hist.* 2000;44:301–322.

Yu M, Zhu X, Li J, Oakley D, Reame NE. Perimenstrual symptoms among Chinese women in an urban area of China. *Health Care Women Int.* 1996;17(2):161–172.

Chapter 2 What Is PMDD?

ACOG Practice Bulletin: Premenstrual Syndrome. ACOG Practice Bulletin No. 15, April 2000.

Bloch M, Schmidt PJ, Su T-P, et al. Pituitary-adrenal hormones and testosterone across the menstrual cycle in women with premenstrual syndrome and controls. *Biol Psychiatry.* 1998;43:897–903.

Chrousos GP, Torpy DJ, Gold PW. Interactions between the hypothalamic-pituitary-adrenal axis and the female reproductive system: clinical implications. *Ann Intern Med.* 1998;129:229–240.

Cleckner-Smith CS, Doughty AS, Grossman JA. Premenstrual symptoms: prevalence and severity in an adolescent sample. *J Adolesc Health.* 1998 May;22(5):403–408.

Condon JT. The premenstrual syndrome: a twin study. *Br J Psychiatry.* 1993;162:481–486.

Giannini AJ, Melmeis SM, Martin DM, Folts DJ. Symptoms of premenstrual syndrome as a function of beta-endorphin: two subtypes. *Prog Neuropsychopharmacol Biol Psychiatry.* 1994;18(2):321–327.

Girdler SS, Pedersen CA, Straneva PA, et al. Dysregulation of cardiovascular and neuroendocrine responses to stress in premenstrual dysphoric disorder. *Psychiatry Res.* 1998;81:163–178.

Girdler SS, Straneva PA, Light KC, et al. Allopregnanolone levels and reactivity to mental stress in premenstrual dysphoric disorder. *Biol Psychiatry.* 2001;49:788–797.

Kasckow JW, Baker D, Geracioti TD Jr. Corticotropin-releasing hormone in depression and post-traumatic stress disorder. *Peptides.* 2001;22(5):845–851.

Kendler K, Karkowski L, Corey L. Longitudinal population-based twin study of retrospectively reported premenstrual symptoms and lifetime major depression. *Am J Psychiatry.* 1998;155:1234.

Kendler KS, Silberg JL, Neale MC, et al. Genetic and environmental factors in the aetiology of menstrual, premenstrual and neurotic symptoms: a population-based twin study. *Psychol Med.* 1992;22(1):85–100.

Parry BL. Psychobiology of premenstrual dysphoric disorder. *Semin Reprod Endocrinol.* 1997;15(1):55–68.

Pearlstein TB, Frank E, Rivera-Tovar A, et al. Prevalence of axis I and axis II disorders in women with late luteal phase dysphoric disorder. *J Affect Disord.* 1990;20(2):129–134.

Rubinow DR, Schmidt PJ. Models for the development and expression of symptoms in premenstrual syndrome. *Psychiatr Clin North Am.* 1989;12(1):53–68.

Schmidt PJ, Nieman LK, Danaceau MA, et al. Differential behavioral effects of gonadal steroids in women with and in those without premenstrual syndrome. *New Engl J Med.* 1998;338(4):209–216.

Taskin O, Gokdeniz R, Yalcinoglu A, et al. Placebo-controlled cross-over study of effects of tibolone on premenstrual symptoms and peripheral beta-endorphin concentrations in premenstrual syndrome. *Human Reprod.* 1998;13(9):2402–2405.

Woods NF, Lentz M, Mitchell ES, et al. PMS after 40: persistence of a stress-related symptom pattern. *Res Nurs Health.* 1997;20:329–340.

Chapter 3 Do You Have PMDD?

Bloch M, Schmidt PJ, Rubinow DR. Premenstrual syndrome: evidence for symptom stability across cycles. *Am J Psychiatry.* 1997;154(12):1741–1746.

Diagnostic and Statistical Manual of Mental Disorders, 4th ed, text revision. Washington, DC: American Psychiatric Association; 2000.

Endicott J, Amsterdam J, Eriksson E, et al. Is premenstrual dysphoric disorder a distinct clinical entity? *J Womens Health Gend Based Med.* 1999;8(5):663–679.

Freeman EW, DeRubeis RJ, Rickels K. Reliability and validity of a daily diary for premenstrual syndrome. *Psychiatry Res.* 1996;65:97–106.

Graze KK, Nee J, Endicott J. Premenstrual depression predicts future major depressive disorder. *Acta Psychiatr Scand.* 1990;81:201–205.

Hardie EA. PMS in the workplace: dispelling the myth of cyclic dysfunction. *J Occup Organiz Psychol.* 1997;70(1):97–102.

Hurt SW, Schnurr PP, Severino SK, et al. Late luteal phase dysphoric disorder in 670 women evaluated for premenstrual complaints. *Am J Psychiatry.* 1992;149(4):525–530.

Kraemer GR, Kraemer RR. Premenstrual syndrome: diagnosis and treatment experiences. *J Womens Health.* 1998;7(7):893–907.

Mortola JF. Issues in the diagnosis and research of premenstrual syndrome. *Clin Obstet Gynecol.* 1992;35(3):587–598.

Parry BL. A 45-year-old woman with premenstrual dysphoric disorder. *JAMA.* 1999;281(4):368–373.

Rapkin AJ, Chang LC, Reading AE. Mood and cognitive style in premenstrual syndrome. *Obstet Gynecol.* 1989;74(4):644–649.

Reid R. Premenstrual syndrome. In: *Current Problems in Obstetrics, Gynecology and Fertility.* Chicago, IL: Year Book Medical Publishers Inc; 1985:1–57.

Robinson RL, Swindle RW. Premenstrual symptom severity: impact on social functioning and treatment-seeking behaviors. *J Womens Health Gend Based Med.* 2000;9(7):757–768.

Rubinow DR, Schmidt PJ. Models for the development and expression of symptoms in premenstrual syndrome. *Psychiatr Clin North Am.* 1989;12(1):53–68.

Society for Women's Health Research. A study of the awareness and attitudes of women toward PMDD. Survey. Sept 2000. www.womenshealth.org.

Sommer B. How does menstruation affect cognitive competence and psychophysiological response? *Women Health.* 1983;8(2–3);53–90.

Steiner M, Streiner DL, Steinberg S, et al. The measurement of premenstrual mood symptoms. *J Affect Disord.* 1999;53:269–273.

Chapter 4 Premenstrual Exacerbation (PME)

Anderberg UM, Marteinsdottir I, Hallman J, Baeckstroem T. Variability in cyclicity affects pain and other symptoms in female fibromyalgia syndrome patients. *J Musculoskeletal Pain.* 1998;6(4):5–22.

Bailey JW, Cohen LS. Prevalence of mood and anxiety disorders in women who seek treatment for premenstrual syndrome. *J Womens Health Gend Based Med.* 1999;8(9):1181–1184.

Basoglu C, Cetin M, Semi UB, et al. Premenstrual exacerbation and suicidal behavior in patients with panic disorder. *Compr Psychiatry.* 2000;41(2):103–105.

Case AM, Reid RL. Effects of the menstrual cycle on medical disorders. *Arch Intern Med.* 1998;158:1405–1412.

Critchlow DG, Bond AJ, Wingrove J. Mood disorder history and personality assessment in premenstrual dysphoric disorder. *J Clin Psychiatry.* 2001;62(9):688–693.

Duncan S, Read CL, Brodie MJ. How common is catamenial epilepsy? *Epilepsia.* 1993;34(5):827–831.

Eliasson O, Scherzer HH, DeGraff AC Jr. Morbidity in asthma in relation to the menstrual cycle. *J Allergy Clin Immunol.* 1986;77(1 Pt 1):87–94.

Facchinetti F, Tarabusi M, Nappi G. Premenstrual syndrome and anxiety disorders: a psychobiological link. *Psychother Psychosom.* 1998;67:57–60.

Fava M, Pedrazzi F, Guaraldi GP, et al. Comorbid anxiety and depression among patients with late luteal phase dysphoric disorder. *J Anxiety Disord.* 1992;6(4):325–335.

Gallagher RM. Menstrual migraine and intermittent ergonovine therapy. *Headache.* 1989;29(6):366–367.

Gladis MM, Walsh BT. Premenstrual exacerbation of binge eating in bulimia. *Am J Psychiatry.* 1987;144(12):1592–1595.

Granella F, Sances G, Messa G, et al. Treatment of menstrual migraine. *Cephalalgia.* 1997;17(suppl 20):35–38.

Hartlage SA, Arduino KE, Gehlert S. Premenstrual dysphoric disorder and risk for major depressive disorder: a preliminary study. *J Clin Psychology.* 2001;57(12):1571–1578.

Hartlage SA, Gehlart S. Differentiating premenstrual dysphoric disorder from premenstrual exacerbations of other disorders: a methods dilemma. *Clinical Psychology: Science & Practice.* 2001;8(2):242–253.

Kane SV, Sable K, Hanauer SB. The menstrual cycle and its effect on inflammatory bowel disease and irritable bowel syndrome: a prevalence study. *Am J Gastroenterol.* 1998;93(10):1867–1872.

Kumar N, Behari M, Aruja GK, Jailhani BL. Phenytoin levels in catamenial epilepsy. *Epilepsia.* 1988;29:155–158.

Lundberg PO. Catamenial epilepsy: a review. *Cephalalgia.* 1997;17(suppl 20):42–45.

Magadle R, Berrar-Yanay N, Weiner P. Long-acting bronchodilators in premenstrual exacerbation of asthma. *Respir Med.* 2001;95(9):740–743.

McMurray RW. Estrogen, prolactin, and autoimmunity: actions and interactions. *Int Immunopharmacol.* 2001;1(6):995–1008.

McMurray RW. Prolactin and systemic lupus erythematosus. *Ann Med Interne.* (Paris) 1996;147(4):253–258.

Morse CA, Dudley E, Guthrie J, Dennerstein L. Relationships between premenstrual complaints and perimenopausal experiences. *J Psychosom Obstet Gynecol.* 1998;19:182–191.

Olfson M, Marcus SC, Druss B, et al. National trends in the outpatient treatment of depression. *JAMA.* 2002;287(2):203–209.

Praschak-Rieder N, Willeit M, Neumeister A, et al. Prevalence of premenstrual dysphoric disorder in female patients with seasonal affective disorder. *J Affect Disord.* 2001;63:239–242.

Rider V, Abdou NI. Gender differences in autoimmunity: molecular basis for estrogen effects in systemic lupus erythematosus. *Int Immunopharmacol.* 2001;1(6):1009–1024.

Rubinow DR, Schmidt PJ, Roca CA. Estrogen-serotonin interactions: implications for affective regulation. *Biol Psychiatry.* 1998;44:839–850.

Sandyk R. Estrogen's impact on cognitive functions in multiple sclerosis. *Int J Neurosci.* 1996;86(1–2):23–31.

Sommerville BW. The role of estrogen withdrawal in the etiology of menstrual migraine. *Neurology.* 1972;22:355–365.

Souza SS, Castro FA, Mendonca HC, et al. Influence of menstrual cycle on NK activity. *J Reprod Immunol.* 2001;50(2):151–159.

Veeninga AT, de Ruiter C, Kraaimaat FW. The relationship between late luteal phase dysphoric disorder and anxiety disorders. *J Anxiety Disord.* 1994;8(3):207–215.

Verri A, Nappi RE, Vallero E, et al. Premenstrual dysphoric disorder and eating disorders. *Cephalalgia.* 1997;17(suppl 20):25–28.

Walsh CH, Malins JM. Menstruation and control of diabetes. *BMJ.* 1977;2(6080):177–179.

Whitehead WE, Cheskin LJ, Heller BR, et al. Evidence for exacerbation of irritable bowel syndrome during menses. *Gastroenterology.* 1990;98(6):1485–1489.

Williams EY, Weekes LR. Premenstrual tension associated with psychotic episodes: preliminary report. *J Nervous Mental Disord.* 1952;116:321–329.

Yonkers KA. Anxiety symptoms and anxiety disorders: how are they related to premenstrual disorders? *J Clin Psychiatry.* 1997;58(suppl 3):62–67.

Yonkers KA. The association between premenstrual dysphoric disorder and other mood disorders. *J Clin Psychiatry.* 1997;58(suppl 15):19–25.

Yonkers KA, White K. Premenstrual exacerbation of depression: one process or two? *J Clin Psychiatry.* 1992;53(8):289–292.

Chapter 6 Serotonin Reuptake Inhibitors

Dimmock PW, Wyatt KM, Jones PW, O'Brien PMS. Efficacy of selective serotonin-reuptake inhibitors in premenstrual syndrome: a systematic review. *Lancet.* 2000;356:1131–1136.

Eriksson E. Serotonin reuptake inhibitors for the treatment of premenstrual dysphoria. *Int Clin Psychopharmacol.* 1999;14(suppl 2):S27–S33.

Eriksson E, Hedberg MA, Andersch B, Sundblad C. The serotonin reuptake inhibitor paroxetine is superior to the noradrenalin reuptake inhibitor maprotiline in the treatment of premenstrual syndrome. *Neuropsychopharmacology.* 1995;12(2):167–176.

Eriksson E, Lisjo P, Sundblad C, et al. Effect of clomipramine on premenstrual syndrome. *Acta Psychiatr Scand.* 1990;81(1):87–88.

Freeman EW, Jabara S, Sondheimer SJ, et al. A pilot study of the effectiveness of citalopram in PMS patients with prior SSRI treatment failure. Poster presented at the 41st Annual Meeting of the New Clinical Drug Evaluation Unit (NCDEU), May 28–31, 2001, Phoenix, AZ.

Freeman EW, Rickels K, Sondheimer SJ. Fluvoxamine for premenstrual dysphoric disorder: a pilot study. *J Clin Psychiatry.* 1996;57(suppl 8):56–59.

Freeman EW, Rickels K, Sondheimer SJ, Polansky M. Differential response to antidepressants in women with premenstrual syndrome/premenstrual dysphoric disorder: a randomized controlled trial. *Arch Gen Psychiatry.* 1999;56(10):932–939.

Freeman EW, Rickels K, Yonkers KA, et al. Venlafaxine in the treatment of premenstrual dysphoric disorder. *Obstet Gynecol.* 2001;98(5 pt 1):737–744.

Gardner DM, Lynd LD. Sumatriptan contraindications and the serotonin syndrome. *Annals Pharmacotherapy.* 1998;32:33–38.

Gitau R, Menson E, Pickles V, et al. Umbilical cortisol levels as an indicator of the fetal stress response to assisted vaginal delivery. *Eur J Obstet Gynecol Reprod Biol.* 2001;98(1):14–17.

Halbreich U, Smoller JW. Intermittent luteal phase sertraline treatment of dysphoric premenstrual syndrome. *J Clin Psychiatry.* 1997;58:399–402.

Joffe RT, Sokolov STH. Co-administration of fluoxetine and sumatriptan: the Canadian experience. *Acta Psychiatr Scand.* 1997;95:551–552.

Michelson D, Fava M, Amsterdam J. Interruption of selective serotonin reuptake inhibitor treatment. *Br J Psychiatry.* 2000;176:363–368.

Misri S, Burgmann A, Kostaras D. Are SSRIs safe for pregnant and breastfeeding women? *Can Fam Physician.* 2000;46:626–628,631–633.

Misri S, Kostaras D, Kostaras X. The use of selective serotonin reuptake inhibitors during pregnancy and lactation: current knowledge. *Can J Psychiatry.* 2000;45(3):285–287.

Parker N, Brown C, Ling FW. Managing PMDD with SSRIs. *OBG Management.* 2000 Mar:67–71.

Pearlstein TB, Halbreich U, Batzar ED, et al. Psychosocial functioning in women with premenstrual dysphoric disorder before and after treatment with sertraline or placebo. *J Clin Psychiatry.* 2000;61(2):101–109.

Rapkin AJ, Edelmuth E, Chang LC, et al. Whole blood serotonin in premenstrual syndrome. *Obstet Gynecol.* 1987;70:533–537.

Singhal AB, Caviness VS, Begleiter AF, et al. Cerebral vasoconstriction and stroke after use of serotonergic drugs. *Neurology.* 2002;58(1):130–133.

Steiner M, Judge R, Brown E, Dillon J. Fluoxetine improves social functioning in women with premenstrual dysphoric disorder (PMDD). Poster #160. NIMH: New Clinical Drug Evaluation Unit Conference, 2000.

Steiner M, Korzekwa M, Lamont J, Wilkins A. Intermittent fluoxetine dosing in the treatment of women with premenstrual dysphoria. *Psychopharmacol Bull.* 1997;33:771–774.

Steiner M, Pearlstein T. Premenstrual dysphoria and the serotonin system: pathophysiology and treatment. *J Clin Psychiatry.* 2000;61(suppl 12):17–21.

Steiner M, Romano SJ, Babcock S, et al. The efficacy of fluoxetine in improving physical symptoms associated with premenstrual dysphoric disorder. *Br J Obstet Gyn.* 2001;108:462–468.

Steiner M, Steinberg S, Stewart D, et al. Fluoxetine in the treatment of premenstrual dysphoria. *New Engl J Med.* 1995;23(332):1529–1534.

Sternbach H. The serotonin syndrome. *Am J Psychiatry.* 1991;148:705–713.

Stone AB, Pearlstein TB, Brown WA. Fluoxetine in the treatment of premenstrual syndrome. *Psychopharmacol Bull.* 1990;26(3):331–335.

Sundblad C, Hedberg MA, Eriksson E. Clomipramine administered during the luteal phase reduces the symptoms of premenstrual syndrome: a placebo-controlled trial. *Neuropsychopharmacology.* 1993;9(2):133–145.

Sundblad C, Modigh K, Andersch B, et al. Clomipramine effectively reduces premenstrual irritability and dysphoria: a placebo-controlled trial. *Acta Psychiatr Scand.* 1992;85(1):39–47.

Sundblad C, Wickander I, Andersch B, Eriksson E. A naturalistic study of paroxetine in premenstrual syndrome: efficacy and side-effects during 10 cycles of treatment. *Eur Neuropsychopharmacol.* 1997;7(3):201–206.

Veeninga AT, Westenberg HG, Weusten JT. Fluvoxamine in the treatment of menstrually related mood disorders. *Psychopharmacology (Berl).* 1990;102(3):414–416.

Walsh MT, Dinan TG. Selective serotonin reuptake inhibitors and violence: a review of the available evidence. *Aca Psychiatr Scand.* 2001;104(2):84–91.

Wikander I, Sundblad C, Andersch B, et al. Citalopram in premenstrual dysphoric disorder: is intermittent treatment more effective than continuous drug administration? *J Clin Psychopharm.* 1998;18:390–398.

Yonkers KA, Gullion C, Williams A, et al. Paroxetine as a treatment for premenstrual dysphoric disorder. *J Clin Psychopharmacol.* 1996;16(1):3–8.

Yonkers KA, Halbreich U, Freeman E, et al. The Sertraline Premenstrual Dysphoric Collaborative Study Group. Symptomatic improvement of premenstrual dysphoric disorder with sertraline treatment. *JAMA.* 1997;278(12):983–988.

Yoshida K, Smith B, Craggs M, Kumar RC. Fluoxetine in breast-milk and developmental outcome of breast-fed infants. *Br J Psychiatry.* 1998;172:172–178.

Chapter 7   Diet and Exercise

Aganoff JA, Boyle GJ. Aerobic exercise, mood states and menstrual cycle symptoms. *J Psychosom Res.* 1994;38(3):183–192.

Alberti-Fidanza A, Fruittini D, Servili M. Gustatory and food habit changes during the menstrual cycle. *Int J Vitam Nutr Res.* 1998;68(2):149–153.

American Dietetic Association. For the food and nutrition professional: a chocolate update. *J Am Dietetic Assn.* 2000;100(2):269.

Bancroft J, Cook A, Williamson L. Food craving, mood and the menstrual cycle. *Psychol Med.* 1988;18(4):855–860.

Blanchard CM, Rodgers WM, Spence JC, Courneya KS. Feeling state responses to acute exercise of high and low intensity. *J Sci Med Sport.* 2001;4(1):30–38.

Bowen DJ, Grunberg NE. Variations in food preference and consumption across the menstrual cycle. *Physiol Behav.* 1990;47(2):287–291.

Bruinsma K, Taren DL. Chocolate: food or drug? *J Am Dietetic Assn.* 1999;99(10):1249–1256.

Bussell G. Premenstrual syndrome and diet. *J Nutr Environ Med.* 1998;8(1):65–75.

Christensen AM, Board BJ, Oei TP. A psychosocial profile of women with premenstrual dysphoria. *J Affect Disord.* 1992;25(4):251–259.

Christensen L. Effects of eating behavior on mood: a review of the literature. *Int J Eat Disord.* 1993;14(2):171–183.

Clementz GL, Dailey JW. Psychotropic effects of caffeine. *Am Fam Physician.* 1988;37(5):167–172.

Danker-Hopfe H, Roczen K, Lowenstein-Wagner U. Regulation of food intake during the menstrual cycle. *Anthropol Anz.* 1995;53(3):231–238.

Dog, TL. Integrative treatments for premenstrual syndrome. *Altern Ther Health Med.* 2001;7(5):32–39.

Dunn AL, Trivedi MH, O'Neal HA. Physical activity dose-response effects on outcomes of depression and anxiety. *Med Sci Sports Exerc.* 2001;33(6 suppl):S587–S597.

Dye L, Warner P, Bancroft J. Food craving during the menstrual cycle and its relationship to stress, happiness of relationship and depression: a preliminary enquiry. *J Affect Disord.* 1995;34(3):157–164.

Hobson ML, Rejeski WJ. Does the dose of acute exercise mediate psychophysiological responses to mental stress? *J Sport Exercise Psychol.* 1993;15:77–87.

Johnson WG, Corrigan SA, Lemmon CR, et al. Energy regulation over the menstrual cycle. *Physiol Behav.* 1994;56(3):523–527.

Kennedy MM, Newton M. Effect of exercise intensity on mood in step aerobics. *J Sports Med Phys Fitness.* 1997;37(3):200–204.

Kurzer MS. Women, food, and mood. *Nutr Rev.* 1997;55(7):268–276.

Lane AM, Lovejoy DJ. The effects of exercise on mood changes: the moderating effect of depressed mood. *J Sports Med Phys Fitness.* 2001;41:539–545.

Meyer T, Broocks A. Therapeutic impact of exercise on psychiatric diseases: guidelines for exercise testing and prescription. *Sports Med.* 2000;30(4):269–279.

O'Boyle M, Severino SK, Hurt SW. Premenstrual syndrome and locus of control. *Int J Psychiatry Med.* 1988;18(1):67–74.

Pearlstein T, Steiner M. Non-antidepressant treatment of premenstrual syndrome. *J Clin Psychiatry.* 2000;61(suppl 12):22–27.

Prior JC, Vigna Y, Sciarretta D, et al. Conditioning exercise decreases premenstrual symptoms: a prospective, controlled 6-month trial. *Fertil Steril.* 1987;47(3):402–408.

Rose DP. Diet, hormones, and cancer. *Annu Rev Public Health.* 1993;14:1–17.

Rose DP, Lubin M, Connolly JM. Effects of diet supplementation with wheat bran on serum estrogen levels in the follicular and luteal phases of the menstrual cycle. *Nutrition.* 1997 June;13(6):535–539.

Rossignol AM, Bonnlander H, Song L, Phillis JW. Do women with premenstrual symptoms self-medicate with caffeine? *Epidemiology.* 1991 Nov;2(6):403–408.

Rossignol AM, Zhang JY, Chen YZ, Xiang Z. Tea and premenstrual syndrome in the People's Republic of China. *Am J Public Health.* 1989 Jan;79(1):67–69.

Roy M, Steptoe A. The inhibition of cardiovascular responses to mental stress following aerobic exercise. *Psychophysiology.* 1991;28:689–700.

Salmon P. Effects of physical exercise on anxiety, depression, and sensitivity to stress: a unifying theory. *Clin Psychology Rev.* 2001;21(1):33–61.

Scully D, Kremer J, Meade MM, et al. Physical exercise and psychological well being: a critical review. *Br J Sports Med.* 1998;32(2):111–120.

Steege JF, Blumenthal JA. The effects of aerobic exercise on premenstrual symptoms in middle-aged women: a preliminary study. *J Psychosom Res.* 1993;37(2):127–133.

Steptoe A, Kimbell J, Basford P. Exercise and the experience and appraisal of daily stressors: a naturalistic study. *J Behav Med.* 1998;21(4):363–374.

Szabo A, Billett E, Turner J. Phenylethylamine, a possible link to the antidepressant effects of exercise? *Br J Sports Med.* 2001;35(5):342–343.

Weisburger JH. Chemopreventive effects of cocoa polyphenols on chronic diseases. *Exp Biol Med (Maywood).* 2001;226(10):891–897.

Wurtman RJ, Wurtman JJ. Do carbohydrates affect food intake via neurotransmitter activity? *Appetite.* 1986;7(suppl):99–103.

Yeung RR. The acute effects of exercise on mood state. *J Psychosom Res.* 1996;40(2):123–141.

Chapter 8 Nutritional Supplements

Barnhardt KT, Freeman E, Grisso JA, et al. The effect of dehydroepiandrosterone supplementation to symptomatic perimenopausal women on serum endocrine profiles, lipid parameters, and health-related quality of life. *J Clin Endocrinol Metab.* 1999;84(11):3896–3902.

Bendich A. The potential for dietary supplements to reduce premenstrual syndrome (PMS) symptoms. *J Am Coll Nutr.* 2000;19(1):3–12.

Chuong CJ, Dawson EB, Smith ER. Vitamin E levels in premenstrual syndrome. *Am J Obstet Gynecol.* 1990;163(5 pt 1):1591–1595.

Collins A, Cerin A, Coleman G, Landgren BM. Essential fatty acids in the treatment of premenstrual syndrome. *Obstet Gynecol.* 1993;81(1):93–98.

De Souza MC, Walker AF, Robinson PA, Bolland K. A synergistic effect of a daily supplement for 1 month of 200 mg magnesium plus 50 mg vitamin B6 for the relief of anxiety-related premenstrual symptoms: a randomized, double-blind, crossover study. *J Womens Health Gend Based Med.* 2000;9(2):131–139.

Eriksson E, Sundblad C, Lisjo P, et al. Serum levels of androgens are higher in women with premenstrual irritability and dysphoria than in controls. *Psychoneuroendocrinology.* 1992;17(2–3):195–204.

Facchinetti F, Borella P, Sances G, et al. Oral magnesium successfully relieves premenstrual mood changes. *Obstet Gynecol.* 1991;78(2):177–181.

FDA: Information Paper on L-tryptophan and 5-hydroxy-L-tryptophan. Feb 2001. http://vm.cfsan.fda.gov/~dms/ds-tryp1.html.

Freeman MP. Omega-3 fatty acids in psychiatry: a review. *Ann Clin Psychiatry.* 2000;12(3):159–165.

Klarskov K, Johnson KL, Benson LM, et al. Eosinophilia-myalgia syndrome case-associated contaminants in commercially available 5-hydroxytryptophan. *Adv Exp Med Biol.* 1999;467:461–468.

London RS, Murphy L, Kitlowski KE, Reynolds MA. Efficacy of alpha-tocopherol in the treatment of the premenstrual syndrome. *J Reprod Med.* 1987;32(6):400–404.

London RS, Sundaram G, Manimekalai S, et al. The effect of alpha-tocopherol on premenstrual symptomotology: a double-blind study. II. Endocrine correlates. *J Am Coll Nutr.* 1984;3(4):351–356.

Mischoulon D, Fava M. Docosahexanoic acid and omega-3 fatty acids in depression. *Psychiatr Clin North Am.* 2000;23(4):785–794.

Pearlstein T, Steiner M. Non-antidepressant treatment of premenstrual syndrome. *J Clin Psychiatry.* 2000;61(suppl 12):22–27.

Penland JG, Johnson PE. Dietary calcium and manganese effects on menstrual cycle symptoms. *Am J Obstet Gynecol.* 1993;168:1417–1423.

Shils ME, Olson JA, Shike M, Ross AC, eds. *Modern Nutrition in Health and Disease,* 9th ed. Baltimore, MD: Williams & Wilkins; 1999.

Thys-Jacobs S. Micronutrients and the premenstrual syndrome: the case for calcium. *J Am Coll Nutr.* 2000;19(2):220–227.

Thys-Jacobs S, Ceccarelli S, Bierman A, et al. Calcium supplementation in premenstrual syndrome. *J Gen Intern Med.* 1989;4:183–189.

Thys-Jacobs S, Silverton M, Alvir J, et al. Reduced bone mass in women with premenstrual syndrome. *J Womens Health.* 1995;4:161–168.

Thys-Jacobs S, Starkey P, Bernstein D, Tian J. Calcium carbonate and the premenstrual syndrome: effects on premenstrual and menstrual symptoms. *Am J Obstet Gynecol.* 1998;179:444–452.

Walker AF, De Souza MC, Vickers MF, et al. Magnesium supplementation alleviates premenstrual symptoms of fluid retention. *J Womens Health.* 1998;7:1157–1165.

Ward MW, Holimon TD. Calcium treatment for premenstrual syndrome. *Annals Pharmacotherapy.* 1999;33:1356–1358.

Wyatt KM, Dimmock PW, Jones PW, O'Brien PMS. Efficacy of vitamin B-6 in the treatment of premenstrual syndrome: systematic review. *BMJ.* 1999;318:1375–1381.

Chapter 9 Complementary Treatments

Benson H, Beary JF, Carol MP. The relaxation response. *Psychiatry.* 1974;37(1):37–46.

Berger D, Schaffner W, Schrader E, et al. Efficacy of *Vitex agnus castus* L. extract Ze440 in patients with premenstrual syndrome (PMS). *Arch Gynecol Obstet.* 2000;264(3):150–153.

Brenner R, Bjerkenstedt L, Edman GV. *Hypericum perforatum* extract (St. John's wort) for depression. *Psychiatric Annals.* 2002;32(1):21–26.

Budeiri D, Li Wan Po A, Dornan JC. Is evening primrose oil of value in the treatment of premenstrual syndrome? *Control Clin Trials.* 1996;17(1):60–68.

Chavez ML, Spitzer MF. Herbals and other dietary supplements for premenstrual syndrome and menopause. *Psychiatric Annals.* 2002;32(1):61–71.

Dog TL. Integrative treatments for premenstrual syndrome. *Altern Ther Health Med.* 2001;7(5):32–39.

Eich H, Agelink MW, Lehmann E, et al. [Acupuncture in patients with minor depressive episodes and generalized anxiety. Results of an experimental study.] *Fortschr Neurol Psychiatr.* 2000;68(3):137–144. [German]

Ernst E. The risk-benefit profile of commonly used herbal therapies: ginkgo, St. John's wort, ginseng, echinacea, saw palmetto, and kava. *Annals Intern Med.* 2002;136(1):42–53.

Ernst E, Rand JI, Stevenson C. Complementary therapies for depression: an overview. *Arch Gen Psychiatry.* 1998;55(11):1026–1032.

Fetrow CW, Avila JR. *Professional's Handbook of Complementary & Alternative Medicines.* Springhouse, PA: Springhouse; 1999.

Goodale IL, Domar AD, Benson H. Alleviation of premenstrual syndrome symptoms with the relaxation response. *Obstet Gynecol.* 1990;75:649–655.

Gunn, JC. *Dr. Gunn's New Family Physician, or Home Book of Health.* New York, NY: Saalfield Publishing Co; 1901.

Hernandez-Reif M, Martinez A, Field T, et al. Premenstrual symptoms are relieved by massage therapy. *J Psychosom Obstet Gynaecol.* 2000 Mar;21(1):9–15.

Hirata JD, Swiersz LM, Zell B, et al. Does dong quai have estrogenic effects in postmenopausal women? A double-blind, placebo-controlled trial. *Fertil Steril.* 1997;68(6):981–986.

Khoo SK, Munro C, Battistutta D. Evening primrose oil and treatment of premenstrual syndrome. *Med J Austr.* 1990;153:189–192.

Lauritzen C, Reuter HD, Repges R, et al. Treatment of premenstrual tension syndrome with *Vitex agnus castus*—controlled, double-blind study versus pyridoxine. *Phytomedicine.* 1997;4:183–189.

Liao JF, Jan YM, Huang SY, et al. Evaluation with receptor binding assay on the water extracts of ten CNS-active Chinese herbal drugs. *Proc Natl Sci Counc Repub China B.* 1995;19(3):151–158.

Linde K, Ramirez G, Mulrow CD, et al. St. John's wort for depression—an overview and meta-analysis of randomized clinical trials. *BMJ.* 1996;313(7052):253–258.

Loch E-G, Selle H, Boblitz N. Treatment of premenstrual syndrome with a phytopharmaceutical formulation containing *Vitex agnus castus. J Womens Health Gend Based Med.* 2000;9(3):315–320.

McKenna DJ, Jones K, Hughes K. Efficacy, safety, and use of ginkgo biloba in clinical and preclinical applications. *Altern Ther Health Med.* 2001;7(5):70–86;88–90.

Meng F-Q, Luo H-C, Halbreich U. Concepts, techniques, and clinical applications of acupuncture. *Psychiatric Annals.* 2002;32(1):45–49.

Perovic S, Muller WEG. Pharmacological profile of Hypericum extract. Effect of serotonin uptake by postsynaptic receptors. *Arzneimittel-Forschuns.* 1995;45:1145–1148.

Pittler MH, Ernst E. Efficacy of kava extract for treating anxiety: systematic review and meta-analysis. *J Clin Psychopharmacol.* 2000;20(1):84–89.

Rennard BO, Ertl RF, Gossman GL, et al. Chicken soup inhibits neutrophil chemotaxis *in vitro*. *Chest.* 2000;118:1150–1157.

Roschke J, Wolf C, Muller MJ, et al. The benefit from whole body acupuncture in major depression. *J Affect Disord.* 2000;57(1–3):73–81.

Schellenberg R. Treatment for the premenstrual syndrome with agnus castus fruit extract: prospective, randomized, placebo-controlled study. *BMJ.* 2001;322:134–137.

Schneider B. Ginkgo biloba extract in peripheral arterial diseases. Meta-analysis of controlled clinical studies. *Arzneim Forschung.* 1992;42:428–436.

Sommer BR, Schatzberg AF. Ginkgo biloba and related compounds in Alzheimer's disease. *Psychiatric Annals.* 2002;32(1):13–18.

Stevinson C, Ernst E. Complementary/alternative therapies for premenstrual syndrome: a systematic review of randomized controlled trials. *Am J Obstet Gynecol.* 2001;185(1):227–235.

Stevinson C, Ernst E. Hypericum for depression. An update of the clinical evidence. *Eur Neuropsychopharmacol.* 1999;9(6):501–505.

Stevinson C, Ernst E. A pilot study of Hypericum perforatum for the treatment of premenstrual syndrome. *Br J Obstet Gynaecol.* 2000;107(7):870–876.

Tamborini A, Taurelle R. [Value of standardized Ginkgo biloba extract (Egb 761) in the management of congestive symptoms of premenstrual syndrome.] *Rev Fr Gynecol Obstet.* 1993;88(7–9):447–457. [French]

Tyler VE, Foster S. *Tyler's Honest Herbal: A Sensible Guide to the Use of Herbs and Related Remedies,* 4th ed. Binghamton, NY: Hayworth Press; 1999.

Volz HP, Kieser M. Kava-kava extract WS 1490 versus placebo in anxiety disorders—a randomized placebo-controlled 25-week outpatient trial. *Pharmacopsychiatry.* 1997;30(1):1–5.

Yakir M, Kreitler S, Brzezinski A, et al. Effects of homeopathic treatment in women with premenstrual syndrome: a pilot study. *Br Homeopath J.* 2001;90(3):148–153.

Chapter 10 Light and Sleep Therapies

Graw P, Recker S, Sand L, et al. Winter and summer outdoor light exposure in women with and without seasonal affective disorder. *J Affect Disord.* 1999;56(2–3):163–169.

Lam RW, Carter D, Misri S, et al. A controlled study of light therapy in women with late luteal phase dysphoric disorder. *Psychiatry Res.* 1999;86(3):185–192.

Maskall DD, Lam RW, Misri S, et al. Seasonality of symptoms in women with late luteal phase dysphoric disorder. *Am J Psychiatry.* 1997;154(10):1436–1441.

Parry BL, Berga SL, Kripke DF, et al. Altered waveform of plasma nocturnal melatonin secretion in premenstrual depression. *Arch Gen Psychiatry.* 1990;47(12):1139–1146.

Parry BL, Berga SL, Kripke DF, et al. Melatonin and phototherapy in premenstrual depression. *Prog Clin Biol Res.* 1990;341B:35–43.

Parry BL, Berga SL, Mostofi, N, et al. Plasma melatonin circadian rhythms during the menstrual cycle and after light therapy in premenstrual dysphoric disorder and normal control subjects. *J Biological Rhythms.* 1997;12(1):47–64.

Parry BL, Cover H, Mostofi N, et al. Early versus late partial sleep deprivation in patients with premenstrual dysphoric disorder and normal comparison subjects. *Am J Psychiatry.* 1995;152(3):404–412.

Parry BL, Hauger R, LeVeau B, et al. Circadian rhythms of prolactin and thyroid-stimulating hormone during the menstrual cycle and early versus late sleep deprivation in premenstrual dysphoric disorder. *Psychiatry Res.* 1996;62(2):147–160.

Parry BL, Hauger R, Lin E, et al. Neuroendocrine effects of light therapy in late luteal phase dysphoric disorder. *Biol Psychiatry.* 1994;36(6):356–364.

Parry BL, Javeed S, Laughlin GA, et al. Cortisol circadian rhythms during the menstrual cycle and with sleep deprivation in premenstrual dysphoric disorder and normal control subjects. *Biol Psychiatry.* 2000;48(9):920–931.

Parry BL, LeVeau B, Mostofi N, et al. Temperature circadian rhythms during the menstrual cycle and sleep deprivation in premenstrual dysphoric disorder and normal comparison subjects. *J Biological Rhythms.* 1997;12(1):34–46.

Parry BL, Mahan AM, Mostofi N, et al. Light therapy of late luteal phase dysphoric disorder: an extended study. *Am J Psychiatry.* 1993;150(9):1417–1419.

Parry BL, Mostofi N, LeVeau B, et al. Sleep EEG studies during early and late partial sleep deprivation in premenstrual dysphoric disorder and normal control subjects. *Psychiatry Res.* 1999;85(2):127–143.

Parry BL, Newton RP. Chronobiological basis of female-specific mood disorders. *Neuropsychopharmacology.* 2001;25(suppl 5):S102–S108.

Parry BL, Udell C, Elliott JA, et al. Blunted phase-shift responses to morning bright light in premenstrual dysphoric disorder. *J Biological Rhythms.* 1997;12(5):443–456.

Shinohara K, Uchiyama M, Okawa M, et al. Menstrual changes in sleep, rectal temperature and melatonin rhythms in a subject with premenstrual syndrome. *Neuroscience Letters.* 2000;281(2–3):159–162.

Terman M, Terman JS. Bright light therapy: side effects and benefits across the symptom spectrum. *J Clin Psychiatry.* 1999;60(11):799–808.

Chapter 11 Psychological Therapies

Beck LE, Gevirtz R, Mortola JF. The predictive role of psychosocial stress on symptom severity in premenstrual syndrome. *Psychosom Med.* 1990;52(5):536–543.

Blake F, Salkovskis P, Gath D, et al. Cognitive therapy for premenstrual syndrome: a controlled trial. *J Psychosom Res.* 1998;45(4):307–318.

Brown MA, Lewis LL. Cycle-phase changes in perceived stress in women with varying levels of premenstrual symptomotology. *Res Nurs Health.* 1993;16(6):423–429.

Fontana AM, Badawy S. Perceptual and coping processes across the menstrual cycle: an investigation in a premenstrual syndrome clinic and a community sample. *Behav Med.* 1997;22(4):152–159.

Fontana AM, Palfai TG. Psychosocial factors in premenstrual dysphoria: stressors, appraisal, and coping processes. *J Psychosom Res.* 1994;38(6):557–567.

Kirkby RJ. Changes in premenstrual symptoms and irrational thinking following cognitive-behavioral coping skills training. *J Consult Clin Psychology.* 1994;62:1026–1032.

Ornitz AW, Brown MA. Family coping and premenstrual symptomotology. *J Obstet Gynecol Neonatal Nurs.* 1993;22(1):49–55.

Stevinson C, Ernst E. Complementary/alternative therapies for premenstrual syndrome: a systematic review of randomized controlled trials. *Am J Obstet Gynecol.* 2001;185(1):227–235.

Walton J, Youngkin E. The effect of a support group on self-esteem of women with premenstrual syndrome. *J Obstet Gynecol Neonatal Nurs.* 1987;16(3):174–178.

Warren CJ, Baker S. Coping resources of women with premenstrual syndrome. *Arch Psychiatr Nurs.* 1992;6(1):48–53.

Chapter 12   Other Medical Treatments

Altshuler LL, Hendrick V, Parry B. Pharmacological management of premenstrual disorder. *Harvard Rev Psychiatry.* 1995;2:233–245.

Brown CS, Ling FW, Andersen RN, et al. Efficacy of depot leuprolide in premenstrual syndrome: effect of symptom severity and type in a controlled trial. *Obstet Gynecol.* 1994;84(5):779–786.

Casper RF, Hearn MT. The effect of hysterectomy and bilateral oophorectomy in women with severe premenstrual syndrome. *Am J Obstet Gynecol.* 1990;162(1):105–109.

Casson P, Hahn PM, Van Vugt DA, Reid RL. Lasting response to ovariectomy in severe intractable premenstrual syndrome. *Am J Obstet Gynecol.* 1990;162(1):99–105.

Deeny M, Hawthorn R, McKay Hart D. Low dose danazol in the treatment of the premenstrual syndrome. *Postgrad Med J.* 1991;67(787):450–454.

Evans SM, Foltin RW, Fischman MW. Food "cravings" and the acute effects of alprazolam on food intake in women with premenstrual dysphoric disorder. *Appetite.* 1999;32(3):331–349.

Evans SM, Haney M, Levin FR, et al. Mood and performance changes in women with premenstrual dysphoric disorder: acute effects of alprazolam. *Neuropsychopharmacology.* 1998;19(6):499–516.

Facchinetti F, Fioroni L, Sances G, et al. Naproxen sodium in the treatment of premenstrual symptoms. A placebo-controlled study. *Gynecol Obstet Invest.* 1989;28(4):205–208.

Fentiman IS, Caleffi M, Brame K, et al. Double-blind controlled trial of tamoxifen therapy for mastalgia. *Lancet.* 1986;1(8476):287–288.

Freeman EW, Kroll R, Rapkin A, et al. Evaluation of a unique oral contraceptive in the treatment of premenstrual dysphoric disorder. *J Womens Health Gend Based Med.* 2001;10(6):561–569.

Freeman EW, Rickels K, Sondheimer SJ, et al. Nefazodone in the treatment of premenstrual syndrome: a preliminary study. *J Clin Psychopharmacol.* 1994;14(3):180–186.

Freeman EW, Rickels K, Sondheimer SJ, Polansky M. A double-blind trial of oral progesterone, alprazolam, and placebo in treatment of severe premenstrual syndrome. *JAMA.* 1995;274(1):51–57.

Freeman EW, Sondheimer SJ, Rickels K. Gonadotropin-releasing hormone agonist in the treatment of premenstrual symptoms with and without ongoing dysphoria: a controlled study. *Psychopharmacology Bull.* 1997;33(2):303–309.

Graham CA, Sherwin BB. A prospective treatment study of premenstrual symptoms using a triphasic oral contraceptive. *J Psychosom Res.* 1992; 36(3):257–266.

Kodesh A, Katz S, Lerner AG, et al. Intermittent, luteal phase nefazodone treatment of premenstrual disorder. *J Psychopharmacol.* 2001;15(1):58–60.

Kontostolis E, Stefanidis K, Navrozoglou I, Lolis D. Comparison of tamoxifen with danazol for treatment of cyclical mastalgia. *Gynecol Endocrinol.* 1997;11(6):393–397.

Landen M, Eriksson O, Sundblad C, et al. Compounds with affinity for serotonergic receptors in the treatment of premenstrual dysphoria: a comparison of buspirone, nefazodone and placebo. *Psychopharmacology.* 2001;155(3):292–298.

Magos AL, Brincat M, Studd JW. Treatment of the premenstrual syndrome by subcutaneous estradiol implants and cyclical oral norethisterone: placebo-controlled study. *BMJ.* 1986;292(6536):1629–1633.

Messinis IE, Lolis D. Treatment of premenstrual mastalgia with tamoxifen. *Acta Obstet Gynecol Scand.* 1988;67(4):307–309.

Mezrow G, Shoupe D, Spicer D, et al. Depot leuprolide acetate with estrogen and progestin add-back for long-term treatment of premenstrual syndrome. *Fertil Steril.* 1994;62(5):932–937.

Miller MN, Miller BE, Chinouth R, et al. Increased premenstrual dosing of nefazodone relieves premenstrual magnification of depression. *Depress Anxiety.* 2002;15(1):48–51.

Mira M, McNeil D, Fraser IS, et al. Mefanamic acid in the treatment of premenstrual syndrome. *Obstet Gynecol.* 1986;68(3):395–398.

Mortola JF. Applications of gonadotropin-releasing hormone analogues in the treatment of premenstrual syndrome. *Clin Obstet Gynecol.* 1993;36(3):753–763.

Mortola JF, Girton L, Fischer U. Successful treatment of severe premenstrual syndrome by combined use of gonadotropin-releasing hormone agonist and estrogen/progestin. *J Clin Endocrinol Metab.* 1991;72(2):252A–252F.

Muse KN, Cetel NS, Futterman LA, Yen SSC. The premenstrual syndrome: effects of "medical ovariectomy." *N Engl J Med.* 184;311:1345–1349.

O'Brien PM, Abukhalil IE. Randomized controlled trial of the management of premenstrual syndrome and premenstrual mastalgia using luteal phase-only danazol. *Am J Obstet Gynecol.* 1999;180:18–23.

Pearlstein T, Steiner M. Non-antidepressant treatment of premenstrual syndrome. *J Clin Psychiatry.* 2000;61(suppl 12):22–27.

Pearlstein TB, Stone AB, Lund SA, et al. Comparison of fluoxetine, bupropion, and placebo in the treatment of premenstrual dysphoric disorder. *J Clin Psychopharmacol.* 1997;17(4):261–266.

Rickels K, Freeman E, Sondheimer S. Buspirone in treatment of premenstrual syndrome. *Lancet.* 1989;1(8641):777.

Sances G, Martignoni E, Fioroni L, et al. Naproxen sodium in menstrual migraine prophylaxis: a double-blind placebo-controlled study. *Headache.* 1990;30(11):705–709.

Schmidt PJ, Grover GN, Rubinow DR. Alprazolam in the treatment of premenstrual syndrome. A double-blind, placebo-controlled trial. *Arch Gen Psychiatry.* 1993;50(6):467–473.

Smith RN, Studd JW, Zamblera D, Holland EF. A randomised comparison over 8 months of 100 micrograms and 200 micrograms twice weekly doses of transdermal oestradiol in the treatment of severe premenstrual syndrome. *Br J Obstet Gynaecol.* 1995;102(6):475–484.

Soares CN, Almeida OP, Joffe H, Cohen LS. Efficacy of estradiol for the treatment of depressive disorders in perimenopausal women. *Arch Gen Psychiatry.* 2001;58(6):529–534.

Vellacott ID, Shroff NE, Pearce MY, et al. A double-blind, placebo-controlled evaluation of spironolactone in the premenstrual syndrome. *Curr Med Res Opin.* 1987;10(7):450–456.

Wang M, Hammarback S, Lindhe BA, et al. Treatment of premenstrual syndrome by spironolactone: a double-blind, placebo-controlled study. *Acta Obstet Gynecol Scand.* 1995;74:803–808.

Wood C, Jakubowicz D. The treatment of premenstrual symptoms with mefanamic acid. *Br J Obstet Gynaecol.* 1980;87(7):627–630.

Wyatt K, Dimmock P, Jones P, et al. Efficacy of progesterone and progestogens in management of premenstrual syndrome: systematic review. *BMJ.* 2001;323(7316):776–780.

Chapter 13 PMDD Game Plan

Chau JPC, Chang AM. Effects of an educational programme on adolescents with premenstrual syndrome. *Health Ed Res: Theory & Practice.* 1999;14(6):817–830.

Morse CA, Dudley E, Guthrie J, Dennerstein L. Relationships between premenstrual complaints and perimenopausal experiences. *J Psychosom Obstet Gynaecol.* 1998;19(4):182–191.

Taylor D. Effectiveness of professional-peer group treatment: symptom management for women with PMS. *Res Nurs Health.* 1999;22:496–511.

Index